Intersections of Law and Culture

Palgrave Macmillan Socio-Legal Studies

Series Editor
David Cowan, Professor of Law and Policy, University of Bristol, UK

Editorial Board

Dame Hazel Genn, Professor of Socio-Legal Studies, University College London, UK

Fiona Haines, Associate Professor, School of Social and Political Science, University of Melbourne, Australia

Herbert Kritzer, Professor of Law and Public Policy, University of Minnesota, USA

Linda Mulcahy, Professor of Law, London School of Economics and Political Science, UK

Carl Stychin, Dean and Professor, The City Law School, City University London, UK

Intersections of Law and Culture

Edited by

Priska Gisler
Berne University of the Arts, Switzerland

Sara Steinert Borella
Franklin College Switzerland

Caroline Wiedmer
Franklin College Switzerland

Published with support of the Swiss National Science Foundation

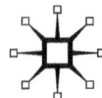

Editorial selection and matter © Priska Gisler, Sara Steinert Borella and Caroline Wiedmer 2012
Chapters © their individual authors 2012

All rights reserved. No reproduction, copy or transmission of this publication may be made without written permission.

No portion of this publication may be reproduced, copied or transmitted save with written permission or in accordance with the provisions of the Copyright, Designs and Patents Act 1988, or under the terms of any licence permitting limited copying issued by the Copyright Licensing Agency, Saffron House, 6–10 Kirby Street, London EC1N 8TS.

Any person who does any unauthorized act in relation to this publication may be liable to criminal prosecution and civil claims for damages.

The authors have asserted their right to be identified as the authors of this work in accordance with the Copyright, Designs and Patents Act 1988.

First published 2012 by
PALGRAVE MACMILLAN

Palgrave Macmillan in the UK is an imprint of Macmillan Publishers Limited, registered in England, company number 785998, of Houndmills, Basingstoke, Hampshire RG21 6XS.

Palgrave Macmillan in the US is a division of St Martin's Press LLC,
175 Fifth Avenue, New York, NY 10010.

Palgrave Macmillan is the global academic imprint of the above companies and has companies and representatives throughout the world.

Palgrave® and Macmillan® are registered trademarks in the United States, the United Kingdom, Europe and other countries.

ISBN: 978–0–230–29383–0 paperback

This book is printed on paper suitable for recycling and made from fully managed and sustained forest sources. Logging, pulping and manufacturing processes are expected to conform to the environmental regulations of the country of origin.

A catalogue record for this book is available from the British Library.

A catalog record for this book is available from the Library of Congress.

10 9 8 7 6 5 4 3 2 1
21 20 19 18 17 16 15 14 13 12

Printed and bound in Great Britain by CPI Chippenham and Eastbourne

Contents

Acknowledgments	vii
Notes on Contributors	viii
Setting the Stage: Reading Law and Culture *Priska Gisler, Sara Steinert Borella and Caroline Wiedmer*	1

Part I The Codification of Culture

1 **Law as Gendered Narratives: Criminal Court Decisions against Left-Wing Terrorists** 17
   Dominique Grisard

2 **Every Picture Speaks a Thousand Words: Visualizing Judicial Authority in the Press** 31
   Leslie J Moran

3 **I Hereby Find You Guilty of Cheating: How Television Judges Give Personal Problems Legal Dimensions** 50
   Anna Krakus

4 **Female Genital Cutting, Migration and the Art of Legal Boundary Maintenance** 66
   Caroline Wiedmer

Part II Performing Resistance

5 **The Actant Doesn't Speak: Configuring a Law for Research on Humans** 85
   Priska Gisler

6 ***Giù le mani dalla mia storia*: Narrating Regional Identity Politics in Ticino** 102
   Sara Steinert Borella

7 **'That's Life': Actualizing the *Non-Lieu* as an Empty Space** 116
   Fabio Ferrari

Part III Shifting Epistemologies

8 'On the Study Methods of our Time': Methodologies of
Law and Literature in the Context of Interdisciplinary Studies   133
Jeanne Gaakeer

9 *The Reader* as Thought Experiment: Character,
Moral Luck and the Contingent   150
Melanie Williams

10 Between the Rational and the Marvellous: Edgar
Allan Poe and the Counter-Enlightenment Origins
of the Modern Detective Story   170
Neil Sargent

11 Law's Life on the Screen   192
Richard K. Sherwin

Index   213

Acknowledgements

The chapters in this volume were first presented in lecture form at a conference entitled Intersections of Law and Culture in 2009 at Franklin College in Lugano, Switzerland. We are very aware of the fact that such a conference cannot be hosted without the dedication and skill of a number of individuals and we would like to thank Calhoun Allen and Jevon Brunk for all their work in marketing and on the website, Tomaso Rizzi for keeping us on the right side of the financial ledger, and Salvatore Bohrer, Alexandra Davis, Meije Gernez and Maggie Humphries, our student assistants, for their energy and willingness to step in whenever asked. Over the years it took to turn those first papers into the fully fledged chapters you have before you, we had the privilege of spending many hours with the thoughts of our authors as they wrote and rewrote their contributions. We are grateful to them for their hard work, their patience and the many conversations in paper and in person that accompanied the writing process. We also had generous financial support from a number of sources: we would like to thank Willem Peppler not only for several excellent risottos at his home but also for his generous backing of our project; we would like to thank Franklin College for dipping into its faculty development fund; and we would like to thank the Swiss National Science Foundation for supporting not only the initial conference but the publication of this volume as well. Our heartfelt thanks go to the series editor and commissioning editor at Palgrave, David Cowan and Rob Gibson, for leading us through the publishing process with patience and good humour. Finally, thanks to our copy-editor Marie Selwood for her judicious and careful editing. We dedicate this volume to our wonderful daughters – Hella, Anna, Lina, Meieli, Mimi and Jeanne – with love.

Priska Gisler, Sara Steinert Borella and Caroline Wiedmer

Notes on Contributors

Fabio Ferrari is Chair of Modern Languages and Assistant Professor of Italian and Comparative Literary and Cultural Studies at Franklin College Switzerland, in Lugano. His areas of critical interest range from Italian cinema of the 'boom' era, French surrealism and the avant-garde, performance and fringe theatre of 1980s and 1990s New York, contemporary queer theory and cultural politics, Italian poetry and prose of the interwar years. Ferrari is currently working on a new book, *Immaculate Reconceptions: Queering International Surrogacy, Querying Cultural Paradigms of Family Values*.

Jeanne Gaakeer is Endowed Professor of Legal Theory and Associate Professor of Jurisprudence at Erasmus School of Law, Erasmus University, Rotterdam, the Netherlands. The focus of her research is on interdisciplinary developments in law and legal theory, more specifically on law and literature and law and the humanities, and their relevance to legal practice. She is co-founder, with Greta Olson (Giessen University), of the European Network for Law and Literature (www.eurnll.org). She also serves as a Justice in the criminal law section of the Appellate Court of The Hague.

Priska Gisler is Professor at the Institute of Transdisciplinarity and Head of the Research Unit, Intermediality, at Bern University of the Arts. She has published in areas such as science and technology studies, gender studies and sociology of law. Her books include *Imaginierte Laien*, a volume about the imaginative powers of the lay-person as scientific expert (Weilerswist: Velbrück 2004), and *Modell Mensch*, a collection of essays on the configuration of the human in the sciences (Zurich: Chronos 2011). She is currently at work on two projects: *Präparat Bergsturz*, a publication of artistic approaches to the phenomenon of the rockslide; and a study on the relations between animals and humans in the zoo.

Dominique Grisard is an Associate Scholar at the Centre for Gender Studies at the University of Basel. Currently on leave, she is a Swiss National Science Foundation Fellow at the New School for Social Research in New York where she is working on two book-length projects: *Pink* weaves a history of gender and sexuality through and around the colour pink; a second project focuses on intimacies and sexualities in nineteenth and twentieth-century European prisons. She is the author of *Gendering Terror*, a history of (counter)terrorism in 1970s Switzerland and Germany (Frankfurt/New York: Campus 2011) and the editor of two anthologies on gender theory (*Gender and Knowledge*, Zürich: Chronos 2004; *Gender in Motion*, Frankfurt/New York: Campus 2007).

Anna Krakus is Assistant Professor of Slavic Languages and Literatures at the University of Southern California. She earned her PhD from New York University (NYU) and holds a BA in literature from Stockholm University where she also attended law school before being awarded a Fulbright Fellowship and coming to NYU. She has published in the journal *Law and Humanities* about the conflation of the literary and the legal in Polish secret police files, and in the Swedish literary journal *Samlaren* on law and literature and various approaches towards it. Her research interests include cold-war literature and cinema in Poland, jurisprudence, archive theory, and modern political thought. She is a sitting member of the board of the Law and Humanities Institute and an original member of the Nordic Network for Law and Literature.

Leslie J Moran is Professor of Law at Birkbeck College, University of London. He has published widely in areas relating to visual culture and law and the judiciary. He is a member of the JILC (Justice Image Language Culture) research laboratory in Paris. He teaches undergraduate and postgraduate courses in a range of areas from criminal justice and corporate law to judicial studies. He is currently engaged in a research project on images of judicial authority across a wide range of media and cultural formats, from painted portraits, photography and cartoons to reality court TV shows.

Neil Sargent is an Associate Professor in the Department of Law and Legal Studies at Carleton University in Ottawa where he teaches courses on introduction to private law relations, the legal regulation of corporate crime, and legal method and social inquiry. His research interests focus on law and literature, the epistemological foundations of detective fiction, corporate criminal liability and alternative dispute resolution. He is co-author of *Private Law: Social Life* (2nd edn with L Atkinson, Toronto: Lexis Nexis 2007) and *The Art and Science of Mediation* (with C Picard, P Bishop and R Ramkay, Toronto: Emond Montgomery 2004).

Richard K. Sherwin is a Professor of Law and Director of the Visual Persuasion Project at New York Law School. He teaches criminal procedure and torts as well as a seminar called 'Visual persuasion in the law'. He is the author of *Visualizing Law in the Age of the Digital Baroque: Arabesques and Entanglements* (London: Routledge 2011) and *When Law Goes Pop: The Vanishing Line between Law and Popular Culture* (Chicago: University of Chicago Press 2000). In 2005, he established the visual persuasion website (www.nyls.edu/centers/projects/visual_persuasion). Its goal is to study and advance visual intelligence and to inspire creative visualizations and informed critique of legal evidence and advocacy.

Sara Steinert Borella is Professor of Comparative Literary and Cultural Studies and Dean of the College at Franklin College Switzerland. She teaches a variety of courses on topics such as migration, cuisine and deception. Her research interests include travel writing and women travellers in Switzerland and Europe, and her book, *The Travel Narratives of Ella Maillart: (En)Gendering the Quest* appeared in 2006 (New York: Peter Lang). Her most recent publications and research focus on law and literature in their Swiss and European contexts.

Caroline Wiedmer is Professor of Comparative Literary and Cultural Studies and Chair of the Department of Literature and Culture at Franklin College Switzerland, in Lugano. She teaches a variety of courses on topics such as gender, poverty, memory, and law and culture. Her books include *The Claims of Memory: Representations of the Holocaust in France and Germany* (New York: Cornell University Press 1999), *Space and Motherhood: Configurations of the Maternal through Politics, Home and the Body* (with Sarah Hardy, Basingstoke: Palgrave Macmillan 2005) and *Inventing the Past: Memory Work in Culture and History* (with Otto Heim, Basel: Schwabe Verlag 2005). Her current research is on street newspapers, and on gender and law in the Swiss context.

Melanie Williams is Professor of Law at the University of Exeter where she teaches across a number of legal theory and socio-legal modules at undergraduate and postgraduate levels. She has published two books on law and literature (*Empty Justice: One Hundred Years of Law, Literature and Philosophy – Existential, Feminist and Normative Perspectives in Literary Jurisprudence* (London: Cavendish 2002) and *Secrets and Laws: Essays in Law, Life and Literature* (London: Routledge-Cavendish 2005). Her research interests focus upon links between law and ethics, especially as these are discoverable via literary and linguistic devices.

Setting the Stage: Reading Law and Culture

Priska Gisler, Sara Steinert Borella and Caroline Wiedmer

Introduction

In November 2009, an initiative calling for a ban on minarets in Switzerland was put to the popular vote and passed by a small but clear margin: ultimately, the vote resulted in a moratorium from that time forth on the construction of minarets on Swiss ground. During the months both before and after the vote, debates about the significance of this initiative dominated discussion in Switzerland and quickly spread to much of the Western and Islamic worlds. Questions about the ban far outnumbered any ready answers. Did the ban constitute a threat to religious freedom? If so, what did it mean for Switzerland to curtail the religious practices of a well-integrated minority? Was the ban an infringement on international law, which forms an inalienable part of the constitution, and hence invalid? How would the Muslim population within and outside of Switzerland react? The posters that appeared on roadside billboards, with their images of minarets rising like rockets out of the Swiss flag next to a black-clad figure in a niqab, proved especially provocative and understandably troublesome to many. Were the posters racist? Sexist? Feminist? Swiss federal councillors appeared flustered in press conferences that were called to assure the world that the Muslim population in Switzerland was well-liked and well-integrated, and meetings in Brussels with European officials were urgently convened to determine the legality of the initiative. At the same time, populist parties in Austria and Germany ambitiously declared that they, too, wanted to ban minarets in their countries. It quickly became clear that the new law, and all of the emotion that went into the discussions, had little to do with the actual construction of the minarets. Few of the Swiss who went to vote on the initiative had, in fact, ever thought about, much less encountered, one of the four minarets that had already been built in Switzerland. Rather, the initiative and the resulting law came down, in their most basic interpretation, to an attempt to reiterate a political right-wing ideology. Simply put, the initiative sought to erect a symbolic boundary that emphasized once more the differences between 'our' culture and 'their' culture. As Ulrich Schlüer, one of the proponents of the minaret initiative, was quoted as saying in *The Guardian*, minarets represented 'a symbol of political power, a prelude to the introduction of sharia law' (Traynor, 2009). Accordingly, the varied reactions to the ban either celebrated this newly drawn boundary or attempted to erase it and return to the status quo that prevailed prior to the new law. Either way, it became clear that the essential spectacle did not concern the construction of minarets, but rather the creation of a new law with the power to reshuffle cultural meaning and to redirect the ways we think about differences. The minarets merely served as a point at which law and culture intersected, and this intersection provoked a potent reconfiguration of the political landscape.

The notion of intersection proves to be quite an elastic concept. It can mean anything from the deliberate marshalling of a minor issue to attain a political end, as we have just seen with the minaret initiative, to the urgent convergence of social and political needs with moments of historical readiness in cases such as *Roe v Wade* or *Brown v the Board of Education*. The societal reactions to such intersections can range from the equivalent of a polite nod between acquaintances to a metaphorical collision that can derail entire social systems. Intersections are, therefore, far from trivial phenomena. Consider, for example, diverse political and social themes that intersect: architecture and religion in the case of the minarets; human experimentation and freedom of research; or homosexuality and parenthood in the case of laws on gay parenting. Our understandings of these issues and, in some cases, the meaning and importance of these issues are forever transformed. Intersections of competing cultural and legal norms may thus inform new discourses, both popular and academic, and create transformed social realities.

The relationship between law and culture

The aim of this volume is to highlight a number of such points of intersection in the form of case studies and to explore how law and culture react and interact in their wake. Depending on how the relations of law and culture are conceptualized, the precise geometry of these intersections can be thought of in various ways: as meeting points; as partially overlapping planes; or as intersecting straight lines with potentially dramatic reiterations of boundaries and the constitution of new realms. In addition to distinct notions of what constitutes intersections, the articles in this volume operate with different definitions of what constitutes culture or how law functions in society.

While we readily speak of law and culture and claim to understand the implications, we acknowledge in this volume that various disciplines read and interpret law and culture from a multitude of perspectives. Culture, for instance, can be defined narrowly as simply an artefact – such as a painting, a music score, a Barbie doll, or a beautifully manicured garden – the product of human activity rather than the activity itself. Law often interprets culture in just this way: a book, for instance, can be treated as an object that is legally contested and might be censored or banned by a legal decision. A broader definition, in contrast, might hold culture to be an all-encompassing field, one composed of all social practices, including the operation of law. Within British cultural studies, Raymond Williams was an early proponent of widening the concept of culture in an attempt to wrest the notion away from an elitist upper class which associated it primarily with the objects and tastes of a high form, such as canonized literature, music and art. 'Yet a culture is not only a body of intellectual and imaginative work,' Williams writes in an article aptly entitled 'Culture is Ordinary', 'it is always and essentially a whole way of life' (Williams, 1958). Anthropologists have also long operated with an all-encompassing notion of culture. Plog and Bates, for instance, write that culture is a 'system of shared beliefs, values, customs, behaviors, and artifacts that the members of society use to cope with their world and with one another, and that are transmitted from generation to generation through learning' (Plog and Bates, 1988, p. 7). Thus, a learned system of culture inevitably depends on one's position in the world. In *Minding the Law*, Anthony Amsterdam and Jerome Bruner describe the entanglements and complexities of culture and its relationship to law. 'Cultures', they write:

> are marked by *contests for control over perceptions of reality*. In any culture, there are both canonical versions of *how things really are and should be* and countervailing visions about *what is alternatively possible*. What is alternatively possible comprises both what is desirable and beguiling and what seems disastrous and horrifying. The statutes and conventions and authorities and orthodoxies of a culture are always in a dialectical relationship with contrarian myths, dissenting fictions and, most importantly of all, the restless powers of the human imagination (Amsterdam and Bruner, 2001, pp. 231–2, emphasis added).

Culture in this volume is conceptualized very much according to these ideas, as an exquisitely complex organism, forever moving in several directions at once and constantly seeking a balance between the possible and the desirable.

Where does that leave law? Within these expansive definitions of culture, law remains a crucial component because it functions as a tool that can be used at once to maintain and frame the way things are while making forays into the way things might be. Indeed, often seen as the system in charge of taming the unruly within a given culture, law maintains and shapes a cohesive whole with pervasive regulations and negotiations that impart values, hierarchies, symbols and ideologies. In Foucauldian terms, law is both a discourse and the complex set of rules, mechanisms and guidelines that direct the ways in which we behave and act. The discourse and the system the discourse engenders inform hierarchies of power, as is the case with our story of Switzerland and its minarets: the new law, absurd as it might seem, belongs to a larger structure of regulations that characterize a specific logic having to do with immigrants; a system, to put it provocatively, that is characterized by a fear of the 'Other'. This fear might be said to be reflected in its overall legislation as a symptom of sorts that pervades regulations having to do with those deemed foreigners, even as particular pieces of legislation actively shape the intransigence of the Swiss border. The minaret proper then becomes a symbol of this fear. Law, in this view, becomes a part of culture, inextricably entangled with social practices and involving meaning-making processes that deeply affect the way we conduct our everyday lives. As Goldberg, Musheno and Bower write, '[t]here is no abstract law, a language of law transcending culture, purged of all spatio-temporal specificity...there is no law, then, that is not at once political in its assumptions and implications' (Goldberg et al., 2001, p. xiv).

Of course, law can also be broken down into its component parts. These include discreet pieces of legislation inscribed in a constitution, or in a civil or penal code; a series of organizations and institutions such as courts, parliaments, lawyers' offices, and police stations; and finally, a range of actors who interpret rules and guidelines, such as judges, juries, lawyers, members of the police and the public. The contributions assembled here focus variously on these discreet parts, examining how the different configurations of the law intersect with culture in its many aspects.

Thus, some of the contributions in this volume concentrate on culture as a *Gesamtkunstwerk*, while others look at particular practices, and still others concentrate on a particular artefact. The same applies to the treatments of the law. While some contributions focus on individual laws and tell the story of their coming into being, others report the manifold ways in which political decisions come to fruition and unfold their agency. What all of the articles have in common, regardless of their particular take on culture and the law, is that they consider law and culture as intrinsically fluid processes of negotiation. They then seek to answer questions about how the overarching culture, or the diverse legal practices, and the wide range of culturally coined objects intersect; how they might be configured by law and culture; and, subsequently, how law and culture mutually constitute each other.

One of the recurring themes throughout the volume, moreover, is that of borders and boundaries: erecting them, shifting them, overstepping them and occasionally tearing them down completely. That law fundamentally operates according to the logic of boundaries has long been recognized: 'In its basic operation', write the editors of a volume on socio-legal culture, 'law attempts to create, police, and occasionally transgress social, spatial and temporal boundaries... Within law's spatio-temporal grid, complex systems of classifications are established, creating boundaries that define individuals, communities, acts and norms.' (Sarat et al., 1998, pp. 3–4) Thus, if we think of our minarets as a place where law and culture meet, we become aware of processes of exclusion and inclusion, a tug-of-war over belonging, identity and legitimacy.

Conversations

Read singly, the contributions in this volume each engage the relation of law and culture from within distinct cultural and disciplinary perspectives, often using novel and unorthodox methodological approaches. Read together, the juxtaposition of disparate topics and ideas develop a synergy of their own across what we have come to think of as behind-the-scenes conversations. The first of these conversations is about what happens to disciplinary and methodological thinking under the aegis of a topic as broad and frankly post-disciplinary as law and culture. While nominally belonging to disciplines such as literature, sociology and history; or cultural, legal and gender studies, each author here delves into areas of scholarship that include law and literature, law and culture and socio-legal studies. The effect is not so much a redrawing of disciplinary boundaries, of a juxtaposition of ideas from others realms of scholarship, as it is the complete erasure of lines between disciplines. The results are insights not only about the relation of law to culture, but indeed about the process of knowledge-making itself.

A second conversation that takes place behind the scenes has to do with the two legal traditions, civil law and common law, which act as a basis for the respective pieces. The civil law tradition, to which European legal systems belong, differs substantially from the common law tradition, which governs, among many others, the legal systems in the United States and Great Britain. These traditions, we suggest, constitute a kind of baseline for the authors' perceptions of law's relation to culture. This second conversation is more akin to an indistinct whispering in the background, because the functioning of the legal tradition in one's particular environment is in general assumed to be a norm by the individual authors and therefore is only faintly reflected in the contributions. Why then is this differentiation among legal traditions important? On the one hand, each has distinct procedures as well as distinct forms of negotiation and dispute resolution that determine the access individuals have to the law and the roles they get to play in its processes. The jury system, for instance, is largely non-existent in the civil law tradition; hence, the audience a lawyer faces is entirely different in European countries from the one that lawyers play to in the Anglo-Saxon system. Thus, when Richard Sherwin calls for a visual jurisprudence in his contribution and bases his call on the visual literacy of his jury, his argument signifies something distinctly different for a civil law court and those involved in it. Depending on the legal tradition in which we write, the arguments we make will be affected accordingly. These differences in legal traditions have implications for more than just scholarship. As John Merryman and Rogelio Perez-Perdomo write, a legal tradition is

> a set of deeply rooted, historically conditioned attitudes about the nature of law, about the role of law in the society and the polity, about the proper organization and operation of a legal system, and about the way law is or should be made, applied, studied, perfected and taught. The legal tradition relates the legal system to the culture of which it is a partial expression. It puts the legal system into cultural perspective. (Merryman and Perez-Perdomo, 2007, p. 2)

The example of the Swiss minarets only serves to reinforce these observations: historically conditioned attitudes to outsiders ultimately shape the latest modifications to the Swiss constitution, highlighting how the legal tradition may then express cultural fears and bias.

Different cultures will thus engender varied perspectives on legal systems and on how these systems are conceptualized and enacted. An approach that highlights these competing traditions can provide not only new grounds for interpretation, but can help remind us that our own positions are inevitably culturally determined. We would like to suggest that the breadth of this volume comes specifically from the diversity of voices represented, from the UK, the US, France, the Netherlands and Switzerland. This provides the reader with the opportunity to read across legal traditions in a comparative fashion. The European legal culture comparison (Van Hoecke and Warrington, 1998, p. 504) provides enough points in common to make such an endeavour useful while the multinational platform creates enough dissonance to offer up new insights into the intersections of different legal traditions.

Chapters and parts

We have organized the chapters in this volume into three parts, each representing different conceptualizations of the relation between law and culture.

Part I, The Codification of Culture, is about containment and norm, about negotiation and memory. It examines the ways in which law regulates the unruly and untamed areas of society by delving into the fraught territory framed by our cultural understandings of gender, class and authority. The contributions in this section analyse some of the attempts for control over the perceptions of reality referred to by Amsterdam and Bruner. Dominique Grisard's opening essay, 'Law as Gendered Narratives: Criminal Court Decisions against Left-Wing Terrorists', addresses constructions of masculinity, nationhood and terrorism in the unlikely context of Switzerland in the 1970s and 1980s. In her analysis of the trials and the subsequent controversial and paradoxical sentencing, she draws on the performative character of gender in court decisions and marks out the narrative space in which the figure of the defendant is simultaneously constructed as a man and as a terrorist. With her argument that court decisions about terrorists are neither gender-neutral nor value-free, but rather that gendered techniques of power exert a normalizing effect on subjects, she posits a system of criminal law that stabilizes a masculine-coded and binary-gendered legal state.

Les Moran's essay, 'Every Picture Speaks a Thousand Words: Visualizing Judicial Authority in the Press', examines the boundaries of legal and judicial authority. Moran argues that news media in various formats – print, television and, more recently, digital documentaries – and a wide variety of fictional visual formats – including film, television and the internet – play a major role in providing information about the judiciary and the people who occupy that role. Focusing upon English news media and more specifically data drawn from established English newspapers in both their print and digital formats, Les Moran explores the image of the English judge produced in and through those sources. In doing so, he addresses an aspect of judicial representation in news culture that many scholars have neglected while still others have actively dismissed as dangerous and distracting. As he points out, in England the appearance of judicial images in newspapers occurs under a particular set of conditions, specifically a continuing legal ban on cameras in the court. This ban, he argues, does not result in the total absence of visual images of judges in newspapers, but it does lead to the popular appropriation of media images that, in fact, lead away from the courtroom. At the same time, he notes a scholarly neglect of the images produced in that arena.

In 'I Hereby Find You Guilty of Cheating: How Television Judges Give Personal Problems Legal Dimensions', Anna Krakus shifts our focus to the US and, in particular, to the issue of legal consciousness as it plays out in real-world courtroom settings, after having passed through the filter of popular culture. To do so, she explores televised 'syndi-courts', with real cases and real judges, to show how the humanities and social sciences can inform one another in the field of legal research. She considers how the concept of legal consciousness can be theoretically elaborated and rendered useful when immersed in the context of popular and aesthetic culture. Exploring the cultural habits and aesthetic preferences of those who go to court can serve to explain some of the questions that socio-legal scholars struggle with, while at the same time a focus on socio-legal questions can help direct humanistic work. Krakus concludes that legal consciousness may be influenced not only by an individual's own interactions with the law, but also by the experiences depicted on courtroom-based television programmes.

In the final selection of the first part, Caroline Wiedmer returns to questions of gender and performance in the context of Switzerland. Her chapter, entitled 'Female Genital Cutting, Migration and the Art of Legal Boundary Maintenance', examines our fundamental understanding of human rights and culturally specific rituals, in particular, female genital cutting. By focusing on our Western and hence unmitigated condemnation of this cultural practice, she examines the cultural and legal conundrum created for immigrants arriving in Switzerland. She takes the first historic court decision on a case of female circumcision in Switzerland as the point of departure to examine the powerful effect media, literature and film have on the codification of laws that prohibit female circumcision even as they reinscribe problematic positions vis-à-vis the black female body. In the process, she brings to the fore the multiple intersecting narratives that crowd the issue of circumcision. She concludes that, while the declared aim articulated in the prohibition of female circumcision is the protection of young girls, the presentation of the laws is entangled in views of sexuality and social rights that go against recent feminist and culturally relative tenets. Ultimately, while Switzerland claims to protect immigrant women and the diversity of beliefs and cultures that accompany them, the author suggests that the constitutional change allows one moral position to categorically triumph over all others while, at the same time, deflecting attention away from Switzerland's problematic relation to the Other.

The second part, entitled Performing Resistance, represents in many ways the opposite side of the coin, focusing on moments of resistance to regulation, and reflecting on the legal vacuum that often follows the collapse of legislation. It also shows alternative possibilities of structuring the everyday in chapters that explore the mutual influence of cultural norms and identities on legislation. By considering the possibilities of questioning, undermining and transforming normative boundaries, it uncovers some of the antagonistic dynamics between law and culture.

Priska Gisler opens Part II with her chapter 'The Actant Doesn't Speak: Configuring a Law for Research on Humans' in which she takes her cue from a controversy over art, specifically a display known as *Ruan*, shown at the Museum of the Arts, Bern, in the mid-1990s. *Ruan*, a human–animal chimera created by the Chinese artist Xiao Yu, opened up a range of questions related to the use of human or non-human bodies. The controversy took place about midway through the creation of a new law, the so-called 'law on research on humans'. In both the debate about the artwork and the discussion about the new legislation, the concept of freedom of research played a key role as the two storylines, the artistic and the bio-political, intersected. In the ensuing parliamentary debates, Gisler argues that the debate on research in humans not only contributed to the closure of a legal gap but also to a potentially powerful reconfiguration of the existing social order.

In *'Giù le mani dalla mia storia*: Narrating Regional Identity Politics in Ticino', Sara Steinert Borella discusses the extent to which the 2008 strike by the local railway machine workers rewrote political and legal history in Ticino, the Italian-speaking, southernmost canton of Switzerland. This regional resurgence spoke not only for jobs past and present that might be lost or gained, but also symbolized the articulation of voices that had long been ignored in national politics and decision-making. Legally, the strike signalled crises on multiple fronts: a rupture in the confederation's dealings with its minority canton; a threat to the uninterrupted and emblematic Swiss rail service; and a direct strike against the confederation's legal code. The author shows how the legal understanding of the strike, the reception of the strike as an *ultima ratio*, and the eventual acceptance of the strike as a legitimate bargaining tool within Switzerland had everything to do with a broader identity narrative. Thus, the chapter reveals how this regional story reproduces what Jerome Bruner calls 'the narrative creation of self', how the political system in Switzerland has enabled and played a role in this performance, and how this strike tale becomes a meta-narrative for the country's own minority position in Europe.

From the fight over the conceptualization of one law, as illustrated by Priska Gisler, we move on to Fabio Ferrari's chapter on planning parenthood ('That's Life': Actualizing the *Non-Lieu* as Empty Space), a cultural drama situated in a legal non-space. This contribution is as much about family-planning, queer fatherhood and the legitimacy and legality of surrogacy as it is about the author's resistance to an all-encompassing normative frame. Ferrari's story is a kind of a 'rough experiment on the theme of queer parenting' and on his experiences in legality. As he argues, the legal loophole that enables parenthood for gay men in many European countries is, ironically, based on their compliance to a heterosexist establishment.

The third and final part of this volume, entitled Shifting Epistemologies, leaves the material world of law and culture and convenes the notion of intersection on the plane of epistemology, asking how the process of thinking across disciplines extends our ideas about the way law is practised and culture is understood.

Jeanne Gaakeer's article 'On the Study Methods of our Time' introduces Part III by questioning one of the general adages in the study of law and literature, namely that the two areas of study are mutually enriching. Indeed, for decades, the Anglo-American claim prominent in law and literature has suggested that reading literature can help mitigate the disciplinary tendencies of legal education, in particular its tendency toward a methodology of reading texts only to find 'the right answer'. Hoping that literary challenges will provide lawyers with new insights and will motivate them to practise law in more reflective, more ethical ways, literature and legal theory have been juxtaposed in the law school curriculum. Given the institutional and scholarly successes of law and literature, law has obviously negotiated its relationship with literature. The salient question would then be whether or not law has an edifying aspect for literature: if literature is a storehouse of topics and claims of meaning to law, what then is law to literature?

In her essay entitled '*The Reader* as Thought Experiment: Character, Moral Luck and the Contingent', Melanie Williams ponders the role of moral luck both in law and in *The Reader*. By tying her argument to thought experiments familiar from mainstream philosophy, the author reminds us that such experiments may help us interpret moments of cultural crisis. Indeed, it is through such tales that we learn to calibrate the moral landscape. According to Williams, the moral luck debate helps us recognize the degree of *investment* necessary to particular expressions of agency. The capital drawn on for that investment may derive from religious, community, or group values, but it cannot arise wholly neutrally and in isolation from the contextual influences that prevail.

Neil Sargent's 'Between the Rational and the Marvellous: Edgar Allan Poe and the Counter-Enlightenment Origins of the Modern Detective Story' examines a founding text in the emergence of detective fiction as a new popular literary genre, Poe's *The Murders in the Rue Morgue*. Published in 1841, and occupying an ambiguous epistemic stance between the rational and the marvellous, the narrative deploys the emergent science of forensic evidence-gathering to establish the 'facts' of a mystery that can otherwise only be explained metaphysically. In establishing the literary conventions governing the production and consumption of this new literary genre, the text also confronts many of the operative assumptions concerning the relationship between proof and truth that are implicit in the criminal trial process, in both its accusatory and inquisitorial forms. As such, the text provides an interesting comparative point of departure from which to examine the ways in which both law and popular culture share a common commitment to what Ian Watt, in *The Rise of the Novel*, has called 'the circumstantial view of life' (Watt, 2000, p. 31).

The final chapter in the book tackles the changes wrought in the practice of law in a culture steeped in visuality. Proceeding from the insight that law is increasingly visualized in the form of pictorial evidence and visual argument, not only in the wider culture but also within the courtroom, Richard Sherwin, in 'Law's Life on the Screen', calls for a rigorous analysis of the aesthetic, cognitive and metaphysical import of this visualization as a way of stocking a toolkit fit to deal with what he terms 'our new visual jurisprudence'. In a tour de force, he walks us through the phenomenology of the sublime and the ersatz sublime, the baroque and what he refers to as the 'digital baroque', arguing for discernment between sheer visual delight that we might experience when beholding a Warhol painting and the ontological excess we experience as an ethical demand. Only a heightened visual literacy, he argues, will take us to the place where we are able to take full responsibility for judgments based on the visual.

The Swiss connection

It will have become obvious from this line-up that the volume presents an emphasis on Switzerland, a potentially intriguing cultural and legal context, as we suggest here at the outset. Switzerland, and Lugano in particular, played host to a conference that led to this publication. Hence, it is perhaps not surprising to see the Confederation Helvetica represented here. Then again, despite the fact that Switzerland is home to myriad international organizations founded at the intersection of law and culture, from the Red Cross to the United Nations, it does not often come to the fore in comparative law or cultural studies discussions. We would like to propose that perhaps it should. Culturally, Switzerland offers a tiny image of the world at large, bringing together four national languages as well as the languages of its nearly 2 million immigrants. These diverse cultural perspectives inform a single legal system, one grounded in a civil code inspired by the Napoleonic tradition and first adopted in 1912.

While this legal context aligns Switzerland to some degree with its continental neighbours and their civil codes, Switzerland still does not belong to the European Union, as do France, Germany, Italy, and the UK; the country struggles with the integration of an important immigrant population despite a tradition linked to international humanitarianism; and it lagged decades behind the rest of Europe in according women's suffrage (the last vestiges of the old system prevailing into the mid-1990s in a few cantons). In fact, the world's oldest democracy goes to battle daily with the same issues that influence the juncture of law and culture in the USA, the UK and the rest of Europe, but on a somewhat smaller scale. The Swiss context offers a focused lens through which to examine these intersections of gender, race, ethics, aesthetics and the law, revealing new perspectives while providing solid points of comparison for traditions with which the reader may be more familiar.

Moreover, the Swiss political system of direct democracy enables us to observe up close some of the legal and political processes that remain largely hidden in other systems. It also enables a very particular relationship between state and subject since, theoretically at least, every citizen who has reached his or her 18th birthday is legally entitled to suggest initiatives that can result in new laws. If we return to the initiative to ban the construction of minarets, discussed above, we see that it took less than a year to collect the 113,540 valid signatures necessary to get the proposal on the federal ballot (13,540 more than the required 100,000). This number may seem tiny to citizens of other countries; in fact, the required 100,000 signatures to start an initiative represents less than 1.5 per cent of the more than 7.6 million people living in Switzerland. Hardly a year after the signatures had been collected, the voters in Switzerland approved the following addition to the Swiss Constitution: 'The construction of minarets is forbidden.' Of course, the construction of minarets never menaced anyone in the Swiss Confederation, nor did it somehow privilege one religion over another. The issue did, however, remind the world of the fragile boundaries drawn between religions, cultures, languages and legal systems.

Conclusion

Today, in the wake of the 2011 federal elections, support for the right-wing Populist Party has begun to wane. We might argue that this reaction against the far right and its anti-minaret campaign came as a result of an epiphany of sorts for the average Swiss citizen. Do the Swiss wish to be represented as allies of neo-Nazi parties in Germany and Austria? Do they want the world to re-examine their commitment to human rights? The most recent vote would suggest that the Swiss do not. Despite this swing in public opinion, the change to the constitution still stands. The minaret initiative created a precedent that will continue to engender discourses about inclusion and exclusion. The most recent example of the episodic nature of this narrative is the September 2011 vote in the lower chambers of the Swiss Parliament where members approved a ban on garments like the burka (which covers the whole body). The Populist Party played on its advantage in Parliament, but could not follow up in the subsequent elections where the people rejected the anti-Islamic platform presented to them. Ultimately, the immediacy of direct democracy pushes contemporary social issues to the fore in Switzerland, thus creating fertile ground for our study of intersections to which this volume – a compilation of studies in an international arena – is dedicated.

Works consulted

Amsterdam, A and J Bruner (2001) *Minding the Law* (Cambridge, MA: Harvard University Press)

Ewick, P and S Silbey (1998) *The Common Place of Law: Stories from Everyday Life* (Chicago: Chicago Series in Law and Society)

Freeman, M (ed.) (2005) *Law and Popular Culture* (Oxford: Oxford University Press)

Goldberg, D T, M Musheno, and L C Bower (2001) *Between Law and Culture: Relocating Legal Studies* (Minneapolis: University of Minnesota Press)

Lemke, T (2001) 'The Birth of Bio-politics: Michel Foucault's Lecture at the Collège de France on Neo-liberal Governmentality' **30**(2) *Economy and Society* 190–207

Merryman, J and R Perez-Perdomo (2007) *The Civil Law Tradition: An Introduction to the Legal Systems of Europe and Latin America* (Palo Alto, CA: Stanford University Press) (3rd edn)

Plog, F and D G Bates (1988) *Cultural Anthropology* (New York: Random House)

Sarat, A, M Constable and D Engel (eds) (1998) *Crossing Boundaries: Traditions and Transformations in Law and Society Research* (Chicago: Northwestern University Press/American Bar Foundation)

Sarat, A and T R Kearns (1999) *Cultural Pluralism, Identity Politics, and the Law* (Ann Arbor, MI: University of Michigan Press)

Sherwin, R (2006) 'Law Frames: Historical Truth and Narrative Necessity in a Criminal Case' in *Popular Culture and Law* (New York: Ashgate)

Traynor I (2009) 'Swiss to Vote on Mosque Minarets Ban', *The Guardian*, 26 November 2009

Van Hoeke, M and M Warrington (1998) 'Legal Cultures, Legal Paradigms and Legal Doctrine: Towards a New Model for Comparative Law' **47**(3) *International and Comparative Law Quarterly* 495–536

Watt, I (2000) *The Rise of the Novel* (London: Pimlico)

William, R (1958) 'Culture is Ordinary' in *Resources of Hope: Culture, Democracy, Socialism* (London: Verso), pp. 3–14

Part I
The Codification of Culture

1
Law as Gendered Narratives: Criminal Court Decisions against Left-Wing Terrorists

Dominique Grisard

Terrorism is a term that today is frequently associated with the attack on the World Trade Center on 11 September 2001. In German-speaking countries, the word also recalls the attacks carried out by the Red Army Faction (RAF) in the 1970s and 1980s. Hardly anyone thinks of Switzerland in the context of terrorism, however, in the 1970s and 1980s, several terrorist trials were held there, which – at least from a contemporary perspective – were largely concerned with so-called 'would-be terrorists' (BAR E 4320 C, p. 2). These trials, which in part led to paradoxical sentencing, raised questions about what a terrorist is, and how the constitutional state can deal with terrorist attacks. This chapter is most concerned with how these trials were informed and structured by gendered narratives. In fact, its focus lies on how the judgments negotiated the relationship between different types of masculinities in 1970s Switzerland.

As is customary in Swiss jurisprudence, court rulings refer to existing laws and previous court rulings. This can be seen in the judgment against Swiss would-be terrorist Jakob Müller: the district court of Zurich referred to previous rulings of the federal court and the cantonal court of Zurich – for example, to the judgment against two young men from Geneva who, in 1972, were sentenced by a federal court to two-and-a-half years in prison for 'endangerment of the constitutional order' – in order to support its choice of the statutory offence ('attacks on the constitutional order') (2216/1972, pp. 16–17).[1] This formal procedure indicates the performative character of court decisions (Künzel, 2004, p. 73; see also Butler, 1993; Bal, 2001): by consulting

---

1 According to my review of Swiss court decisions of the 1970s and 1980s, leftist terrorism first became a topic in Swiss court decisions in 1972 when two young men from Geneva were convicted of endangerment of the constitutional order by a federal court. In 1973, various members of the Bändlistrasse Group were brought before Zurich cantonal, district and youth courts, which had been assigned the case through an executive order of the *Bundesrat* (Swiss Federal Council).

and interpreting previous judgments, judges, lawyers and legal scholars confirm the juridical process in general, and, more specifically, legitimate the juridical evaluation of the accused person.

In the tradition of the 'law as narrative' approach to reading court decisions, I will show – using the case of Jakob Müller – how narrative conventions construct deviant and dominant masculinities (Brooks, 1996, p. 16). Drawing on my own historical research on court decisions against left-wing terrorists in 1970s Switzerland, I will mark out the narrative space in which the figure of the defendant is simultaneously constructed as a hypermasculine terrorist and as a failed man. In this context, hypermasculinity refers to 'an oversaturation of signs of the masculine' (Weber, 1999, p. 11) which arises when dominant white bourgeois masculinity is threatened. Hypermasculinity naturalizes and rationalizes the privileges and permanence of dominant masculinity. I thus contend that court decisions are neither gender neutral nor value free, but gendered techniques of power that exert a normalizing effect on subjects (Holzleithner, 2002).

Law as gendered narratives

My interest in law's stories may be situated within a larger field of inquiry commonly referred to as cultural criticism of law, located at the intersection between cultural and legal studies (Binder and Weisberg, 2000, p. 461; Porter Abbott, 2008, p. xiii; Brooks and Gerwitz, 1996). This approach reads law as a cultural practice of representation, critique and negotiation of conventions and norms (Brooks, 1996, pp. 15–17). According to Amsterdam and Bruner, the law hinges on the (re)construction of facts, and facts are constructed in and through narratives (2000, p. 111). They infer that the law, because it depends on facts, is grounded in narratives. This conclusion about the law in general also applies to the legal judgment in particular: deeds must be styled into facts, attributed to the defendant, and subsumed under the norm of the statutory offence according to its elements. German legal scholar Thomas Seibert argues along the same lines when he claims that the judgment is allotted to narrative and rhetorical elements because it always must narrate a deed, that is, 'establish' it (1996, p. 87). A selection is made from a vast quantity of data in order to enable a coherent and seemingly self-contained rendition of the facts. This coherence comes at a price: certain events are systematically blocked out and specific statements are excluded, whereas other statements and events are granted exceptional expository power.

The judgment is a legal decision that concludes a criminal proceeding. It is written following the main hearing, which takes place in court, and is concerned, on the one hand, with determining the criminal nature of the conduct, and on the other, with allocating punishment. As a rule, the text of the judgment begins with an introduction and exposition of the charge. Then, the facts of the case are delineated and subsumed under the category of a criminal offence as outlined by the law. It is necessary to explain why the conduct of the accused, as expressed in the facts of the case, has been allotted to the elements of a particular criminal offence.[2] The final part of the judgment is the sentence, which takes into account the biography and motives of the perpetrator as well as the circumstances of the crime.

From a 'law as narrative' perspective, the legitimating power of the judgment can be traced back to its integration within legal discourse, and to narrative set-pieces that plausibly link a sequence of events to the charge and to the biography of the accused person. Further, the often unquestioned authority of the judgment can be explained by the ascription of the criminal act to a typified perpetrator figure, and this stock character being located within a clichéd biography.

Descriptions of perpetrators and their life stories in judgment texts reveal that gender is one of the structuring principles of law's stories. Indeed, feminist legal scholars conceive the classification of accused persons into women and men, and the inscription of the figure of the defendant within a gendered life course as legal constructions of gender (Smaus, 2010). These classifications and ascriptions are discursively produced and confirmed in the repetitions of the narrative conventions of the judgment text (Butler, 1993, p. 206; 1997, p. 309). From this perspective, the narratives of a legal decision are not simply 'stories told within social contexts; rather, narratives are social practices, part of the constitution of their own context' (Ewick and Silbey, 1995, p. 211). Court rulings are performative acts that produce bourgeois conventions of gender by elevating certain narratives to facts while ruling out others. This performative character also harbours the potential for change: in that existing law texts can be interpreted in founding a judgment, the semantic content of legal discourse can shift imperceptibly. However, in this essay, I concentrate on the stabilizing effects of judgments: 'Performativity is thus not a singular "act", for it is always a reiteration of a norm or set of norms, and to the extent that it acquires an act-like status in the present, it conceals or dissimulates the conventions of which it is a repetition', argues Butler in *Bodies that Matter* (1993, p. 12). In this sense, in the legal judgment as well, there is no legitimating authority of a subject that intentionally repeats the conventions of gender (Bal, 2001,

---

2 While the elements of the statutory offence comprise general descriptions of possible cases that are punishable in Switzerland, the facts of the case designate what has 'in fact' occurred and how it has occurred 'in reality'. Thus, it must be determined whether the objective and subjective elements of the offence as described in the law have been met, and whether the defendant's actions are illegal and punishable.

p. 200). Instead, it is the repeating narratives of a judgment, together with their principles of ordering, inclusion and exclusion, that both grant the court ruling its plausibility and legitimacy, and also reproduce the bourgeois gender order. In what follows, my aim is to focus on the repertoire of narratives that create juridical facts, and to question the typified figures and clichéd situations that underlie them (Amsterdam and Bruner, 2000, p. 142).

The case of Jakob Müller

By means of armed combat, Jakob Müller[3] and five other members of the same group planned to abolish the state and bring about new forms of communal life, according to the introduction to the judgment made against Jakob Müller by the Zurich district court in 1973 (2216/1972, pp. 16–17). Jakob Müller was brought to trial because of assaults on the constitutional order, Article 275 of the Swiss criminal code.[4] As explained in the charge, Müller was one of the two main actors in a group of male and female 'terrorists' who maintained loose ties to the RAF and, at the time of their arrest, were in possession of enough explosives to carry out regular terrorist attacks and contribute to the disruption of state institutions (2216/1972, p. 72).

The cultural context for this trial against Müller is a period of West German (and Italian) terrorism commonly seen to have emerged from the radical periphery of the waning student movement of the 1960s (Passmore, 2009, p. 34). The Baader-Meinhof Group, or RAF as it called itself, was formed in 1968 in the aftermath of arson attacks and the arrest and subsequent liberation of one of the perpetrators of the attacks, Andreas Baader. The group existed underground until 1998, robbing banks, carrying out bombings and kidnapping high-profile public figures. In the 1970s, the Swiss mass media incessantly covered (potential) terrorist attacks by the RAF and other German terrorist factions. If that weren't enough, RAF wanted posters, featuring an unusually high number of images of scowling female terrorists, adorned the walls at Swiss customs posts (Melzer, 2009; Grisard, 2011). Unsurprisingly, there was avid community involvement in reporting terrorist suspects to the Swiss police, even after the initial leaders and figureheads of the RAF (Andreas Baader, Gudrun Ensslin and Ulrike Meinhof) had been arrested in 1972. In this light, it does not come as a surprise that big neighbour Germany and its framing of the RAF as a serious threat to

---

3 The names of all parties have been changed.
4 Article 275 of the Swiss Penal Code: 'Persons who undertake an action directed at disrupting or changing the constitutional order of the Federation or the Cantons are punished with a prison sentence of up to five years.'

state security influenced how the Swiss courts dealt with Müller and the other members of the Bändlistrasse group.

On the very first page of the 100-page judgment against Müller, the nature of the offence to be judged is designated as 'potential terrorist attacks', and the defendant is introduced as Müller, Jakob, from Zurich, 'no profession', born in 1952, 'single', with a 'criminal record', 'not enlisted', 'currently in a psychiatric clinic'. As an introduction to the decision, this sketch of the defendant as both a masculine perpetrator figure with clear terrorist motives and a disoriented youth who failed to become a proper man implies a tension that I will pursue in the next section of this paper. On the one hand, the person of the accused is the protagonist of a narrative about terrorism and a threat to the state. For this purpose, the defendant is portrayed as a rational man conscious of his destructive acts. On the other hand, Jakob Müller's characterization as 'not enlisted' and 'no profession' implies that he does not satisfy the image of a Swiss male citizen in the early 1970s: having no profession and not performing military service stands in marked contrast to the Protestant work ethic and the civic duty to defend the 'Vaterland'.[5] A narrative is constructed around the stereotype of the disoriented young tough.

Not only do these two narrative threads, each promoting a different type of masculinity, run through the decision as a whole. Müller's case also resonates in others. In fact, my analysis of 17 court decisions against left-wing terrorists in Switzerland in the 1970s and early 1980s reveals that his case is typical for the way Swiss penal courts dealt with so-called terrorists at the time.

Rationality and dilettantism: two narratives

What is only implied in the introduction to the judgment is shown for the first time with perfect clarity in the determination of the statutory offence: Müller's deeds are embedded in a narrative that underscores their danger to the Swiss constitutional state. According to the charge, the planned 'abduction of important personages, blackmail of authorities, use of explosives to attack government buildings, military compounds, and banks' were intended to bring about the disintegration of existing social and governmental structures (2216/1972, pp. 18–19). In what follows, I will refer to this as a 'narrative of rationality'. In this narrative, Müller's actions are woven into a threat scenario and classified as the preparation of crimes against the constitutional state. The narrative of rationality is best characterized by the frequent distinction between the 'existing order' and the 'endangered

---

5 The explicitly gendered, paternalistic sense of the German expression 'Vaterland' (literally, fatherland) seems lost in the English translation as 'one's own nation'.

order' (2216/1972, pp. 16–18). The stated threat to the status quo is amplified through the court's repetition of the phrase 'existing order' in immediate proximity to the phrase 'armed combat'. The wording of the charge illustrates this well:

> Likely around November 1971 and no later than February 1972, the defendant Jakob Müller started working towards establishing the logistic conditions for operating an organization of the extreme left, that, similarly to foreign revolutionary groups such as the Baader-Meinhof-group in Germany and the Tupamaros in Uruguay, intended to eliminate the existing order and structures and bring about new forms of cohabitation by means of armed combat. (2216/1972, p. 17)

According to the court, from a certain point in time onwards, Müller was occupied solely with preparing for illegal armed combat and committed himself entirely to the intentional endangerment of the existing order. Hence, the narrative of rationality situates the defendant's crimes within a militaristic and thus also (inter)national and political context. The terrorist attacks were understood as a declaration against the integrity of the constitutional state. Thus, actions that could have been punished according to criminal law became politicized as threats against the nation state. In turn, this nationalization and politicization of the narrative of rationality enabled the court to hold Müller responsible as a citizen distinctly coded as masculine. It is to be noted that the responsible citizen was still very much a masculine concept at the time (Ludi, 2005): in fact, in Switzerland, women's suffrage was only introduced in 1971, men's right and duty to bear arms having long served as a reason for excluding women from full citizenship (Frevert, 1991, p. 120; Wecker, 1999). Up until this time, the direct democratic structure of Switzerland had managed to guarantee optimal integration into the political system – to Swiss men at least (Blattmann and Meier, 1998, p. 12). Indeed, the political model of concordance and compromise bolstered a homosocial bond among the different players involved (Blattmann, 1998, pp. 29–30). This brotherhood across party, professional and class lines was fortified by the shared experience of serving in the army and by providing the family income. In 1970, only 10.4 per cent of all Swiss married women worked outside the home (Wecker, 1984, p. 332). As a result, men's role as breadwinners remained largely unquestioned. A congressman's call to introduce draconian laws to counter terrorism illustrates this point: 'Had one of us lost a wife or child in such a terrorist act or one's own life as breadwinner of his family, it would have meant facing completely new circumstances,' conservative congressman Heinrich Müller reminded his colleagues in Congress (Müller, AB 1974 N). To him it was more than unjust that terrorism forced a man to live two lives, as a civilized citizen on the one hand, and as a threatened, innocent victim on the other (Müller, AB 1974 N). Not only is it telling that Müller forgot to include the ten congresswomen present in his statement (after three years, women's presence in Parliament was apparently neither normal nor the norm), it seems even more significant, however, that the terrorist threat quite obviously undermined both the male congressman's – and by extension all male citizens' – ability to govern the state and to protect the family (Müller, AB 1974 N).

However, it was not just terrorism that contested the hegemony of the male citizen and his bourgeois mores. In 1970s Switzerland, with women's new presence as voters and political representatives, and the extra-parliamentary left and women's movements establishing a different political culture outside conventional political spaces, bourgeois men's political privileges became uncertain. To give an example: an increasing number of young men criticized the use of (legal) violence against so-called enemies of the state, and some even opted to boycott the conscript army altogether. These men were not only seen as consciously paralysing the army, a pillar of the Swiss nation state, but by refusing to comply with the citizen-soldier's duty to defend the fatherland, they also threatened a pillar of bourgeois masculinity. It is in this context, that the meaning of the gender marking of Jakob Müller unfolds. Now that bourgeois masculinity was perceived as exceedingly fragile, his gender-specific classification bolstered the subject type of the rationally operating, politically reflective and responsible adult man.

Since the defence pleaded not guilty to the charge 'attacks on the constitutional order', the court found itself prompted, first, to explain again with precision the elements of the criminal offence as outlined in the law, and second, to justify at length why the conduct of the defendant met the elements of this crime against national security. The defence's objections were a part of court practice, that is, part of a narrative strategy that allows the decision of the court to appear credible (Amsterdam and Bruner, 2000, p. 113).

At this point, the narrative of rationality is interrupted, and a second narrative is introduced, which seems at first glance to contradict the rhetorical logic of the narrative of rationality. This second narrative ties in with the first pages of the judgment, which reported on the defendant's criminal record and stated that he was presently being housed in a psychiatric clinic. In this narrative, another image of the defendant is presented: in view of his criminal past, he now appears as an unstable good-for-nothing. The facts that Müller has already come into conflict with the law and that he was in psychiatric treatment at the time of the trial also become a repeating topos of this narrative. This impression is enhanced by what is described next – the chaotic behaviour of the group, their spontaneous stealing of luxury cars and unsuccessful attempts to manufacture explosives – which leads the federal prosecutor to raise the question of whether such dilettantish, spontaneous actions can possibly be credited with having endangered the constitutional order. Various speculations are formulated in the judgment: the group's explosives might have been of a sufficient quantity to carry out regular terrorist attacks, and the connection to other terrorist groups such as the German Baader-Meinhof Group could have escalated into a situation of threat to the state (2216/1972, p. 72). In effect, this new narrative affects how later remarks about Müller are read.

The lynchpin of this narrative of dilettantism, as I call it, is provided by the events that lead to the arrest of the group: the police's attention was drawn to the group because, on the day that the group had planned an assault on the couriers of the bursar of the Swiss Federal Institute of Technology, Jakob Müller, under the influence of drugs, fell out of the window of his apartment. Thus, initially, this second narrative seems fundamentally to call into question the narrative of rationality and the type of masculinity it promoted.

Because of the close formal adherence of the judgment to the narrative conventions of its genre, it is almost expected that the dimension of the crime that comprises its threat to the state be challenged in the first part of the judgment. However, the scepticism, once it has arisen, must be instantly rebutted: thus, Müller's statements and those of his co-defendants are brought into consideration. The judgment refers to scientific findings, presents psychiatric evaluations, and exposes Müller's development since the beginning of primary school, in order to demonstrate persuasively 'that he was engaged in preparing for armed combat against the state' all along (2216/1972, p. 76). In this process, Müller's crimes are causally linked with selected biographical events: a connection is produced between his childhood and youth and the crimes under discussion. For example, juridical facts lend credibility by referring to Müller's instability and 'negative attitude' towards school. Built into the (re)construction of the facts of the case, the review of Müller's biography thus represents a narrative strategy typical of penal court cases in general. The judgment aims to link his criminal activities to his difficulties in primary school. Furthermore, the court refers to earlier judgments in order to dispel the doubts that have been expressed as to the state-threatening dimension of Müller's deeds. According to the judgment, it is not only actions that in fact cause a disruption of the constitutional order (or that comprise attempts to do this) that are punishable by law, but, as the court goes on to stress, mere preparatory actions are also punishable. In fact, it is sufficient if the attack against the state is only one uncertain goal among others of greater importance (2216/1972, p. 70).

Article 275 of the Swiss criminal code becomes a catch-all for whatever legal and illegal actions point to the preparation for 'armed combat', so the 'dilettantish' actions can in this way be given a political dimension while it is also possible to represent Jakob Müller's life as one single action of preparation for 'armed combat'.[6] The doubt as to the rightness of the juridical classification of the facts of the case can be dispelled, and the objective elements of the offence can be considered met. In this process, the narrative of dilettantism is subordinated to the narrative of rationality, and the dominant narrative of rationality is concluded with the 'indisputably' punishable nature of the facts of the case. This subordination to the narrative of rationality in the establishment of the facts of the case in turn enables Müller's dilettantish, spontaneous actions to be construed as potential actions of preparation for a 'revolution' (2216/1972, pp. 18–19).

Denial of masculinity

In contrast to the determination of the punishable nature of the conduct, the allocation of punishment is grounded in the frame of what I have called the narrative of dilettantism. The strictly formalized, chronological narrative begins with the defendant's birth and ends with his arrest. Unlike in the narrative of rationality, here the image is evoked not of a politically menacing terrorist, but instead of an uncontrollable young man. This is first accomplished through a class-specific devaluation of Müller's masculinity, in that his childhood and youth are judged against the background of bourgeois conceptions of gender and family (Kersten, 1995). From this point of view, Müller's father, the male guardian in the family, is a wholly unsuitable role model. The judges write that he 'lacks self-control', is 'contentious and short-tempered' (2216/1972, p. 85). Müller's mother, too, who should have taken care of the domestic and physical well-being of her children, from the point of view of the court did not fulfil the responsibilities of a mother, since she worked outside of the home and neglected the household. Moreover, according to the psychiatric evaluations, clinicians observed that Müller unconsciously identified with his short-tempered father. With this characterization as violent and quick to anger, the court not only codes Müller's father as a simple labourer, but also suggests a familial propagation of this deviant masculinity. Essentially, the court describes Müller as the victim of a squalid childhood, for whom there was never any possibility of escaping his milieu. Thus, in the judgment, the belief is manifest that masculine socialization can only succeed in a 'reliable' family and a sheltered home

---

6 As early as the 1970s, the Basel legal scholars Günter Stratenwerth and Magdalena Rutz pointed out that Article 275 presents 'extraordinarily indeterminate' elements of the offence. They consider it problematic that this statute incorporates preparation into what is punishable without providing a more precise delineation of scope (Rutz, 1973, p. 198; Stratenwerth, 1978, p. 263; also Stratenwerth, 1982).

(2216/1972, p. 87). This requires a gender-specific division of labour within the family according to the bourgeois model, or so the tenor implies.

Second, Müller is characterized as infantile. The judicial assessment of motive, mainly founded in psychiatric evaluations, emphasizes Müller's 'insecure', 'infantile' disposition (2216/1972, pp. 88–9). In the judgment, multiple psychiatric evaluations are cited or paraphrased:

> It is evident that as a result of the massive harm inflicted upon the patient by his milieu, and the related impossibility for identification, the patient was not able to develop normally, and in many respects retained an infantile disposition. (2216/1972, p. 94)

Thus, from the perspective of the court, the process of becoming a man was already substantially disrupted in childhood. Conflicts in school, severe problems at work and serious criminal activity predetermine the 'crisis' that led to his being committed to a home for troubled youths (2216/1972, p. 86). The opinion of the court, in compliance with the psychiatric evaluations, is that, because of a lack of a suitable role model in his father, he never became, or has not yet become, a proper man. For this reason, Müller never succeeded in keeping his 'drives' under control (2216/1972, p. 91). Consequently, the judge concludes that the crimes are grounded in a 'very substantial lack of self-restraint and a pronounced criminal will' (2216/1972, p. 91).

Third, Müller is effectively denied a political will. Instead, it is implied that because of his lack of a paternal role model and a proper education, he was positively compelled to take on a 'criminal will'.[7] The judges expressed serious doubts as to whether Müller's motives were indeed political, especially where his luxury car thefts were concerned. Even though Müller himself underlined the politics of stealing what is deemed a status symbol in capitalist societies, the court was unable to count the group's car robberies as political acts. Instead, the judges emphasized peer pressure as the driving force. The court's inability to acknowledge Müller's political incentive reveals how deeply ingrained the bourgeois understanding of politics was. Accordingly, in the allocation of punishment in the second part of the judgment, it is noted that the defendant himself considers his offences as politically motivated, but the text of the judgment leaves no doubt that the 'real motive' for his deeds is an 'inclination to criminal activities' (2216/1972, p. 86). The court contends that Jakob Müller is not lying when he justifies his crimes with political motives. However, to the judges, the defendant possesses a 'marked capacity for repression' which allows him after the fact to rationalize his crimes politically. Consequently, the construction of the politically motivated terrorist,

---

7 Foucault refers to the connection between the male subject and politics in *The Use of Pleasure*. According to him, the exercise of political power requires the control of the subject over him or herself as an interior principle of regulation (Foucault, 1989, p. 107; see also Maihofer, 1995; Lorey, 1996).

which allows the court to determine the punishable nature of the conduct in the first part of the judgment, is completely disavowed when it comes to allocating the punishment. In fact, in the second part of the judgment, it is seen as incomprehensible that Jakob Müller could act as a result of political motivation (Grisard, 2011, p. 129).

In the end, Jakob Müller was sentenced to three-and-a-half years in prison. However, the court arranged to suspend enforcement of the sentence and commit him to a psychiatric clinic. As follows logically from the sentencing, the lack of a male guardian in childhood impeded his development into an adult man. This is also attested to by the young defendant's 'role model problem' diagnosed by the psychiatrists (2216/1972, p. 89). Meanwhile, the political motivation of the defendant continues to be taken seriously within the narrative of rationality. It is thus evident that the text of the judgment skilfully alternates between the narrative of dilettantism and the narrative of rationality: while, in the second part of the judgment, the primary objective is to pathologize the political motives of the defendant within the narrative of dilettantism, the judges have recourse to the narrative of rationality at the moment in which they seek to affirm Müller's intellectual capacity for rationalization (2216/1972, pp. 16–17).

Pathologizing the perpetrator, depoliticizing the crime

There may be several reasons why the court argues differently during the determination of the criminal nature of the case than it does during the sentencing. One explanation may be that, according to the principles of the constitutional state, Müller needs to be held responsible for his actions as a rationally acting perpetrator-subject. The narrative of rationality enables the court to invoke the defendant as an adult man and a citizen. It is the universal aspect of the bourgeois subject – we are all the same – that is invoked in the determination of the criminal nature of the case, and embedded in the narrative of rationality (Scott, 1996). Seen in this way, the concept of the rational and intentional doer behind the deed provides the context necessary to pronounce Jakob Müller guilty of a crime against national security. By contrast, the narrative of dilettantism is expressly dedicated to the individual aspect of the subject – we are all unique – and here, to the pathologizing of the perpetrator. The introduction of his individuality makes it possible, in the second part of the judgment – the sentence – for the defendant to be portrayed as a child lacking in self-restraint because of the harm done to him by his milieu, and thus for him to be denied his own political will. The conception of the subject as both a unique and a universal being underlying the sentence thus clarifies the premises according to which persons such as Jakob Müller are judged in court.

In the sentence, the pathologized individual plays a significant part in the constitution of the legally responsible citizen – specifically because the critical attributes of the citizen, such as acting like a rational adult and possessing a political will, have been denied to him. The repeated marking of difference that is enacted through the pathologizing of the perpetrator in the sentence can thus be understood as an 'articulatory practice' (Hall, 2000) fundamental to the construction of the citizen-subject. With reference to the judgment of a 'terrorist' discussed here, this also explains why the narratives of dilettantism and of rationality are referred to one another. They represent a performative articulation of the discourse of gender and of law. In the more dominant narrative of rationality, Müller is styled as a politically acting, rational man, while in the narrative of dilettantism, he is styled as deviating from this bourgeois ideal.

In one and the same judgment, the defendant is, so to speak, awarded and deprived of bourgeois masculinity. From this point of view, the (re)construction of this case of left-wing terrorism points to a tension that generally characterizes legal proceedings against people of the extreme left in Switzerland in the 1970s. On the one hand, they are taken seriously as hypermasculine legal persons and political perpetrators. On the other hand, it is made clear that the intention of these failed men to overthrow the state cannot be taken seriously by the courts. In Jakob Müller's case, this leads to depoliticizing the crime and pathologizing the perpetrator.

References

2216/1972 Bezirksgericht Zürich [District Court of Zurich] i. S. Bezirksanwaltschaft und Jugendanwaltschaft Zürich gegen Müller Jakob und Käser Jürg betreffend Angriffe auf die verfassungsmässige Ordnung, 21.9.1973, 104 pages

BAR E 4320 (C) [Swiss Federal Archive], 1995/392, 229, (018)39/868, Aktion Jet-Funke, 3.12.1981: Kantonspolizei Zürich, Rapport Dienststelle Nachrichtendienst/Extremismus, Aktion Funke, an Schweiz. Bundesanwaltschaft, Kantons- und Stadtpolizei, 5 pages

Amsterdam, A and J Bruner (2000) *Minding the Law* (Cambridge, MA: Harvard University Press)

Bal, M (2001) 'Performanz und Performativität' in J Huber (ed.), *Kultur-Analysen: Interventionen*, 10 (Wien and New York: Springer Verlag)

Binder, G and R Weisberg (2000) *Literary Criticisms of Law* (Princeton, NJ: Princeton University Press)

Blattmann, L (1998) 'Männerbund und Bundesstaat' in L Blattmann and I Meier (eds), *Männerbund und Bundesstaat: Über die politische Kultur der Schweiz* (Zürich: Orell Füssli)

Blattmann, L and I Meier (1998) 'Introduction' in L Blattmann and I Meier (eds), *Männerbund und Bundesstaat: Über die politische Kultur der Schweiz* (Zürich: Orell Füssli)
Brooks, P (1996) 'The Law as Narrative and Rhetoric' in P Brooks and P Gerwitz (eds), *Law's Stories: Narrative and Rhetoric in the Law* (New Haven and London: Yale University Press)
Brooks, P and P Gerwitz (eds) (1996) *Law's Stories: Narrative and Rhetoric in the Law* (New Haven and London: Yale University Press)
Butler, J (1993) *Bodies that Matter: On the Discursive Limits of Sex* (New York and London: Routledge Chapman & Hall)
Butler, J (1997) *Körper von Gewicht* (Suhrkamp: Frankfurt am Main)
Ewick, P and S Silbey (1995) 'Subversive Stories and Hegemonic Tales: Toward a Sociology of Narrative' 29(2) *Law and Society Review*
Foucault, M (1989) *Der Gebrauch der Lüste: Sexualität und Wahrheit 2* (Frankfurt am Main: Suhrkamp Verlag)
Frevert, U (1991) *Ehrenmänner: Das Duell in der bürgerlichen Gesellschaft* (München: C H Beck)
Grisard, D (2011) *Gendering Terror: Eine Geschlechtergeschichte des Linksterrorismus in der Schweiz* (Frankfurt am Main and New York: Campus Verlag)
Hall, S (2000) 'Postmoderne und Artikulation' in N Räthzel (ed.), *Cultural Studies: Ein politisches Theorieprojekt: Ausgewählte Schriften* (Hamburg: Argument Verlag) (3rd edn)
Holzleithner, E (2002) *Recht Macht Gender: Legal Gender Studies. Eine Einführung* (Wien: Facultas Universitätsverlag)
Kersten, J (1995) 'Junge Männer und Gewalt' 7(1) *Neue Kriminalpolitik*
Künzel, C (2004) 'Zwischen Fakten und Fiktionen: Überlegungen zur Rolle des Vorstellungsvermögens in der richterlichen Urteilsbildung' 25(1) *Zeitschrift für Rechtssoziologie*
Lorey, I (1996) *Immer Ärger mit dem Subjekt: Theoretische und politische Konsequenzen eines juridischen Machtmodells: Judith Butler* (Tübingen: Edition Dischord)
Ludi, R (2005) 'Gendering Citizenship and the State in Switzerland after 1945' in V Tolz and S Booth (eds), *Nation and Gender in Contemporary Europe* (Manchester: Manchester University Press)
Maihofer, A (1995) *Geschlecht als Existenzweise: Macht, Moral, Recht und Geschlechterdifferenz* (Frankfurt am Main: Ulrike Helmer Verlag)
Melzer, P (2009) 'Death in the Shape of a Young Girl: Feminist Responses to Media Representations of Women Terrorists during the "German Autumn" of 1977' **11**(1) *International Feminist Journal of Politics*
Müller, AB 1974 N, 'Schutz vor Gewaltverbrechen', Postulat vom 27 June 1974, *Amtliches Bulletin der Bundesversammlung* (Nationalrat), 12.053, 10.12.1974

Passmore, L (2009) 'The Art of Hunger: Self-Starvation in the Red Army Faction' **27**(1) *German History*

Porter Abbott, H (2008) *The Cambridge Introduction to Narrative* (Cambridge: Cambridge University Press)

Rutz, R (1973) *Einige Überlegungen zum Verhältnis zwischen Strafrecht und Politik* (Basel: University of Basel Faculty of Law)

Scott, J W (1996) *Only Paradoxes to Offer: French Feminists and the Rights of Man* (Cambridge, MA: Harvard University Press)

Seibert, T M (1996) *Zeichen, Prozesse: Grenzgänge zur Semiotik des Rechts* (Berlin: Duncker & Humblot)

Smaus, G (2010) 'Welchen Sinn hat die Frage nach dem Geschlecht' des Strafrechts?' in G Temme and C Künzel (eds), *Hat Strafrecht ein Geschlecht? Zur Deutung und Bedeutung der Kategorie Geschlecht in strafrechtlichen Diskursen vom 18. Jahrhundert bis heute* (Bielefeld: Transcript)

Stratenwerth, G (1978) *Schweizerisches Strafrecht, Besonderer Teil II: Straftaten gegen Gemeininteressen* (Bern: Stämpfli Verlag)

Stratenwerth, G (1982) *Schweizerisches Strafrecht, Allgemeiner Teil I: Die Straftat* (Bern: Stämpfli Verlag)

Weber, C (1999) *Faking It: US Hegemony in a 'Post-Phallic' Era* (Minneapolis: University of Minnesota Press)

Wecker, R (1984) 'Frauenlohnarbeit – Statistik und Wirklichkeit in der Schweiz an der Wende zum 20. Jahrhundert, *Schweizerische Zeitschrift für Geschichte* 34

Wecker, R (1999) 'Ehe ist Schicksal, Vaterland ist auch Schicksal und dagegen ist kein Kraut gewachsen: Gemeindebürgerrecht und Staatsangehörigkeit von Frauen in der Schweiz 1789–1998' **10**(1) *L'homme*

2
Every Picture Speaks a Thousand Words: Visualizing Judicial Authority in the Press

Leslie J Moran

Domestic policy debates in the UK have noted that mass media, and visual media in particular, play an important role in generating experiences and understandings about the courts and the justice system more generally (Hough and Roberts, 2004; Falconer, 2005; Moorhead et al., 2008; Stepniak, 2008; Lambert 2011). News and more factual reports delivered by way of print and screen technologies have been identified as a particularly important source of popular information (Page et al., 2004, p. 7).[1] UK research on the interface between the news media and the justice system has been preoccupied with representations of crime, the depiction of perpetrators of crime and police image-making and image management activities (Cohen and Young, 1973; Chibnall, 1977; Schlesinger and Tumber, 1994; Mawby, 2002; Leishman and Mason, 2003). Studies of the depiction of the judiciary are most notable by their absence. This is a surprising omission. As Papke notes (2007), in common law legal systems the judge is a key figure in the justice system being a decision-maker who symbolizes and embodies some of its fundamental values and virtues such as impartiality, rule-based and substantive justice and legitimate authority. As few members of the public experience or learn about the judiciary from direct observation (Mulcahy, 2011, ch. 5), mass media potentially plays an important role in shaping perceptions and understandings of the judiciary and the justice system more generally. My particular research interest is visual images of the judiciary. In this chapter, the objective is to embark upon a preliminary exploration of visual images of the judiciary used in news reports in the press.

The study of the nature, use and effect of visual images of the judiciary is underdeveloped (Moran, 2009; 2012). Various factors contribute to

---

1 Fictions and dramas also play an important role (Falconer, 2005).

this state of affairs. One parochial factor is the ongoing domestic ban on cameras in courts. In England and Wales, section 41 of the Criminal Justice Act 1925 makes it an offence to take or attempt to take in or in the environs of a court any photograph, or to make a portrait or sketch of any person, being a judge of the court or a juror or a witness in or a party to any proceedings before the court, whether civil or criminal (Rubin, 2008). In 2005, the Constitutional Reform Act introduced an exception allowing cameras into the UK Supreme Court. Government has announced an intention to now allow cameras into the courts in England and Wales. Until this reform takes place, the current regime potentially limits the opportunity and shapes the capacity to make visual images of the judiciary currently available for use in news stories (Nead, 2002). A more general and enduring challenge is the subject itself. The judiciary is said to be a difficult subject to depict visually (Gregory, 2005, p. 102). Judicial work has little visual appeal being static, cerebral. But my earlier research has found a long history of visual images of judges and a contemporary practice that is diverse spanning many different visual media (Moran, 2008a; 2009; 2010; Moran et al., 2010).

In undertaking this study of contemporary judicial images in the press, I want to address a number of questions. What images of judges are used in the news stories that are made under the current prohibitions on image-making in courts? What aesthetic traditions do these images draw on? What role do these judicial images play in telling (and selling) news stories? What do pictures of the judiciary in newspapers tell us about the judiciary and judicial authority? I will provide some provisional answers to these questions by way of a small selection of news stories that refer to named judges and use images of the judiciary to tell the news. They have been drawn from a larger set of news reports that make reference to the judiciary using both text and image. In turn, this subset is part of a bigger archive of randomly collected news stories that refer to the judiciary that I am continuing to develop. The examples used here come from two mainstream English newspapers and their related websites. The *Daily Mail* is one of the country's most popular newspapers, attracting the attention of successive governments as the voice of 'middle England'. *The Times* is a centre-right broadsheet-style newspaper that is more closely associated with the establishment and particularly with the legal profession. One of its distinguishing characteristics is that it is the only daily newspaper that from time to time includes brief law reports summarizing court decisions and judgments. All of the news stories and images analysed here are contemporary, spanning a period from 2007 to 2009. The selected news stories use what I have identified as two main types of judicial image: the courtroom sketch and the judicial portrait.

Figure 1: In the newspaper reproduction of this sketch a caption was incorporated into the frame of the sketch, in the top right hand corner. It read, 'The mother and father centre right and left in court yesterday.' It offers the reader guidance on how to read the sketch. Reproduced with the permission of the artist.

The judge and the courtroom sketch

'Let my little boy die' is the front page banner headline attached to the first news story/image, published in the *Daily Mail* (Hale, 2009a). The report is about the first day of contested civil proceedings before the Family Division of the High Court in London. A hospital applied to the court for approval to withdraw a life-support machine from a severely disabled child. The effect of the withdrawal would be the death of the child. The child's mother supported the application. It was contested by the child's father. The report includes several short extracts from the opening statement by counsel for the hospital, Mr Mylonas. It presents summaries of evidence, about the child's condition and the impact the withdrawal will have, that is to be presented to the court during the case. The judge who is hearing and deciding the case is named in the report: Mr Justice McFarlane.[2]

The print version of the story includes one visual image.[3] It is a courtroom sketch.[4] It appears on the inside pages (p. 4) and takes up about one-third

---

2 The judge is also mentioned in other newspaper reports of the first day of the case. See, for example, in the tabloid newspaper *The Sun* (Haywood, 2009) and in the left-of-centre *Guardian* newspaper (Jones, 2009).
3 The online version of the story has an additional image, being a photograph of the entrance to the Royal Courts of Justice on the Strand in London.
4 The sketch has been repeatedly used in stories about the hearing published in the *Daily Mail*. The artist is not identified in the hard copy version of the news story. She is identified, Priscilla Coleman, in the online version of the report. Her name appears adjacent to a copyright symbol. For more about her work, see Coleman and Cheston, 2010. See also the artist's website. www.priscilla-coleman.co.uk/index.html (accessed 24 April 2012).

of the story on that page (Figure 1). Mr Justice McFarlane occupies a prominent place in the sketch. He is the sole figure in the top half of the image, positioned left of centre. He rises over the other figures in the sketch, shown in the well of the court. The judge is sitting, with head and shoulders above the line of the judicial bench. He is dressed informally; a business suit, shirt and tie. He displays none of the traditional paraphernalia of judicial office. He is shown full face, intently observing one of the other figures in the well of the court who, shown in profile, engages the judge. Three other figures are shown in profile. The composition singles out two other figures, but they are unidentifiable, shown facing the judge with their backs to the viewer.

The courtroom sketch is a practice of legal image-making that has various important characteristics. Its contemporary domestic roots are in the ongoing statutory prohibition on visual image-making in courts. Because of this ban it is a visual image of what takes place in court that can only be made out of court. It is based on the artist's memory of events in the courtroom (Coleman and Cheston, 2010, p. 7). It is produced at speed, not only to capture that memory but also to meet the dictates of news deadlines (Church, 2006).

The contrast between a sketch and a photographic image offers further insights into a courtroom sketch's distinctive qualities and function. With the sketch, the marks of the process of making the image are visible and are part of the image. With a photograph, there is rarely anything in the image that evidences the process of image-making and more specifically the decisions informing composition and its manipulation, such as editing. The sketch is more obviously manipulated.

Photographic images still tend to engage what Tagg calls 'realist assumptions' which he describes as:

> an existential connection between 'the *necessarily* real thing which has been placed before the lens' and the photographic image: 'every photograph is somehow co-natural with its referent'. What the photograph asserts is the overwhelming truth that 'the thing has been there': this is a reality which once existed. (Tagg, 1998, p. 1)

These assumptions express the epistemological qualities ascribed to a photograph: its indexical qualities. The photograph has factual and evidential associations attached to it. In contrast, the artist's sketch, being a more obvious fabrication, may struggle to produce or sustain similar epistemological effects. The sketch used in the 'Let my little boy die' report is more clearly authored, a more obviously particular view of the court and the judge within it, whether the artist is named or not.

But the signs of the hasty composition of this sketch may also enhance its epistemological status as telling the truth. The artist's marks are a constant reminder of the presence of the artist in court. She is our 'eye on the proceedings' (an eyewitness) scrutinizing the court and the judge, overcoming both the statutory prohibition restricting image-making in court and the viewer's absence (Newton, 2008). Moreover, the technique of the artist, manipulating the perspective, attaches the epistemological qualities that attach to the image to a privileged viewing position in the court (Clover, 1998; Barnhurst and Nerone, 2001, p. 126). The artist has foreshortened the perspective bringing the judge closer to the plane of the image. It makes him loom slightly larger than the figures below him. The red back of his chair, framing his head and shoulders, singles out the judicial figure. These techniques bring the judge, usually physically remote in the court, closer to the plane of the image and thereby closer to the viewer, inviting close scrutiny.

In order to examine the role this image plays in telling and selling the news story, I begin with an insight drawn from journalism scholars. The interrelationship of pictures and text and the spatial design of the page are important to understanding the use of visual images and their meaning (Huxford, 2001; Domke et al., 2002, p. 133). What are the textual and visual devices that help to make the meaning of this courtroom sketch of a judge (Figure 2)?

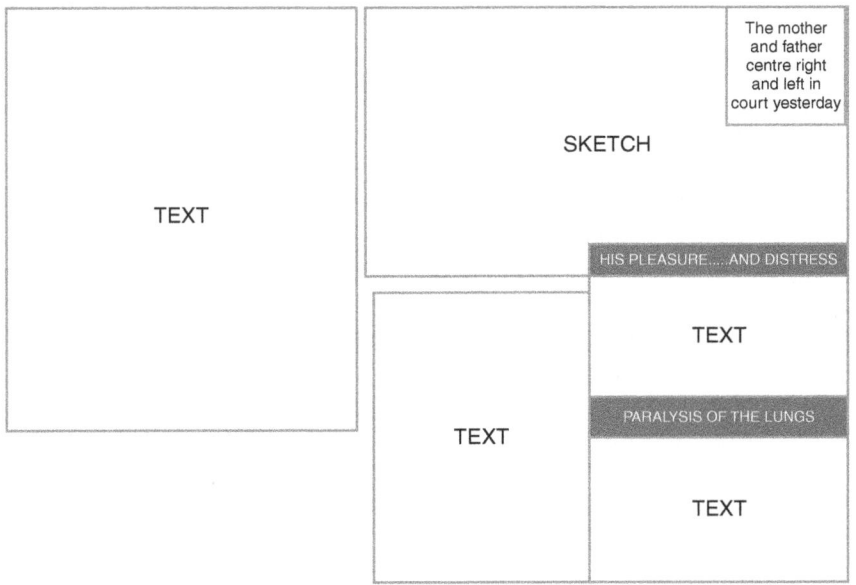

Figure 2: Layout showing the courtroom sketch and accompanying overlapping texts.

One textual device used to generate the image's meaning is the caption that accompanies the image. The online version reads 'Judge Justice McFarlane listens to the case as Baby RB's father (centre) and mother (centre right) look on.' A different, shorter, caption is used in the hard-copy version. It is now incorporated into the sketch at the top right hand corner. It reads: 'The mother and father centre right and left in court yesterday.' Both offer guidance to the viewer on how to read the image. Their common focus, naming the two faceless (anonymous) figures centre right, the mother and father, is perhaps unsurprising. The caption reduces the effect of the ban on naming parties to the dispute in order to protect the child's identity. But why is there no reference to the judge in the hard copy caption?

One answer lies in the layout of the paper version of the story. The sketch is attached at the bottom right-hand corner to a boxed text which is literally inserted into the sketch, bottom right. The box functions as an extended double caption. Three devices achieve this effect and add emphasis to its content; headings in a larger font, the use of bold lettering and background shading. The first heading, 'His pleasure...and distress', sits within the frame of the sketch. What follows in the accompanying text are described as 'key factors' about the child's condition presented to 'the court'. The box literally attaches to the sketch a summary of evidence presented and to be presented to the judge. It has the effect of animating the courtroom sketch that gives a prominent place to the judge. The second boxed heading adds another layer of drama, picking out a key dimension of the child's physical condition.

Research exploring news values and their impact upon the generation of law and order news can further assist in understanding the nature and use of this judicial image and the meanings it generates about the judiciary and judicial authority. Chibnall describes news values as 'the criteria of relevance which guide reporters' choice and construction of newsworthy stories...tacitly accepted and implicitly understood' (Chibnall 1977, p. 13). Dramatization, simplification and personalization are three of the news values I want to focus on here. Dramatization emphasizes the importance of attention-grabbing action, of spectacle. Simplification tends to point to the use of stark binary oppositions. The front-page banner headline 'Let my little boy die', which is followed by 'Heartbroken mother fights father for right to switch off disabled baby's life support', weave these together with personalization. The story appears to be of a mother against father literally locked in a life-and-death courtroom battle over their child, the ideal innocent victim.

But a ban on naming the parties has the potential to compromise the personalization of this stark drama. The story manages this ban by use of the more general subject positions of 'mother', 'father', 'baby' and 'child'. All offer much potential for identification. However, their dramatizing potential is potentially compromised as the reader is told the mother and father are 'on good terms'.

Another news value, novelty, can help us to understand how this works to shift the drama in the direction of the judge:

> If the hospital's application is successful it would be the first time a British court has against the will of the parent determined that life support can be withdrawn from a child who is not suffering brain damage.

In this extract novelty is associated with the substance of the application before the court. But the judge is not named: or is he? The key word here is 'court'. In the text of the story, the journalist makes repeated use of the word 'court' in the following way, 'the court was told'. The term 'court' works as a metaphor that names the judge by way of emphasizing the institutional qualities of the judge, the adjudicative role and judicial decision-making. While the judge is named in the body of the news report, his name only appears once. He is named in the context of listening to descriptions of the activities of the disabled child on the ventilator. Other characters seem to have a more prominent place. For example, counsel for the hospital, Michael Mylonas, is named more frequently and is quoted extensively. But the judge is referred to many times through the repeated use of the phrase 'the court was told'. He is personalized, or my preferred term would be personified, by way of a more anonymous and institutional title, 'the court'. It is through this device and the news value of 'novelty' that the judge is given a prominence in this story.

The courtroom sketch offers a vivid depiction of the key role of the judge in this story. The format of the sketch, a landscape format where the horizontal axis is longer than the vertical axis, is associated with pictures that have a strong story-telling function (Moran, 2008b). In this composition, the judge is placed literally at the centre of that narrative. The artist has distorted the perspective which has the effect of positioning the judge at the top of a triangular arrangement of faces. The judge is the only subject shown full face, fully revealed. His is the only face that engages the viewer. These compositional factors together work to draw the viewer toward the judge and towards the role the judge is playing in the proceedings; listening to the opposing parties. The inserted boxed text adds the detail of the imagined dialogue that the judge is shown listening to intently.[5]

---

[5] Many of the 191 comments attached to the online version of the story offer evidence of reader attachment to the position of the judge: 'I don't envy the judge having to make a decision here.' After the sixth day of the hearing, the father agreed to the withdrawal of the life-support facility, bringing the proceedings to a close. See Hale, 2009b. See *In the matter of RB (A Child)* for Mr Justice McFarlane's 'Words of Endorsement'.

Portraying the judge (1): 'Mother who forced her girls to marry is jailed'

Published on the 22 May 2009 in the *Daily Mail*, the second news story/image I want to examine is about serious criminal proceedings in the Crown Court Manchester (Narain, 2009).[6] The story reports the conviction and sentencing of a woman on charges relating to various sex offences and attempts to pervert the course of justice that involved her children. The report provides a summary of the incidents that are the subject of the criminal charges. Much of the text is taken up with quotations drawn from comments made by the judge during the course of sentencing. The judge is named several times in the text: Judge Clement Goldstone QC. The report incorporates a picture (Figure 3).

Column-wide, the visual image sits immediately under the headline and at the top of the story's second column. It occupies approximately 25 per cent of the story's total space. It is, as the caption accompanying the image announces, an image of the judge, 'Judge Goldstone'. What type of image is this?

This is a very different form and style of picture. First, it is a photograph. Second, it is a portrait. It is dominated by the subject's head and face respectively covered and framed by a full-bottom wig. Below the face is a large white lace-edged scarf called a 'lace stock' which is ceremonial court dress. It is a composition that brings the face close to the plane of the image. The subject gazes into the camera's lens directly engaging the viewer.

The portrait format, a longer vertical than horizontal axis, is less associated with narrative and more with contemplation of the subject of the image. It has strong associations with the representation of accurate likeness and the subject's character and personality.

The origins of this particular picture tell us something about its function and the aesthetic traditions it draws upon. One clue as to its source is the credit that appears at the bottom left-hand corner of the version of the picture used in the online version of the story, '© © UPPA Ltd'. Its source is Universal Pictorial Press & Agency Limited (UPPA). UPPA, now owned by Photoshot, is described in that company's promotions literature as 'the photography business of record for royalty, politicians and the judiciary, also photographing the ... appointments of judges.' (Anon, n.d., 4) It continues on to say that UPPA is one of a small group of agencies chosen to represent these subjects by those responsible for these institutional figures. This suggests

---

6 The online version has a different headline, 'Muslim mother who forced her school-age daughters to marry their cousins is jailed for 3 years'. The hard copy photograph is more closely cropped and the online version has no speech bubble or text.

Figure 3: The layout of 'Mother who forced her girls to marry is jailed', showing the position of the image and accompanying text.

that the image is an authorized or official image. Its original function is to record the individual's occupation of an institutional position. This is clearly expressed in the text that accompanies images of Judge Goldstone that appear on Photoshot's website:

> His Honour Judge Goldstone QC (Leonard Clement Goldstone QC) A Circuit Court Judge Assigned to the Northern Circuit... Date Created 02/24/2002... (Anon, 2002)

The particular composition, the head and shoulders shot, is one now commonly found on court websites on pages dedicated to judicial biographies. The portrait's preoccupation with the full face is an aesthetic associated with identification (Tagg, 1998) and with personalization (Moran, 2009). However, the presence of the wig and other items of ceremonial legal clothing works against the easy identification of the sitter. Personal characteristics, such as head shape and other defining physiognomic features, hair style, fashion items or props, have no place in this type of picture.

Despite the importance of the face, this image gives emphasis to particular items of clothing and dress: the wig, scarf and dark clothing. As such it is a style of portraiture and a long aesthetic tradition associated with the depiction of state officials and members of professions. Judicial portraits are a fine example of this type of portrait. In judicial portraits, the picture tends to be dominated by judicial paraphernalia associated with judicial office. Through these symbols the individual subject of the image, the named judge, is shaped by the values and virtues associated with the judicial institution and judicial office more generally: of majesty, independence, integrity, gravity, dispassion, impartiality, continuity, endurance and consistency (Moran, 2009, p. 300). The potential of portraits to individualize and personalize the sitter for the prospective audience are downplayed in judicial portraiture. The photographic portrait used in this news report has all the hallmarks of a portrait that seeks to depict Judge Goldstone as the personification of the values and virtues of judicial authority.

Turning now to the interrelationship of the picture, text and page design, the image is intimately connected to a boxed text that wraps around the top half of the picture and extends out to the right of it (see Figure 3). The (larger) font size and white lettering on a black background have been used to give emphasis. The position of the box, the use of quotation marks and the attribution of the quote turn the box into an angular speech bubble. The combination of direct gaze and speech bubble produce an effect of direct communication of judge to reader. The speech bubble isolates and reinforces a particular comment and sentiment that is embedded in the body of the text and turns it into the essence of the news report: 'Those who choose to live in this country must not abandon our laws in the practice of their beliefs.' The speech bubble literally and metaphorically attaches the symbols of legitimate judicial authority displayed in the picture to the sentiments highlighted in the news story. The face and name also personalizes the dramatic moment that is the focus of this story; passing sentence. In addition, as a photograph, this particular image contributes epistemological qualities to the experience of engagement with the judge. It adds truth to the experience.

The judicial portrait uses a particular aesthetic and epistemological effects to conjoin a whole set of values and virtues – majesty, independence,

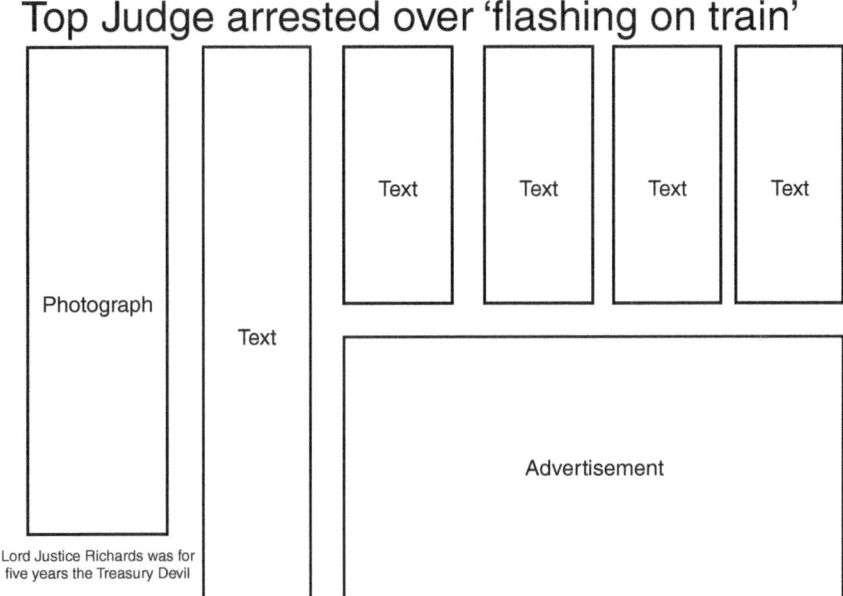

Figure 4: Layout showing the shape and position of the photographic image of the judge.

integrity, gravity, dispassion, impartiality, continuity, endurance and consistency – to the moral and political sentiments extracted from the sentencing comments. The image taps their potential to generate popular deference to and compliance with that authority and thereby deference to and compliance with the sentiments expressed in the news story, so eloquently captured in the quotation selected from the judge's comments (Davis, 1994, p. 3).

Portraying the judge(2): 'Top judge arrested over "flashing on train"'

The third and final news story/image dates from 22 January 2007 and comes from *The Times*. The story is about allegations of indecent exposure (O'Neill, 2007). A photograph occupies the whole of the first column and 25 per cent of the total news report (Figure 4). It is a portrait of a subject in ceremonial robes. An arrest and the subsequent release on bail of a man under investigation provide the events that animate the news story. Two short paragraphs in the first column of the story provide the detail of the arrest and release. The person arrested is repeatedly named as Lord Justice Richards. (He was subsequently tried and found not guilty. The trial was extensively reported in the press.) This is a rather different type of news report about a judge. It is not ostensibly a story about a judge carrying out judicial activities in court or otherwise. It is a story about a man who has been arrested and bailed who is a judge in his professional life.

The majority of the text focuses on that professional life, providing a biographical sketch of 'One of the most senior judges in the country'. It details his legal career at the Bar and on the bench. Particulars of his educational background are included. Special attention is given to his role as judge in a high-profile Court of Appeal case relating to the death of Jean Charles de Menezes, an innocent man killed by police during operations in response to terrorist attacks on the London Underground. The biographical sketch sandwiches his professional life between some information about his marital status and family details, 'married with three children', and his leisure pursuits, 'walking and relaxing in the Welsh hills'. The biographical focus of the text suggests the report is particularly shaped by a preoccupation with personality.

The unattributed source of the image is Photoshot and UPPA Ltd. The original photograph dates from 1998, almost 10 years earlier. The original picture shows the judge surrounded by fellow judges. The description that accompanies the image on the Photoshot website explains that it records the judge carrying out ceremonial activities; taking part in a religious service and subsequent celebration that mark the beginning of the new legal year.[7] Gregory calls occasions such as these opportunities to take some 'easy pictures' (2005, p. 102) of an otherwise challenging and difficult subject.

The picture editing cuts out the entire context and results in a portrait. If it shares that in common with the picture of Judge Goldstone, it is also very different from that portrait. There is less emphasis on the face. Despite close cropping, bringing the subject close to the plane of the image, the face takes up a much smaller part of the image and is further obscured by the full-bottom wig. The body now dominates, occupying 75 per cent of the surface of the image. The gently crossed hands, holding an unidentifiable black object, cut the body in two. Above, the body is covered by a scarlet robe adorned with white fur cuffs, trim and collar. Below, it is covered by a geometric pattern of black and white horizontal and vertical blocks made up of a black belt and scarf and a continuation of the white fur trim. Background is minimal, orientating the eye towards the symbols of judicial office that cover the body. The subject's gaze to the right of the viewer is a

---

7 The service is described as a private event only open to members of the judiciary, other senior figures of the legal establishment, such as the Lord Chancellor and Queen's Counsel, and their staff and invited guests. See www.westminster-abbey.org/worship/special-services and, for more information see, www.parliament.uk/about/how/occasions/lcbreakfast.cfm (both accessed 24 April 2012).

pose that enables the viewer to contemplate the subject of the image without the troubling experience of being confronted by the subject's direct gaze.

Curiously, the editing works against the depiction of Lord Justice Richards as a man, as an individual character and personality. It has the effect of portraying him as the embodiment of the values and virtues of judicial office. It is a picture that echoes an aesthetic tradition that puts those symbols on display for the purpose of acknowledging their meaning and reflecting upon them.

What role does this judicial image play in telling and selling the story? First a few words about the contribution the text and graphic design make to the meaning of this image. The first two words of the headline 'Top judge' sit over the picture and provide an informal caption. They also work to link the picture to the rest of the headline, 'arrested over "flashing on train"'. The subtitle has a more specific job, identifying the individual subject by name. The layout of the story, the juxtaposition of picture, headline, subtitle and text, all orientate the story's movement from that of a mundane story about one man's arrest and release on bail into a news report dominated by biographical detail with a strong institutional focus. The visual image vividly reinforces this institutional preoccupation.

One of the news values Chibnall identifies is titillation (Chibnall, 1977, pp. 31–2). It is a news value associated with fascination and condemnation. The subtitle attached to the picture, stating that the judge was 'for five years the Treasury devil', draws attention to the work titillation does in the making of this particular story. 'Treasury devil' is a legal colloquialism that refers to a highly prestigious position, being counsel to the government in civil disputes. But, in this context, it is put to work to exploit the sinful and lustful connotations of the word devil. It is a phrase that provides a prompt inviting a reader to examine and identify the symbols of judicial authority as evidence of immorality. The scarlet of the robe, a colour associated not only with high status but also with immorality, provides another prompt in this direction, this time visual. The picture is an image of institutional respectability. At the same time, it exploits the archaic symbols as an image of an institution that is not only elite but is also a secret and mysterious world. The picture and text work to facilitate a voyeuristic interest in this elite institutional world. The illicit, the salacious and the voyeuristic dynamic of the story enables and feeds an audience's sense of its own self-righteousness, indignation and moral rectitude.

As a photograph, the image plays another role. It brings to the story the indexical qualities of the image; the assumptions of the objective truth of what it represents. In this case, the epistemological message is put to work not only to express but also to challenge the truth of the values and virtues of judicial office represented by the symbols of legitimate judicial authority and institutional respectability. The photograph works as fact and evidence not only of the positive values and virtues of judicial office but also of their opposite. The virtuous is now base. The moral is immoral. Consistency and continuity are also corruption, incontinence and inconsistency. The dispassionate is now also a sign of hidden and not so hidden passions. Through the violent hierarchy of these binary relations, the picture works to generate the truth of the exotic and scandalous associations and the rightness that it opens up for the audience.[8]

A few methodological notes

In the space available here, I can only briefly comment on the methodologies used in this chapter and point towards some of the limitations and alternatives. One approach used in the selection and examination of the examples featured here is content analysis, identifying types of judicial images, cataloguing some key and recurring compositional characteristics and noting some differences. A second methodological approach draws upon semiology (sometimes called semiotics). Again the focus has been on the image itself, but this time the objective is to explore and analyse the particular way the aesthetics, the technologies of image-making and their use work to generate meanings. A particular emphasis in this study has been the importance of context and, more specifically, the generation of the picture's meaning though the juxtaposition of the visual and the textual aspects of press reporting.

There are limitations to this study, including the role of the audience/reader in making meaning. In the process of presenting the material that makes up this chapter and the accompanying images at various seminars, I have become acutely aware of the multiplicity of readings judicial pictures may generate, some of which have been incorporated into this analysis. Much more work is needed to explore how readers make the meaning of news stories and the meaning of the visual aspects of those stories in particular.

In order to explore news reports about judges and reports that use images in a more systematic way, a larger sample of stories/images and a sample more systematically collected becomes necessary. This would enable consideration of the relative importance of judicial images. It would also enable an exploration of the wider variety of judicial images being made and facilitate further study of the use and effect of different types of visual image on judicial news stories. Further research needs to be undertaken to identify and

---

8 The truth of the story is also made by reference to a number of experts, a spokesman of the British Transport Police, the Judicial Communications Office and authentic sources, such as *Who's Who*. Last but by no means least, the judge himself 'spoke to reporters'.

catalogue the range of contexts in which judges appear in news stories and the meaning of the visual aspects of those stories in particular. More work needs to be undertaken on the impact of digital formats on news stories also published in hard copy. This is far from being an exhaustive list. While this study offers some insights into the visual representation of the judiciary in mass media, it raises many more questions than answers.

Conclusions

The size of the sample of images used in this study inevitably means that any conclusions must be cautiously drawn and preliminary. However, while the sample is small, it offers a disproportionately rich point of departure. The news reports/pictures studied here provide some evidence of the nature and use of visual images of the judiciary in the press at a time when the law continues to prohibit the making of visual images of all the legal proceedings reported in these stories. One important finding is that visual images of the judiciary are used to tell and sell news stories involving the judiciary not only in a criminal justice context but also in civil justice settings. The inclusion of stories and pictures that relate to the judiciary in a civil justice context is particularly important as it is an aspect of the justice system that is frequently neglected in all types of research on justice and, in particular, in work on representations of justice (Genn 1999; 2009). As this chapter shows, to neglect this aspect of justice in media analysis and visual media analysis would be an error. Images of the judiciary in civil justice contexts not only represent them in that context, but may also contribute to more general understandings of the nature and role of legitimate judicial authority.

Another important feature of the stories analysed here is that visual representation is not only about the depiction of judges in courtroom settings. Judges may also become the object of visual representation in other contexts, some of which may appear to be extra-judicial.

The pictures considered here draw on two different aesthetic traditions of picture-making: one that utilizes narrative and another that has a strong focus on personality and character. The sketch of Justice McFarlane puts the judge at the heart of a life-and-death dilemma as the figure authorized to hear and resolve a conflict. Judge Goldstone's portrait calls for the reader to contemplate moral and institutional legitimacy that are attached to a news story about crime, punishment and just deserts.

Another contrast in the stories considered here is the source of these images. One, the sketch, is commissioned by and for a news organization. The others have a different origin and more generic function, being officially commissioned and made for the purpose of recording those who hold office. They have a more formal function. When they are used in a news context they have the quality of being ready-made or found images. Both of the officially commissioned pictures studied here have been manipulated in the process of being used in a news context. The picture captioned 'Lord Justice Richards' is the most severely edited. The aesthetics, and meaning change dramatically, from a picture that records a ceremonial event to one that represents a set of institutional values.

Last but by no means least, the use of the two Photoshot images raises another issue. Neither photograph is an image of what the respective subtitles attached to each image in the news reports suggest. So, the image entitled 'Judge Goldstone' in the *Daily Mail* story is not in fact an image of Mr Goldstone as a judge. The narrative that accompanies that image on the Photoshot website explains the picture is a record of his appointment as a senior advocate, as Queen's Council, in April 1993 (Anon, 1993). It is not a picture of a judge at all. Likewise if you go to the webpage of Photoshot containing the original of the photograph used in *The Times* story about Lord Justice Richards you will discover it is a picture of him as a judge of the High Court, not a judge of the Court of Appeal. Photoshot does have appropriate judicial portraits of both Judge Goldstone and Lord Justice Richards. How are we to make sense of these errors?

One answer might be that those responsible for the choice and use of the image share a common ignorance of official legal paraphernalia and legal institutions more generally. Another might be that there is a certain indifference to the image. Timelines of news production may limit the opportunities for picture research or for the development of expertise. A third factor might be the time pressures that are imposed upon those who produce the news reports. The story is produced using what is readily accessible.

But it remains the case that the misuse of these images is rather surprising. Photoshot webpages clearly indicate what the pictures record, including the institutional role depicted. Another answer to this conundrum is that to focus on the image alone is to miss the point. The meaning is not generated just by the picture. The caption and wider context does a lot of the work of making what may or may not be a picture of a judge into a picture of a judge. While the visual image may do important work in telling and selling the story, those who use the image may be relatively ignorant about what is in the image and relatively indifferent to its content. In the final instance, neither may work to the disadvantage of the story. Whether they work to the disadvantage of public understanding of the judiciary and the justice system more generally is a bigger question that needs to be explored further.

Cases cited

In the matter of RB (A Child) [2009] EWHC 3269 (Fam), available at www.bailii.org/ew/cases/EWHC/Fam/2009/3269.html (accessed 24 April 2012)

References

Anon (n.d.) *Photoshot: The World of Photography on the Web TM*, available at www.photoshot.com/pdfs/photoshot_about_us.pdf (accessed 30 April 2012)

Anon (1993) 'Leonard Clement Goldstone QC New Queen's Counsel', available at www.photoshot.com/view_image.jsp?img_id=1567518&srch_keywords=Goldstone QC&srch_numImages=57 (accessed 24 April 2012)

Anon (2002) 'Judge Goldstone QC', available at www.photoshot.com/view_image.jsp?img_id=1569520&srch_keywords=Judge Goldstone QC&srch_numImages=12 (accessed 24 April 2012)

Barnhurst, K G and J Nerone (2001) *The Form of News: A History* (New York: Guilford Press)

Chibnall, S (1977) *Law and Order News: An Analysis of Crime Reporting in the British Press* (London: Tavistock Publications)

Church, M (2006) 'Introduction' in M Church and L Young, *The Art of Justice: An Eyewitness View of Thirty Infamous Trials* (Philadelphia: Quirk Books), pp. 7–9

Clover, C (1998) 'Movie Juries' **48** *De Paul Law Review* 389–406

Cohen, S and J Young (1973) *The Manufacture of News: Deviance, Social Problems and the Media* (London: Constable)

Coleman, P and P Cheston (2010) *Court Scenes: The Court Art of Priscilla Coleman* (London: Wildy, Simmonds & Hill Publishing)

Davis, R (1994) *Decisions and Images: The Supreme Court and the Press* (Englewood Cliffs, NJ: Prentice Hall)

Domke, D, D Perlmutter and M Spratt (2002) 'The Prime of our Times? An Examination of the "Power" of Visual Images' **3**(2) *Journalism* 131–59

Falconer, Lord (2005) 'Introduction', *Broadcasting Courts Seminar 10 January 2005* (London: Department of Constitutional Affairs), www.dca.gov.ac.uk/consult/courts/seminar.htm (accessed 24 January 2011)

Genn, H (1999) *Paths to Justice: What People Do and Think about Going to Law*, (Oxford: Hart Publishing)

Genn, H (2009) *Judging Civil Justice* (Cambridge: Cambridge University Press)

Gregory, P (2005) *Court Reporting in Australia* (Cambridge: Cambridge University Press)

Hale, B (2009a) 'Let My Little Boy Die', *Daily Mail*, 3 November 2009, available at www.dailymail.co.uk/news/article-1224486/Baby-RB-Tug-love-babys-mother-says-life-support-turned-father-goes-court-stop-it.html (accessed 24 April 2012)

Hale, B (2009b) 'Goodbye, My Beloved Son: Father Gives up Court Battle to Keep his Disabled Boy Alive', *Daily Mail*, available at www.dailymail.co.uk/news/article-1226451/Mothers-views-childs-care-outweighs-father-says-senior-paediatrician.html (accessed 24 April 2012)

Haywood, L (2009) 'Mum: It is Cruel to Keep our Tot Alive', *The Sun*, 3 November 2009, available at www.thesun.co.uk/sol/homepage/news/2711087/Agony-of-mum-in-battle-to-turn-off-babys-life-support-machine.html (accessed 24 April 2012)

Hough, M and J V Roberts (2004) *Confidence in Justice: An International Review*, ICRP Research Paper No 3 (London: Institute for Criminal Policy Research)

Huxford, J (2001) 'Beyond the Referential: Uses of Visual Symbolism in the Press' **2**(1) *Journalism* 45–71

Jones, S (2009) 'Parents Clash in Court over Taking Child off Life Support', *The Guardian*, 3 November 2009, available at www.guardian.co.uk/society/2009/nov/02/parents-court-clash-over-child (accessed 24 April 2012)

Lambert, P (2011) *Courting Publicity: Twitter and Television Cameras in Court* (London: Bloomsbury)

Leishman, F and P Mason (2003) *Policing and the Media: Facts, Fictions and Factions* (London: Willan Cullompton)

Mawby, R (2002) *Policing Images: Policing Communication and Legitimacy* (London: Willan Cullompton)

Moorhead, R, M Sefton and L Scanlan (2008) 'Just Satisfaction? What Drives Public and Participant Satisfaction with Courts and Tribunals' in Research Series 5/08 (London: Ministry of Justice)

Moran, L J (2008a) 'Projecting the Judge: A Case Study in the Cultural Lives of the Judiciary' in A Sarat (ed.), *Law and Film: Essays on the State of the Field*, special edn, **46** *Studies in Law, Politics and Society* 1–24

Moran, L J (2008b), 'Judicial Bodies as Sexual Bodies: A Tale of Two Portraits' **29** *Australian Feminist Law Journal* 91–108

Moran, L J (2009) 'Judging Pictures: A Case Study of Portraits of the Chief Justices Supreme Court New South Wales' **5**(3) *International Journal of Law* 61–80

Moran, L J (2010) 'Walking Here Between the Past and the Future: A Review Essay' **8**(2) *Entertainment and Sports Law Journal*, available at www2.warwick.ac.uk/fac/soc/law/elj/eslj/issues/volume8/number2/moran/ (accessed 24 April 2012)

Moran, L J (2012) 'Legal Studies after the Cultural Turn: A Case Study of Judicial Research' in S Roseneil and S Frosh (eds), *Social Research after the Cultural Turn* (London: Palgrave Macmillan)

Moran, L J, B Skeggs and R Herz (2010) 'Ruth Herz Judge Playing Judge Ruth Herz: Reflections on the Performance of Judicial Authority' **14** *Law, Text, Culture* 198–220

Mulcahy, L (2011) *Legal Architecture: Justice, Due Process and the Place of Law* (London: Routledge)

Nead, L (2002) 'Visual Cultures of the Courtroom: Reflections on History, Law and the Image' 3(2) *Visual Culture in Britain* 119–41

Narain, J (2009) 'Mother Who Forced her Girls to Marry is Jailed', *Daily Mail*, 22 May 2009, available at www.dailymail.co.uk/news/article-1185589/Muslim-mother-forced-school-age-daughters-marry-cousins-jailed-3-years.html (accessed 24 April 2012)

Newton, J (2008) *The Burden of Visual Truth: The Role of Photojournalism in Mediating Reality* (New York: Routledge)

O'Neill, S (2007) 'Top Judge Arrested over "Flashing on Train"', *The Times*, 22 January 2007

Page, B, R Wake and A Ames (2004) 'Public Confidence in the Criminal Justice System', Home Office Findings 221 (London: Home Office)

Papke, D R (2007) 'From Flat to Round: Changing Portrayals of the Judge in American Popular Culture' 31 *Journal of the Legal Profession* 127–51

Rubin, G (2008) 'Seddon, Dell and Rock and Roll: Investigating Alleged Breaches on the Ban on Publishing Photographs Taken within Courts or their Precincts, 1925–1967' *Criminal Law Review* 874–87

Schlesinger, P and H Tumber (1994) *Reporting Crime: The Media Politics of Criminal Justice* (Oxford: Clarendon)

Stepniak, D (2008) *Audio-visual Coverage of Courts: A Comparative Analysis* (Cambridge: Cambridge University Press)

Tagg, J (1998) *The Burden of Representation: Essays on Photographs and Histories* (Basingstoke: Macmillan)

3
I Hereby Find You Guilty of Cheating: How Television Judges Give Personal Problems Legal Dimensions

Anna Krakus*

Introduction

In this chapter, I explore how legal consciousness may be influenced by television court shows. I try to bridge a gap between studies in the humanities and socio-legal studies as I account for some theories about why people go to court, and attempt to answer the question of whether television courts work as motivating factors for people to turn to address specific problems.

In the field of law and literature, there exists a certain tension between literary scholars and lawyers. For instance, Julie Stone Peters describes a mutual disappointment between lawyers and literary scholars when faced with each others' intentions and views of the law (Peters, 2005, pp. 442–53). Likewise, this kind of separation persists between the broader fields of socio-legal studies and law and humanities. Divided by theory and methodology that guide their questioning, literary scholars may find socio-legal empirical method too reductionist when examining only a small group or attempting to find answers using quantitative method. Likewise, socio-legal scholars may find general humanistic thinking, and the humanists' quest to find answers in books rather than collected data, too simplistic.

In attempting to offer a reconciliation between these two points of view, the main point of what follows is that the socio-legal term 'legal consciousness' may be influenced not only by an individual's own interactions with the law (as originally proposed by, among others, Susan Silbey and Patricia Ewick, and Sally Merry),[1] but also by the experiences depicted in courtroom-based television programmes – the kind of material often examined by scholars in the humanities. I argue that close reading of popular culture can help answer questions asked about real-life attitudes and investigate how the two

---
* Many thanks to Sara Steinert Borella, Priska Gisler and Caroline Wiedmer for their helpful comments.
1 For example, Merry 1990; Ewick and Silbey, 1992.

fields, separated by basic methodology, assumptions and research questions, can inform each other when struggling with the problem of the creation of legal consciousness. I attempt to show how the humanities and social sciences can inform one another in the field of legal research, and how the concept of legal consciousness can be theoretically elaborated and rendered useful when put in the context of popular and aesthetic culture. Exploring the cultural habits and aesthetic preferences of those who go to court can serve to explain some of the questions that socio-legal scholars struggle with, while at the same time a focus on socio-legal questions can help direct humanistic work.

Following a long line of courtroom ethnographies[2] the basis and starting point of my argument is an ethnography of the West Los Angeles Superior Court. Upon entering the court, I was immediately struck by the impossibility of escaping television and other forms of popular culture as points of reference for ordinary people dealing with real-life courts. This then necessitated a turn to my second source of material, popular television courts depicting real people presenting real cases. These shows are called 'syndi-courts', since their rights are bought on the syndication market, and I argue that their simple, everyday approach to legal disputes helps form people's beliefs about the law. This move to research popular culture as a means of inspiration for legal consciousness is inspired by, among others: Peter Goodrich's work on linguistics law, images and law, and law and literature law (i.e. 1987; 1990); Austin Sarat and Jonathan Simon's approach to law through cultural studies (Sarat and Simon, 2003); Leif Dahlberg's analysis of courtroom emotions (Dahlberg, 2009); Richard Sherwin's work on how popular culture influences the law (Sherwin, 2000); and, finally, Helle Porsdam's account of *The People's Court* (Porsdam, 1999).

In *When Law Goes Pop,* Richard Sherwin writes about how the legal system is influenced and needs to conform to ideas expressed in popular culture. For instance, lawyers must act in accordance with jury members' expectations in order to be convincing. Another example of this is Jeffrey Heinrick's exposé of juries and the so-called CSI effect (referring to the *Crime, Scene Investigation* television series). He writes that juries are inspired and feel educated by television shows about forensic investigators (Heinrick, 2006). Sherwin writes that '[a]ny attempt to understand adequately the way law works in contemporary society requires that popular culture be taken into account' (Sherwin, 2000, p. 17) and that 'law cannot be adequately understood without a careful examination of specific cultural practices' (Sherwin, 2000, p. 235). I see a similar relationship between law and popular culture in how people construct an idea of the law and construct a legal consciousness.

---

2 Such as Feeley (1992); Conley and O'Barr (1998); Richland (2005); (2008).

Learning to understand the law

'I think he wants to do his Perry Mason thing again, you know, he does this imitation of Perry Mason,' a man in front of me whispers to the woman next to him. He was referring to their attorney, who was arguing their case concerning a $20,000 debt and some valuable property in the Santa Monica Mountains. His comment about the attorney's strategy was one of the first things I heard after entering the West Los Angeles Superior Court in January 2008 for a day of observations. The case had been going on since 2003, yet the plaintiff found the best way to describe his attorney's actions and strategies was by reference to a long-gone fictional courtroom drama. I immediately wondered if television courts not only help explain to laypeople the workings of the law, but perhaps even function as motivating factors for people to turn to the courts in the first place.

Literary, social and legal scholars all face the paradox of 'law in action' versus 'law in the books'. Starting in the 1980s, socio-legal scholars began approaching the problem by examining legal consciousness. In 'After Legal Consciousness', anthropologist Susan Silbey asks, 'Why do people acquiesce to a legal system that, despite its promises of equal treatment, systematically reproduces inequality?' (Silbey, 2005 p. 326) The question concerned ordinary people, not lawyers or judges. Why would they turn to courts that promised little but mistreatment and injustice? By examining people's everyday lives and interactions with the law, and the formation of a legal consciousness, socio-legal scholars believed that they could find what law truly meant to people and society, and that they could help answer the question of why people keep turning to a legal system that does not seem to be able to provide justice. The litigious culture of America seemed to contradict actual courtroom experience, hinting that the legal consciousness of Americans should prevent them from searching for help from the law. But why didn't it?

In 'The Management of Disputes', Takao Tanase lays forth a model to explain the low level of litigiousness in Japan. He dismisses the notion that the Japanese are non-litigious by nature, and instead suggests that 'the Japanese refrain from litigation because the institutions are structured to discourage it' (Tanase, 1995, p. 60). He explains that Japanese courts are understaffed, and that the law and its decisions are rarely enforced. There is thus little incentive to go to court in Japan. One could say that this is not very different from the American legal situation that Silbey has pondered, nor from Malcolm Feeley's ethnographic account of a lower criminal court in New Haven in *The Process is the Punishment*. Yet levels of litigation in the USA are not low. It seems that, despite similar courtroom experiences, Japanese and Americans have differing legal consciousnesses, which implies that the experience of the court is not the only place where legal consciousness is formed. The New Haven court that Feeley examines conducts its business in a bureaucratic yet informal way. Decisions are made based on costs and on who knows whom, and hallway discussions on the way to court can be more important than the actual trial. Feeley argues that there is little incentive for criminal defendants to invoke due process rights since plea-bargaining is more efficient in terms of costs. If an attorney sees a career opportunity in a case, it is likely it will go to court, but if the case is what Feeley explains is labelled as 'garbage, junk, trash, crap, penny ante and the like' and deemed not worthy of the attorney's or prosecutor's time, it is more likely that the attorney would encourage the client to settle (Feeley, 1992, p. 30). Feeley's analysis of cost concerns shows that the court experience should be frustrating at the very least. He goes so far as to say that the process itself is the punishment, since being dragged into the court system will cost money, time and other efforts:

> For each dollar paid out in fines, a defendant is likely to have spent four or five dollars for a bondsman and an attorney...For every defendant who has lost his job because of a conviction, there are probably five who have lost their jobs as a result of simply having missed work in order to appear in court...The time, effort, money and opportunities lost as a direct result of being caught up in the system can quickly come to outweigh the penalty that issues from adjudication and sentence. (Feeley, 1992, p 30)

Feeley's ethnography thus corresponds to the paradox of the cold and unfair courtroom experience and the excessive use of the courts expressed by Silbey. Based on courtroom experience alone, people should not be going to court.

Perhaps the answer to why litigiousness persists lies in one of Richard Sherwin's observations: 'law's stories and images and characters leach back into the culture at large. In this way, law is a coproducer of popular culture' (Sherwin, 2000, p. 5). People are made comfortable with the law the way they see it on TV. My thesis is that popular culture can produce the legal subject. People who turn to the courts know less about the problems Silbey and others find with courts and more about their favourite legal personas on the television screen. Helle Porsdam suggests that the viewers of the show *The People's Court*, which ran on television in the United States between 1981 and 1997 and depicted real people and real cases, may have believed that they were getting free legal advice when watching the show (Porsdam, 1999, p. 96). Perhaps people are learning about the law more from popular culture than from their own rare, actual courtroom interactions?

West Los Angeles Superior Court: traffic court arraignments

During my observations of courtroom proceedings in the West Los Angeles Superior Court, I saw similar examples to those of Malcolm Feeley. During arraignments in the traffic court, a strict judge decided that whoever did not start their plea with either a 'guilty' or 'not guilty' statement had to sit back down and wait until everybody else was done. A man I will call Mr Maxwell[3] stood up and began by proclaiming 'I didn't do it,' and was thus asked to sit back down. One-and-a-half hours later, he was asked again and this time he pleaded 'guilty'. I asked Mr Maxwell why he changed his plea from not guilty to guilty. 'The fine was just $35,' he reasoned, although with taxes in the state of California the total of his fine would be closer to $100. He explained to me: 'I didn't do it, but I would rather pay $35 and have it over with, go back to work, than to come back here again – I've already wasted half a workday.' Mr Maxwell's reasoning is found throughout Feeley's book, in which he compares lower criminal courts to a marketplace where normative justice is followed rather than procedural. Mr Maxwell may not have done anything wrong but his decision to plead guilty has nothing to do with justice or the law. It is a normative consideration with a legal outcome.

Furthermore, Judge Robert, the judge in the traffic court I observed, took on the role of a moral teacher. The process in his courtroom was not only the punishment, but also an attempt at reform. Julia, a girl in her early twenties, had been caught driving without a licence. As some others in court had done, she failed to begin by pleading 'not guilty' and instead said 'I *have* a licence,' while holding it up for the bailiff to see. Two hours later, when she had had her second chance to properly plead not guilty, I talked to her. 'The judge acted very unprofessionally,' she said. 'He treats people like they are children in school and when they misbehave they get sent to the back of the line. He does not even listen to us. This is part of our punishment for being bad.' Although I tried to stay objective during my observations in the court, I cannot claim to disagree with Julia's comment about the judge's role as teacher and punisher in this hearing. Judge Robert constantly made sure that he had everybody's attention: I myself, was even told to pay attention at a point when I was looking down in order to take careful notes on what he was saying. My not looking straight at him was understood to be disobedient and unacceptable behaviour.

A third example of the judge's powerplay was evident in the case of Miss Caruso. She was back in traffic court after having completed community service for a prior offence, but not having completed the assigned traffic school for the same violation. The judge said that whoever gave her that

---

3 All names used in this paper are pseudonyms.

ruling was incompetent: according to Judge Robert, you cannot order community service *and* traffic school for one violation – either/or and a fine would be the proper procedure. Based on this, Judge Robert overruled the old decision and sentenced Miss Caruso to pay fines instead of going to traffic school, reminding her that 'traffic school is a privilege not a right!' Miss Caruso was unemployed, and afterward expressed distress to me over having to pay money she does not have when originally all she had to do was show up in traffic school. She said: 'So one guy told me one thing and now this judge says something else, and *I* get punished for it?! They punish us so much! But I won't argue, what's the point?'

The courts cannot always offer justice, as these cases exemplify – at least for the participants themselves – and they can discourage people from turning to them, and may even punish people through their very workings. So, to echo Susan Silbey, why are people still turning to the courts?

Money and conflict 'management'

One reason to endure the courtroom's potential abuse is that there might be monetary gain at the end of the process. On the cover of the 15th edition of Ralph Warner's *Everybody's Guide to Small Claims Court in California,* going to court and collecting money become intimately linked as the book supposedly offers 'Step-by-step advice on how to prepare your case, how to file it, and *perhaps most importantly, how to collect if you win.*' The most important part of filing small claims suits, the book's cover teaches, is to get your money. However, upon actually reading the book one finds that the bulk of the text instead makes it clear that going to small claims court might not be worth the money at all. In fact, according to this book, the monetary gain should act as a rather weak motivator. Writing about 'judgment-proof' defendants or, as he calls them 'deadbeats', the author claims that 'a significant percentage of Californians who are not homeless are nevertheless "judgment proof." You can sue and get judgment against these deadbeat defendants until red cows dance on a pink moon, but you won't be able to collect a dime.' (Warner, 2003, p. 3/2)

In her 1979 article 'Going to Court', Sally Merry accounts for some residents of the urban neighbourhood that she calls Dover Square and their frequent use of the courts. Merry shows that the outcomes of disputes were rarely successful, but nonetheless worked effectively as a means of intimidation and an alternative to violence. Indeed, Merry argues that conflicts are only *managed* in court, not settled. The only satisfactory way for a conflict to end, Merry demonstrates, is for one party to physically leave. Residents of Dover Square kept returning to court even though they had little or no reason to believe in its workings. Their reason to use the court was largely for intimidation purposes, and their experience had shown them that the court was indeed effective in that regard. Merry shows that this had the effect of opening up the legal arena for women in the neighbourhood: 'They turn to the court as a form of power in dealing with others who are more physically powerful than they are' and that 'the prevailing alternative to court is violence' (Merry, 1979, p. 62). The court can thus be a powerful weapon for those who are not physically strong enough to win a physical fight. This finding coupled with the ideas that the court victimizes and punishes leads to a paradox – the courts both give power and take it away from the people who use it. The question of why people choose to turn to the courts in spite of their inefficiency, injustice and violence might thus be that there exists a desire and viable possibility to put someone else through that very treatment and violence.

Responding directly to this problem of the negative experiences a person may have, one possibility is that the motivation could be something not personally experienced but something seen on television, especially when what is shown is categorized as documentary or reality. For that reason I will look into the workings of television courts, such as *Judge Judy*, *Judge Greg Mathis*, and *Judge Joe Brown* that show real people and real cases being settled before a judge. Besides offering entertainment, these shows offer unrealistic expectations of real courts and perhaps bring into existence a belief in a legal system that is on the side of the righteous.

Syndi-courts

In syndi-courts, cases are presented to the television audience as *real* legal disputes settled by a *real* judge inside a televised, *real* courtroom. The judge in the shows wears a robe and has a gavel and the parties, who are sworn in by the bailiff, must rise as the judge enters the courtroom. This spectacle takes on the aesthetics of, supposedly, real litigation, but is in fact simple arbitration.[4] The parties must agree in advance to resolve their dispute according to the arbitrator's ruling, and the decisions of the judge cannot be appealed. An obvious difference from typical arbitration, however, is that it does not take place in private, even though the cases themselves concern quite private matters. Although most of these shows use real judges, the role of the judge is in fact that of an arbitrator in a staged setting:

> The props on syndi-shows, including the gavel, the judge's robe, and the bailiff, all give the impression that the disputes are trials, being decided by a judge. Yet these props are all that the public

---

4 For more about the presentation of arbitration in Syndi-courts, see Kimball (2005).

sees and syndi-shows, as arbitration proceedings under the guise of trials, lack all that makes a trial a trial. (Lang, 2007, p. 781)

What we see is not litigation but arbitration dressed up as litigation. As Erika Lang points out, this is a form of dual misrepresentation, as the shows depict arbitration as well as trials. And this misrepresentation of the legal process is seen by millions of people every day. Consistently beating Oprah Winfrey in ratings, Judge Judy has approximately 6.4 million daily viewers – some sources even claim that she has as many as 10 million viewers a day.[5]

In an interview with Larry King, the television judge phenomenon was explained by some of the on-air judges themselves. One of them was Mablean Ephriam, at the time the host of *Divorce Court*, who was repeatedly presented as *not* being a judge: 'She's an arbitrator and not a judge,' King clarified (*Larry King Live*, 18 January 2000). This clarification seems redundant, as all the television judges act as arbitrators on the shows, but this explicit reminder that Ephriam is *not* a judge, unlike the other hosts, obscures that fact from the public.

The most striking part of what goes on in the syndi-courts, however, is the importance that the judge gives to the personal aspects of the dispute. Whereas traditional courtrooms focus on the law in question and legal procedure, the syndi-courts dwell on the personal, the self. Helle Porsdam writes about the early days of syndi-courts, pointing out that the show *The People's Court* 'dealt primarily with the most mundane aspects of daily life: sick pets, improperly cleaned laundry, overcharging repairmen, and the like', and that 'it seems to be precisely the everyday nature of the litigants and their grievances that made it so popular' (Porsdam, 1999, p. 91). Not only is the nature of the cases personal, the way they are treated follows the same model. The arbitrator only has about 15 minutes per case, and yet most of that time goes into establishing personal relationships and personal problems potentially underlying the cause of the dispute. These are often cases about debts of some sort, but before the legal aspects are brought out, the judge will usually try to find out what the parties' personal history is together. Court shows invoke a legal imagery in which the law follows everyday morals and the bad guy is humiliated and forced to pay, both in shame and in money. The judges on these shows make it seem clear who is right and who is wrong based on the personal character and moral high ground of the parties. If someone has cheated on their spouse, then they are likely also guilty of fraud, and if the personal fault can be brought to light, the legal matter is practically solved.

In *Everybody's Guide to Small Claims Court in California*, attorney Ralph Warner makes it clear that plaintiffs and defendants should keep private

---

5 See, for instance, Judge Judy Ratings on cnn.com and Judge Judy Ratings in Post-Gazette.

matters out of the dispute and act professionally. The book advises the plaintiff which terms to use when describing the person he or she is suing, and argues that a 'good case' is defined as having a strong legal basis and good evidence (Warner, 2003, p. 3/2). Warner gives an example of a dispute in which the parties wrote each other nasty letters and then tried to use them against each other in court: '[since they were not businesslike] both letters were worthless [as evidence]' (Warner, 2003, p. 6/14).

By contrast, in syndi-courts personality and private matters are the only things that are treated as interesting. In an example from *Judge Greg Mathis*, the dispute is presented as follows: 'The ex agreed to pay her rent but since their break up he hasn't paid a dime...He gave money toward the rent and is counter-suing for the money he loaned her to give her breast implant surgery.' (*Judge Greg Mathis*, 17 May 2007) So it is a matter of two possible debts, but the details of the breast implants change the tenor of the complaints. How is the matter handled by the judge?

Judge Mathis: Tell me about the relationship and what you want me to know.
Plaintiff: Me and Jerry started to date in December 2003, and a month later I moved him and three kids in, in addition to my four kids. Within a year my home was a dysfunctional Brady Bunch. His kids were awful to me.

Instead of changing the subject to that of the money, Judge Mathis allows the parties to proceed to tell him about the various ways their children have misbehaved, something completely unrelated to the case. However, these details are quite entertaining, and can potentially bring out the worst in both parties.

Another TV judge, Judge Mills Lane, explicitly states that his rulings are final and may be swayed by his personal opinions:

Plaintiff: The defendant, Zale, used to be my best friend, but now [expletive deleted].
Judge Lane: Hey, hey, hey! You, sir, are a jackass. Let's start out with that observation. You say something like that one more time – and let me tell you something else, *I am not necessarily final because I am right. I am right because I'm final. I'm it.* (shown on *Larry King Live*, 18 January 2000).

On his show, the judge may decide against you if you are being 'a jackass' and, whatever he rules, right or not, it is final.

Payback

Ralph Warner has warned us that small claims courts might be a waste of time if you're just in it for the money. There is, however, one place where if you win you can be certain to get paid. In television courts, the broadcasting company pays for the expenses and fines of the parties who appear. Helle Porsdam, when going over critiques against *The People's Court*, mentions how even the judge on the show, Judge Wapner himself, recognized some undesired side effects: 'To the extent that people don't realize that they must pay if they lose or that they presume the award will be executed immediately if they win, the show is giving litigants a misimpression of life in small-claims court.' (Porsdam, 1999, p. 97) If you win the case, the broadcasting company pays you the fine, and if you lose then they pay it for you, so you have nothing to lose. Porsdam writes that in *The People's Court*, since the production company covered the costs, 'no one lost except in principle' (Porsdam, 1999, pp. 94–5). But then why do the defendants put up a defence? Since they have no monetary obligation, why does it matter if they win or lose? It seems as if this 'principle' in which a party can win or lose is quite powerful. An example of this from Greg Mathis depicts a defendant putting up a fight:

Defendant: [The plaintiff's brother-in-law and landscape architect] She only thinks I did a bad job because she was high all the time, and if there are plants missing, it's because she smoked them! (*Judge Greg Mathis*, 16 December 2007).

This argument is not necessarily presented in order to win the case or the money, but rather to direct the embarrassment that follows a syndi-court appearance onto the other party. It bears witness to how powerful the loss in principle can be. Even though the losing parties in television courts have no money to lose, they are publicly shamed on national television: and who wants their whole town to know that they do their jobs poorly, that they are bad boyfriends, or bad people in general? The television courts offer a game of humiliation where the payback is not monetary but very much real and felt. The monetary gain seems like a weak motivator in these courts, as well as in the regular courts.

Merry's paradox about courtroom violence being used to the parties' advantage is even further enhanced by the possibilities that follow from the special nature of the syndi-courts: the public spectacle, the focus on personal flaws and, also, the circumvention of potentially abusive legal speech that in fact opens the floor for much more hurtful and damaging kinds of conversations.[6] In the television court, the only legal attributes are props and sets. The judge uses everyday language which the parties understand, and the parties get to talk essentially however and about whatever they want. But this, combined with the judges acting more aggressively than they do in a regular court, illustrates that everyday speech can be far more abusive than

---

6 See, for instance, Conley and O'Barr (1997).

legal speech. The judges can be overtly hostile, take sides and make parties feel inferior. In a case over an Ebay scam, Judge Judy yells at the defendant:

Judge Judy: You are an idiot! And a scammer! And the reason your husband isn't here today, what is your first name?
Defendant: Kelly
Judge Judy: Kelly, the reason that your husband isn't here today is that he sent you here to the lying stand because he is a coward! (*Judge Judy* (2008) 'Davenport vs Filkins')

Later, in the same case, Judge Judy repeatedly calls the defendant 'an outrageous person' and 'a thief' and yells at her not to speak. The judge accuses her of preferring to make babies instead of working, and finally comments on the defendant's being overweight.

Another example of the judge attacking a defendant can be seen in *Judge Joe Brown*:

Judge Joe Brown: Well, what do you call yourself?
Defendant: I'm a man. I'm a young man.
Judge Joe Brown: You ain't no young man. You ain't doing what a man's supposed to do…You can't look at your mama. She sitting up there about as mad at you as I am, because you've been giving her a good, hard time, haven't you? She's trying to tell you something, been sacrificing her life for you, and what are you doing? Trying to throw it away, acting like you don't know what a man is all about! (shown on *Larry King Live*, 18 January 2000).

In this verbal bullying, the judge not only attacks the defendant's illegal action, but his very manhood. Besides the judge being given rights to verbally abuse the parties who appear on the syndi-court shows, the production team ultimately has the means to edit out completely someone, or something someone said. Ultimately, no one on these shows can be held responsible for how they are presented. The victimizing violence from the court thus seems to be even harsher and more violent in the televised setting than the overlooked victims in Feeley's ethnography.

Corresponding to Merry's analysis of Dover Square, these examples illustrate that the winning party in a syndi-court has an even greater violent power than a party in a normal court. If someone wants somebody else to feel humiliated or embarrassed enough to move away, there are few greater means of persuasion than shaming them on television in front of millions of people. These disputes may not be about the money (sometimes people on these shows sue over less than $100), but they sure can be about payback.

In 'Going to Court', Sally Merry tells the story of two boys who used to be friends, until one day one of them beats up the other and steals his bike.

Billy, the owner of the bike, sues his aggressor. He wins the case, but is still unhappy. First, because he will not receive the money he has been promised and, second, he had stolen the bike to begin with, so his concern was not actually about lost money. He was upset, Merry explains, because his former friend treated him so badly, and that they were no longer friends. The court has addressed the wrong issue – the television court, on the other hand, would certainly have allowed the boys to let out their feelings about each other and their broken friendship, and perhaps even offered some emotional healing.

One reason why people, such as Billy, take cases with underlying personal motives to court might be that they think that is what courts are for because 'they have seen it on TV'. The television courts offer false expectations on what the role of a judge is and what the role of justice is, as well as an alternative for where to turn to blow off steam. They create false expectations about real courts, as well as a real, legal option for people with small claim disputes.

The strength and danger of these shows is that they let people talk. People get to express themselves and they are led to believe that in a court of law they can talk about their emotions. In the regular courtroom, individuals are transformed into parties, their suffering becomes a 'case', their story a number, and their experience reduced to general, legal terms. Indeed, there is no room for the particular or the self. With the television courts, in contrast, the very focus is instead on the self, and the more particular the better. The television courts are even more violent and more mundanely normative and moral in their message than is a regular court, but they do give people the opportunity to talk about what they find important, and they spread a message that the bad guy must also be wrong *legally speaking*, and may be punished through humiliation. So, although these courts do offer a place for parties to air the private nature of their dispute, the price paid for this televised therapy session is high: for the parties who end up disappointed and dissatisfied; and for the legal system left to handle so-called 'garbage cases' that show up as a result of the legal consciousness formed on a false picture of justice that can make people believe that in court they can prevail if they have strong emotional or moral grounds for their case.

Helle Porsdam writes that:

> Changes have unmistakably come about in the past fifteen years as a result of *The People's Court*. Not everyone agrees that these changes are for the better, though. It may well be that the program has helped increase public awareness of the law, critics concede, but what has also increased is the caseload of once-obscure small-claims courts. (Porsdam, 1999, p. 97)

She quotes Judge Abner J Mikva's critique of syndi-courts: 'Lawsuits over the thickness of a slice of pizza, for heaven's sake' and asks 'how much more frivolous can it get?' (Porsdam, 1999, p. 97)

Just talk

Three cases in the West Los Angeles Traffic Court leave me wondering about emotional aspects of people who show up in court. First there is Julia, who was silenced by the judge and later told me how unprofessional she thought he was. I asked her what she wanted the judge to do differently, 'Just let me explain,' she said and looked down.

Another woman in the same courtroom is sitting behind me. She is crying and has been during the whole hearings. I offer her some tissue and she tells me, without my asking, that her grandmother passed away earlier that day and 'they probably think I am crying because of the fines'. I ask if she wishes the judge would know this, if it might be important for her case, but she says 'no'. Later on, the judge actually lets her off remarkably lightly. 'Thank you!' she exclaims, 'I really needed some good news today,' she continues, and doesn't move. I could not help but think that standing still and looking at the judge was an expression of her hoping that he would ask her why she needed good news this very day. Her telling me all about it a little while before certainly showed that she felt a need to talk about it.

My third example is a woman I call Ms Yun, an Asian woman in her forties. She pleads not guilty, but then tries to force the judge to hear her story about what happened: 'You seem like a very kind and smart judge. Maybe you could give me some advice?' The judge explains why it is illegal for him to advise her in her case. 'But just let me explain in two sentences what happened!' she begs. She is told to 'save it for the trial, that's what the trial is for'. She tries again and explains to the judge that if he could just hear her out, they could solve this whole misunderstanding today. 'I cannot solve the problems of the world here, just register your plea and assign you a trial date, but if you are not guilty then you should always plead not guilty, you are absolutely right about that,' he tells her, as he rushes out and the bailiff asks her to leave. I talk to Ms Yun afterwards and ask her if she has ever been to court before. Before she even answers that question she goes on for quite a while about how she did indeed stop for the stop sign, and tells me the whole story about the unfair policeman, and how she was in a hurry because she runs her own business. I get the whole story first, and only afterwards is she willing to answer any questions. Before she can even begin to talk about anything else, she needs to get her story out and off her chest. All that Ms Yun, the crying woman, Julie and Billy wanted was to be heard.

Judge Robert in traffic court acted much like a syndi-court judge with his own strict rules. One woman even suggested to me that he was fishing for his own show: 'This is LA!' she tells me, 'Everybody's going to Hollywood!' I ask her if she would watch it if he did have his own show: 'I want to say no, because he acted like a real jerk, but honestly, I probably would.' Most people left the court feeling disappointed, having arrived with the belief that they would be allowed to talk. Only one person leaves the judge with a positive impression. Ms Yun tells me she really liked the judge. 'He inspired me,' she tells me. 'He was different and does things differently, I think I can also do things differently! He gave me advice without knowing it!' Even though Ms Yun had not understood the meaning of an arraignment and was annoyed with the fact that she had to come back again, she was happy with her day in court, thanks to the 'lovely, funny and inspirational judge'. When asked if she watches syndi-shows, Ms Yun first answers reluctantly saying that she did not like them. 'They over-exaggerate,' she says, but, when she continues to describe why she feels that way, it becomes clear that she is an avid viewer of more than one show and that she forms a deep personal connection with many of the people on them. I ask all the people I speak with during my visits to the traffic court if they watch syndi-courts, and sure enough, they all do. They all have their favourites and can even recall the latest cases they have seen. They are happy to compare the judge they met with the judges they know and like, or even dislike, from TV.

Concluding notes

The people I interviewed were of different genders, ages, ethnicities and social classes. Some frequented traffic courts or small claims courts often, others were there for the first time. I asked them all if they had read the leaflets or online information that the court provided with details about what to expect and how to prepare, and most of them had not. There was only one question that they all answered the same way: namely whether or not they watched syndi-court shows – which each and every one of them did. Furthermore, they all enjoyed them, even if more or less openly.

Unquestionably, popular culture is being influenced by law, and I believe that it is also true that our legal consciousnesses and expectations are being informed by popular culture. Who knows which came first? Did Perry Mason act like an average lawyer or did lawyers at some point begin acting like and were influenced by Perry Mason? Regardless, courts are full of people who think that they know what they are in for based on what they have seen on TV. When trying to piece together the puzzle of why people address courts with 'garbage cases', personal issues, poor preparation, and inexplicable expectations, it is time to consider the real impact of those real judges, and real cases, in the phony, but real, television courts.

References

Conley, J M and W M O'Barr (1998) *Just Words, Law, Language, and Power* (Chicago: University of Chicago Press)

Dahlberg, L (2009) 'Emotional Tropes in the Courtroom: On Representation of Affect and Emotion in Legal Court Proceedings' **21** *Nordic Theatre Studies* 129–52

Ewick, P and S S Silbey, (1992) 'Conformity, Contestation, and Resistance: An Account of Legal Consciousness' **26**(3) *New England Law Review* 731–49

Feeley, M (1992 [1979]) *The Process is the Punishment: Handling Cases in a Lower Criminal Court* (New York: Russell Sage)

Goodrich, P (1987) *Legal Discourse: Studies in Linguistics, Rhetoric and Legal Analysis* (London/New York: Macmillan and St Martin's Press)

Goodrich, P (1990) *Languages of Law: From Logics of Memory to Nomadic Masks* (London: Weidenfeld & Nicolson)

Heinrick, J (2006) 'Everyone's an Expert: The CSI Effect's Negative Impact on Juries' (autumn) *The Triple Helix*

Kimball, P Z (2005) 'Syndi-Court Justice: Judge Judy and Exploitation of Arbitration' **4**(1)*Journal of American Arbititration*

Lang, E (2007) 'The Reality of Courtroom Television Shows: Should the Model Code of Judicial Conduct Apply to TV Judges?' (summer) *Georgetown Journal of Legal Ethics* 779–3

Merry, S (1979) 'Going to Court: Strategies of Dispute Management in an American Urban Neighborhood' **13**(4) *Law and Society Review* 891–925

Merry, S (1990) *Getting Justice and Getting Even: Legal Consciousness Among Working-Class Americans* (Chicago: University of Chicago Press)

Peters, J (2005) 'Law, Literature and the Vanishing Reel: On the Future of an Interdisciplinary Illusion' **112**(2) (March) *PMLA* 442–53

Porsdam, H (1999) *Legally Speaking, Contemporary American Culture and the Law* (Amherst, MA: University of Massachusetts Press)

Richland, J B (2005) 'What are You Going to Do with the Village's Knowledge? Talking Tradition, Talking Law in Hopi Tribal Court' **39** *Law and Society Review* 235–71

Richland, J B (2008) *Arguing with Tradition: The Language of Law in Hopi Tribal Court* (Chicago and London: University of Chicago Press)

Sarat, A and J Simon (eds) (2003) *Cultural Analysis, Cultural Studies, and the Law: Moving Beyond Legal Realism* (Durham, NC: Duke University Press)

Sherwin, R S (2000) *When Law Goes Pop: The Vanishing Line Between Law and Popular Culture* (Chicago: Chicago University Press)

Silbey, S (2005) 'After Legal Consciousness' **1** *Annual Review of Law and Social Science* 323–68

Tanase, T (1995) 'The Management of Disputes: Automobile Accident Compensation in Japan' in R Abel (ed.), *Law and Society Reader* (New York: New York University Press)

Warner, R (2003) *Everybody's Guide to Small Claims Court in California* (Berkeley, CA: Nolo)

Television shows

Divorce Court, Twentieth Century Fox Film Corporation, 1999–2008

Judge Greg Mathis (17 May 2007, 16 December 2007) Blackpearl Productions, 1999–2008

Judge Joe Brown, CBS Paramount Television, 1998–2008

Judge Judy (2008) 'Davenport vs Filkin', *Judge Judy, Second to None* (DVD), CBS Paramount Television, 1996–2008

Larry King Live, 'TV Judges Take their Stands' (18 January 2000, 9 pm) CNN, 1985–2010

Websites

Judge Judy Ratings on cnn.com, available at http://marquee.blogs.cnn.com/2010/06/10/judge-judy-tops-oprah-in-rankings/

Judge Judy Ratings in Post-Gazette, available at www.post-gazette.com/pg/08359/937221-42.stm

4
Female Genital Cutting, Migration and the Art of Legal Boundary Maintenance

Caroline Wiedmer

Introduction

A constantly evolving swirl of competing discourses, stories, images and scripts shape both our sense of the world we inhabit and who we are in this world. Jerome Bruner has referred to this assemblage of shifting narratives as a 'communal tool kit', a fund of knowledge that keeps us updated about ways in which our culture changes and how we should behave in order to get on in the world (Bruner, 2003). Not surprisingly, the idea of the nation and of national belonging or national identity continues to provide a tidy and compelling frame for how we think about culture – despite numerous attempts to reveal the constructed, indeed invented, nature of the nation and of nationhood. And speaking from within this frame, one obvious way to delineate national belonging has always been via stories about those who do not belong, namely a nation's immigrants.

Our communal toolbox, I would like to suggest, has a special compartment for stories about the 'Other', and these stories are often made compelling because they cast this Other variously as threatening, or pitiful, or primitive – as characters at any rate, who in their perceived otherness not only confirm, but also constitute, our own legitimacy, our own normalcy and our own innate sense of belonging. If these cultural practices are so at odds with prevailing customs that they must be regulated or even 'fixed' by a national legal system in a court of law, all the better. For the many public discussions leading up to the creation of a piece of legislation – in such forums as the parliament, in the tools of direct democracy, the referenda and popular initiatives, and in the omnipresent media – combine to offer a public drama in which everyone is invited to participate, and which, in fact, no one can escape. And often this participation is a way to imagine, perform and rehearse not only one's national identity and one's position within the social hierarchy, but also one's attitudes with regard to race, sexuality and gender.

Moreover, the emotions one gets to experience while playing in the drama, be they righteous indignation at a perceived wrong or pity for perceived victims, tend to reflect one's cultural bias. Quite aside from the content and aims of any given legislation concerning the Other, the negotiation, representation and application of law is a useful instrument with which to conserve societal norms and values, shape forms of relative belonging, fill fissures in societal inconsistencies, and cast one's own government as protector and objective arbiter of right and wrong.

I propose to embark on an exploration of the mechanism by which law works to negotiate the fragile line between them and us by way of recent legislation regarding female genital cutting (FGC) in Switzerland. And since legislation of this nature never comes to pass in a cultural vacuum, I will read the emerging discourse that surrounded this particular piece of legislation within two contexts: first, within the international debates about female cutting; second, within the national debates about foreigners which have in recent years resulted in rather astounding examples of xenophobia and racism in Switzerland. What is particularly striking about the various stories that animate these contexts are the recurring figures of victim, villain and hero that tend to anchor the protagonists in the public imaginary in ways that reproduce social hierarchies and confirm national boundaries. These recurrences raise the following questions: how does the victim discourse construct both the harmed and the healers, the victims and the persecutors in the context of female genital cutting, and what effect do these constructions have beyond the stated aim of protecting children and women? How does the law function as a forum for staging the drama of victimization and heroism and what are the implications of this drama for maintaining a 'civilized state'? And, finally, how is the victimized Other used at once to shore up the notion of the emancipated woman and to elide vexing issues in Switzerland's gender order?

Methodologically, I explore the interplay of discursive strategies across a number of narrative locales, in order to consider three interlocking issues. In the first section, I consider the mechanism and ramifications of the victim discourse. In the second section, I look at how the victim discourse plays in the global debates among Western and non-Western critics of FGC which form the background to the Swiss debate. In the last section, I analyse how the discourse plays itself out on the national stage, on the one hand, in the legislation of FGC and, on the other hand, in two political initiatives which were brought to a vote during roughly the same time period in Switzerland – one concerning the expulsion of criminal foreigners, the other a ban on minarets. In this last section, I am particularly interested in the way the legal system is harnessed to construct what I will suggest are cover narratives that deflect attention away from, rather than focusing on, the fragile state of gender equity and the controversial asylum practices in Switzerland.

The discursive economies of injury and protection

Most of us are familiar with stories of FGC, often told from a first-person perspective by children, teenagers and adults who have undergone or participated in the act of cutting. Their accounts typically are framed as tales of helplessness, violence, agonizing pain and life-altering consequences. They are tales of quintessential victimhood which appear, in more or less graphic detail: in youth books such as Cristina Kessler's story about Sierra Leone, *No Condition is Permanent* (Kessler, 2000) and Pat Lowery Collins' *The Fattening Hut* (Collins, 2003); in novels, such as Alice Walker's *Possessing the Secret of Joy* (Walker, 1993); in documentaries, such as *Warrior Marks*, which Walker produced with film-maker Pratibha Parmar (1993b); and in made-for-TV documentaries, such as Linda May Kallenstein's *The Cut* on FGC in Kenya which was aired on CNN's Voices of Africa (Kallenstein, 2009). They appear in the literature of aid organizations such as the World Health Organization, the United Nations and UNICEF; they appear in medical reports, in newspaper accounts, in the minutes of parliamentary discussions and in courtroom judgments. How do these stories work to frame the discourse around FGC, to produce subject positions, and to create a docking station for the imagination?

The genre of first-hand accounts of atrocities is familiar from progressive movements ranging from the abolitionist movement in the mid-1900s (which used the reports by runaway slaves to mobilize sympathy for its cause), to more contemporary feminist and postcolonial movements (which marshalled the autobiographical to underscore the personal in the political). It has been used widely by those in power to give voice to the oppressed, to garner support and to bring about political change. And those in power have most often been Westerners living in democratic societies who react when addressed on an affective plane that appeals to the liberal sensibilities of the modern democratic subjects. The stories of the marginalized and victimized work to galvanize us because they can offer the attractive subject positions of helper and saviour. This mechanism becomes problematic when, in order for the helpers and saviours to stay permanently in these attractive positions, victims are required to stay permanently in theirs.

The typical Western framing of reports on FGC have over the last two decades assumed a certain gruesome narrative sameness whether they are told in Egypt, in Sierra Leone or in the Gambia, and they have a certain ineluctability to them: a young girl is delivered to an elderly female cutter who wields a rusty instrument. The girl is then held down by people she trusts and her genitals are cut in such a way that she will suffer for the rest of her life. Her legs are then bound together and she is accepted back into her community, a person robbed of her sexuality and her agency. The narrative sequence is usually the same, giving the impression that no matter where the cutting occurs, how it is performed and for what reason, there is a universality to the victim that smooths over any cultural or religious differences. In this sense, the narratives render the protagonist oddly ahistorical and acultural: she is stripped of her individuality. The sameness of these reports and images also informs us Western readers how to think about all women who have migrated to the West from countries in which FGC is practised, regardless of whether these women are cut or not. In other words, the narratives have become part of the white imaginary of the black or brown immigrant female.

There have been a number of publications that explore the discursive positioning of the Muslim woman as victim that are helpful in thinking through the theoretical implications of the mechanisms at play with regard to FGC in Switzerland (Kahf, 1999; Abu-Lughod, 2002; Razack, 2008; Kilic, Saharso and Sauer, 2008; Jacobson and Stenvoll, 2010). In comparing the figures of the Muslim woman and the foreign sex-worker in Norway, Christine Jacobson and Dag Stenvoll draw on Wendy Brown's concept of tolerance as a crucial component in the 'civilizational discourse' that counterposes the free, tolerant and civilized West to the unfree, intolerant and barbaric non-West. Brown writes in this context:

> In the mid-nineteenth through the mid-twentieth centuries, the West imagined itself as standing for civilization against primitivism, and in the cold years for freedom against tyranny; now these two recent histories are merged in the warring figures of the free, the tolerant, and the civilized on the one side, and the fundamentalist, the intolerant and the barbaric on the other. (Brown, 2008, p. 6)

Some people, by falling outside the norm, Brown concludes, are marked as subject to being tolerated while others constitute the norm by their very ability to tolerate difference. Those who are marked as being tolerated are less autonomous, less able to participate in the universal and are, ultimately, less free (Jacobson and Stenvoll, 2010, p. 273).

As Jacobson and Stenvoll point out, the victim discourse operates much like the tolerance discourse: it creates social hierarchies that demarcate the helpers and healers and protectors from the injured and harmed and threatened (Jacobson and Stenvoll, 2010, p. 273). These tend to be hierarchies that are very difficult to escape, especially since they are not only gendered but also racialized and as such they work with visual cues that are specific to place and time. For instance, in the West, today's discursive regimes will often automatically mark women with black skin, veils and burkhas as associated with victim status whereas white women in Western clothing will not be, regardless of their particular histories. The racialized aspect of the marking is particularly robust. By contrast, when the victims are white, and victim status results from acts of rape or domestic violence, then the status is seen to be temporary, particular and individualized. In the case of genital cutting, the victim status becomes permanent, a marker of a group identity that lies outside of the norm (Jacobson and Stenvoll, 2011).

Within the context of law, victim status has been of great import: it has served as a significant recourse for women and minority groups to acknowledge rights and injuries in areas such as domestic violence and rape. In the case of female cutting, and other cases of gender-based persecutions, such as honour killings and forced marriage, a number of jurisdictions have created laws and policies that help women gain political asylum and legal entry. In the USA and France, for instance, FGC was added to the roster of possible grounds for asylum claims, while the practice in many European countries, Switzerland among them, has been codified as a punishable crime (Oxford, 2005). While these changes in various legal institutions have obvious merits for women fleeing gendered harm, Connie Oxford has argued that their implementation often produces a sense of victimization in the migrant women where before there was none, even as they make visible cultural assumptions about femininity and masculinity, sexuality and women's agency (Oxford, 2005, p. 18). Victim status then is a double-edged sword: while it can aid individuals in gaining rights and protection, it also sometimes suggests victimhood where none is perceived on the part of the 'victims', and when women willingly or out of necessity don the role of victim, it tends to adhere to them permanently and as such affect their standing in society.

Competing discourses: female genital cutting

The sheer mass of recurring accounts of personal experience across diverse narrative and geographical locales seems to imply a consensus among Western and non-Western critics regarding the discursive framing of FGC. This impression, however, proves to be inaccurate. In fact, the manner in which knowledge about FGC – variously also referred to as female circumcision or female genital mutilation – has been framed, represented and distributed has been a hotly debated topic for decades among Western (Daly, 1978; Hosken, 1979; Walker and Parmar, 1993a; Nussbaum and Glover, 1995; Nussbaum, 2000; Goldberg, 2009), non-Western (Narayan, 1997; Mohanty, 2003; Ahmadu, 2007) and so-called transnational (Gruenbaum, 2001; Boddy, 2007; Smith, 2011) feminists, academics, intellectuals and activists. The very language that is used to describe the procedure heralds the range of opinions currently polarizing the debate: while critics who speak of female genital mutilation are seen, often by non-Western critics, to take a judgmental stance that is informed by Western ideas of gender and agency; those who take an international feminist stance often speak of cutting; while those who want to be seen as taking a neutral position refer to circumcision.

Though the positions of the two dominant strands of discourse are clearly different, no position denies that FGC may be harmful to the girls and women affected, and most of the participants in the debate fight against the practice from within their own intellectual and cultural contexts. The currency of the debate is representation and the central question is about who frames and controls the rhetoric of FGC and what subject positions are made available to women who practise it. According to recent critical voices from non-Western or transnational intellectuals, Western or 'First World' critics of the practice have controlled the rhetoric on female cutting since colonial times (Gruenbaum, 2001; Boddy, 2007; Smith, 2011). The practice of cutting first came to the attention of the Western world in reports from colonial administrators in the 1930s, who uniformly described it as barbaric and primitive, yet another example in a long line of cultural practices that marked the colonial subject as inferior. Knowledge about cutting became widespread in the West only in the 1970s when feminists such as Gloria Steinem and Mary Daly turned their attention to the practice in the context of second-wave feminism (Bell, 2005). The real reason for genital mutilation, Steinem wrote in her explosive 1980 article in *Ms* magazine, using feminist language of the time, 'can only be understood in the context of the patriarchy: men must control women's bodies as the means of production, and thus repress the independent power of women's sexuality' (Steinem, 1980). This origin of public discourse about FGC in part gave rise to today's commonly held and quickly reproduced interpretation that FGC is above all else a means by which men control women by regulating their sexual agency, an interpretation that is not uniformly shared by women who have undergone the procedure.

The 1990s saw a veritable explosion of attention to the topic in which contributions were made on a number of fronts: by international organizations, such as the United Nations, which condemned 'female genital mutilation' as a violation of the person and called for a ban on the practice in 1994, despite outcries by African feminists; and by the World Conference for Women, which in its meeting in Beijing in 1995 issued a call for an immediate end to the practice. The medical community itself was somewhat divided: on the one hand, it had begun to publish reports on the prevalence and risks associated with the practice, while other reports suggested that the risks said to be associated with female genital cutting might have been exaggerated (Obermeyer, 1999; Morison, 2001; Obermeyer, 2005). The legal systems of various countries, in the meantime, began to consider measures by which to address the issue (Rahman and Toubia, 2000).

Conversely, non-Western or internationalist intellectuals tend to criticize the Western discourse that was produced and disseminated by the powerful institutions of Western medicine, law and aid organizations as judgmental, ethnocentric, universalist and voyeuristic – a powerful framing of FGC that fails to take into account the differences in ethnicities, religions, classes and beliefs of the women directly involved in the practice (Ahmadu, 2007; Boddy, 2007; Gruenbaum, 2001; Smith, 2011). Instead, Western critics are perceived as leaping to conclusions about circumstances that:

> they've only presumed to understand, citing unverified statistics culled from other disparaging publications, relying on self-reference and reiteration to create the truth of their cause. Their typical verdict: that female genital cutting regularly kills, has no valid meaning, and is inflicted on ignorant and powerless women by sadistic men. (Boddy, 2007, p. 3)

As cultural anthropologist Richard Shweder sums it up, 'the global campaign against what has been gratuitously and invidiously labelled "female genital mutilation" remains a flawed game whose rules have been fixed by the rich nations of the world' (Shweder, 2002, p. 38).

Moreover, the Western discourse is said to control the global debate without appreciably affecting or changing the prevalence of the practice itself. In fact, it would seem that neither the rhetoric nor the legislation of the West has come close to fulfilling its aim of eradicating FGC: the practice of cutting continues not only in those societies where it forms part of the tradition but in the diaspora as well (Coleman, 1998; Thomas, 2000; Robertson, 2002, p. 196). In this context, Obioma Nnaemeka speaks of the failure of Western feminists to create a site of true collaboration and partnership with so-called 'Third World' women.

> A crucial dimension of collaborative schemes and viable strategies [she writes] entails developing a rapprochement with the affected population, tapping into the perspective of the indigenous perspectives about the rhythms of change and conceding the local women the right to take the lead in identifying their needs and formulating their solutions. (Nnaemeka, 2005, p. 192)

A more productive and ethical discourse, according to Courtney Smith, 'would thus be based upon the experiences, desires and interests of women who undergo FGC, *as they define them*, rather than employing a universal category of woman, built upon the bodies of normalized Western women' (Smith, 2011, p. 28, emphasis in original).

The case of FGC, then, is far more complex than consumers of mainstream Western media have been led to believe: it is a debate that carries with it struggles over the meaning of sexuality, subject position, agency and gender within different cultural spheres, and it highlights the continued power differential between the mainly white, Western activists and intellectuals who want to help and whose voices are heard on a number of cultural platforms, and the mainly black, African activists who are affected and whose voices have tended to be drowned out in the West. As I turn to the Swiss context to explore how this global debate over the meaning of FGC is inflected through the prism of a recent trial in Switzerland and a new piece of legislation, my focus returns to the questions posed at the outset. How does the discourse surrounding FGC cast immigrant and Swiss women? What does the victimhood status imply for the relationship of citizens to state and to the outsider of the state? And, finally, what sorts of deficits does the victimhood discourse cover up in those who get to play saviour to its victims?

The Swiss context

Every law has its history, and it is with the history of the new legislation on FGC in Switzerland that I want to start this section, especially since this particular piece of legislation begins with a curious fact: when, in 2005, a first attempt was made to draft it, there was already what many considered a perfectly serviceable law in place, namely the law against bodily harm, set out in Article 122 of the Swiss Criminal Code. (Schweizerisches Strafgesetzbuch (StGB)). This law states that FGC constitutes a punishable action against physical intactness, whereby types II and III in the current four-tier classification scheme of female circumcision articulated by the World Health Organization (excision of the clitoris and infibulations, see Article 122 StGB) constitute grievous bodily injury, and types I and IV (removal of the clitoral foreskin and 'diverse practices', see Article 123 StGB) constitute simple bodily injury.

The impulse to change this law ostensibly came from the publication of a 2004 legal study commissioned by UNICEF, which estimated that, at that time, approximately 7000 women and girls living in Switzerland were either circumcised or were at risk from the practice, and that in all probability female circumcision was also being performed in Switzerland (Trechsel and Schlauri, 2004). In March 2005, National Councillor Maria Roth-Bernasconi submitted a parliamentary motion demanding that the federal government propose a law explicitly outlawing all forms of female circumcision. She based her argument not only on the UNICEF report, but also on a report issued by the European council in 2001 that called for an information campaign to enlighten medical personnel and refugee women about the 'dangerous consequences of sexual mutilation for the health, physical integrity and dignity of the woman and her right to self-realization, as well as about customs and traditions that go against human rights' (Roth-Bernasconi, 2005). With this language, Roth-Bernasconi aligns herself squarely with the hegemonic Western discourse on the issue of FGC, which positions the African immigrant woman as a victim whose physical integrity and dignity have been breached, whose agency is endangered, and who comes from a culture that contravenes some of the most dearly held tenets of the Western world, namely human rights.

In 2008, three years after the initial motion was filed by Roth-Bernasconi, the first case of female cutting came before a Swiss court of law. The trial was based on an incident that had occurred some 12 years earlier, in 1996, in the canton of Zurich, and its main protagonists were a two-year old girl and her parents, originally from Somalia. These are the basic facts of the case: the parents, who at the time of the incident had lived in Switzerland for two years as asylum seekers, had had their daughter cut by an itinerant Somalian cutter because, as they would say later, they were not sure that they were going to be able to stay in Switzerland and they wanted to ensure that their daughter would have equal chances in Somalia should their request for asylum be turned down. In September of 2007 – some 11 years after the cutting – the parents, who had been granted asylum and were now applying for citizenship, were asked during an interview for the citizenship application whether their daughters had been circumcised. They answered truthfully that they had indeed had their eldest daughter circumcised in 1996. The girl, 13 by the time of the interview, was subsequently examined by a gynaecologist and the fact that she had undergone cutting was reported to the social services. The latter in turn filed charges with the cantonal court against the girl's parents; the parents were arrested, and a suit was brought against them by the canton of Zurich. In June 2009, the couple was found guilty of incitement to grievous bodily injury by the highest court of the canton of Zurich and sentenced to a two-year conditional jail term. As a result, the citizenship process for the entire family was put on hold.

The case was broadly reported in newspapers and television reports across Switzerland. To show how the mechanisms of the victim discourse operate I will focus on one report of the trial, published in June 2008 by the *Neue Zürcher Zeitung* (NZZ, 2008), one of the leading Swiss newspapers, generally known for its measured tone and its rather conservative positions. While all of the reports I read were very similar in tone and attitude, I will focus on this report in particular because the NZZ has one of the highest circulations in Switzerland and tends to be instrumental in forming opinion across the political spectrum. In my analysis, I focus on the following questions: how is the black female subject – positioned as she is at the critical intersections of ethnicity and gender, on the one hand, and guilt and victimhood on the other, and between the cultural expectations of two societies – put on display both in the newspaper report and in the courtroom drama? To what extent are black women's voices and social realities respected, contained or elided? What sort of ideological slant does this kind of reporting have, and what sort of discursive aims are pursued by it?

The newspaper report begins dramatically:

> Rarely were consternation and dismay so palpable in the chambers of the Zurich cantonal court, so close together, and shared by all those present, as during yesterday's trial. The Somalian husband and father of eight wept during the summation and stammered words of apology over and over again. His wife, who as a child had been tortured with the most invasive form of circumcision in her country of origin, spoke of the honour and purity of cut women, how she had been proud of the mutilations she had suffered and had not known until 1998 that there even existed women who were not circumcised, or that the procedure was not required by any religion. She had only learned this in her country of refuge, Switzerland, but that insight had come two years too late. (*NZZ*, 2008, my translation)

What we find here at the very beginning of the report is a happy ending of sorts: regret, insight and enlightenment on the part of the parents, empathy on the part of the reporter, and a catharsis that unifies everyone in the courtroom, eliding whatever differences might have existed among the various protagonists. The complex and layered story of the Somalian woman is at the centre of the narrative. She is the embodiment of traditional femininity as codified by her culture of origin even as she is portrayed as the ultimate victim of a custom deemed barbaric by her new cultural surroundings, which are presumed to have enlightened her. Because her story spans two cultures, each with its own contradictory gendering mechanisms, she pivots from innocent victim, who had understood FGC as bestowing value upon her and her daughter's womanhood, to enlightened but guilty perpetrator, who has had to accept her own circumcision, and, more importantly, that of her daughter, as mutilation. The verdict of the judge is relatively mild: two years' conditional instead of the possible ten years of prison for incitement to grievous bodily harm. Although the judge, according to the newspaper report, showed 'a great deal of understanding for the good intentions of the couple based on their cultural background and on what they knew in 1996, three years after they had entered Switzerland as asylum seekers', he emphasized that 'such procedures constitute a grievous injury to the bodily integrity and dignity of a woman'. The mother's crime, then, is represented as a misreading of a proper performance of femininity in her new cultural context, and the trial a reminder of the proper performance, not simply to her, but, more importantly, to a wider audience.

If circumcision in Somalia symbolizes purity and promises successful integration into society, in Switzerland it mutates into its opposite and becomes an actual hindrance to successful integration. Recall that what Swiss law defined as a criminal act had been discovered during the process of becoming citizens: in other words, at exactly the moment at which the parents' full social and political integration should have been achieved. Hence, according to the judge, who lauds the fact that the two younger daughters had not been circumcised, the trajectory of successful integration can be charted from the missing clitoris of the eldest daughter to the intact organs of the two younger children – a symbol for the internalized transformation in the transition from one cultural context to another.

But in the end the daughter's missing clitoris – its excision a radical symbol of otherness – cannot simply be contained in a pleasing happy end, at least not for the Somalian family. While the outcome of the trial was relatively mild, the real punishment was meted out by the immigration officials: hearing of the verdict, they decided to halt the immigration process and, at least temporarily, deny the applicants Swiss citizenship. The applicants had, after all, become convicted criminals. Their conviction on charges of FGC then, marked the defendants as irredeemably Other and criminal, not worthy of belonging. The story of the courtroom drama, as reported in the *NZZ*, in which all participants were consolidated into a community of likeminded persons, was thereby transformed into a story of expulsion in the aftermath of the trial. Of course, the voice we never hear at all in this story is that of the young girl on whose behalf the parents were charged. The closest we come to her is in a detailed description of the procedure, which was performed for 250 Swiss francs on a kitchen table when she was a toddler (*NZZ*, 2008). In that sense, she is the ultimate victim, doubly punished: first with a procedure that will forever mark her as mutilated in her country of residence; second, by a decision that takes this very mutilation as a reason to keep her safely on the outside of the society in which she grew up by denying her not only citizenship rights, but a voice as well.

It is a story that confirms the power on the part of the host country to be able to determine which narrative is legitimate and which is not. It is, moreover, the story of the ignorant and primitive immigrant who has learned a lesson from the host culture, an immigrant who apologizes and promises not only to act as the dominant culture demands, but to assume its values. In this process, it is not only and perhaps not primarily the black female body that is protected but the host country's ability to dictate what it means to be feminine and to articulate the paternalistic relationship to the Other in such a way as to appear generous and just.

In December 2010, some two years after the first court case, the Swiss Parliament met to vote on a new piece of legislation outlawing all forms of genital mutilation on persons living in Switzerland, even if the circumcision was performed outside of Switzerland and even if an adult woman chooses to be cut. This last clause is striking and bears repetition: even if a woman wishes to be cut, the law forbids this, thereby taking away her agency over her own body. This, we may recall, is precisely the same gesture the act of genital cutting is usually accused of. This clause in fact marks this new law as a further evolution from the one it has replaced, not only because it goes further in its jurisdiction, but – more importantly – in that it articulates more clearly the relationship between victim and protector/state. Whatever autonomy is left to the migrant woman is conditional upon its fit within the dominant standards of behaviour. Rather than coming to the rescue of victimized migrant women, as Roth-Bernasconi's motion is generally read, the new law accentuates the social hierarchy that places the marked migrant women at the bottom, a move which, if anything, manages to further victimize her.

But if the new law on FGC in Switzerland does not (only) rescue the migrant girls and women who are thought to be threatened, whom or what does it rescue? As Brown argues, victim discourses can be interpreted as means to depoliticize democracies by 'removing a political phenomenon from comprehension of its *historical* emergence and from a recognition of the *powers* that produce and contour it' (Brown, 2006, p. 15, emphasis in the original). The causalities that are found in narratives such as the one about the Somalian family tend to explain injury as resulting from crime or from backward customs in primitive cultures, or as ignorance – all causes that place the responsibility outside of the nation state – rather than issuing from a government's position on topics such as asylum politics, immigration law, gender equity and so forth (Jacobson and Stenvoll, 2010, p. 280). In the case of the Somalian family, the narrative as presented in the *NZZ*, or any of the other media reports, neither lingers on the fact that the parents had to live in Switzerland as asylum seekers in difficult circumstances and without counselling or support before hearing whether they could stay, nor does it delve into the fact that they were denied citizenship in the end because they had acted in what they considered their daughter's best interest at the time. The victim discourse instead rescues the state and its functionaries from having to take responsibility for at least part of the suffering and from the necessity to confront difficult issues having to do with their asylum policies.

There is another figure that the victim discourse rescues, and that is the idealized figure of the emancipated Swiss woman. By using her allotted political power, Roth-Bernasconi and others in Parliament (recall that the vote to accept the the new legislation was unanimous) appropriated the saviour position, speaking as feminists on behalf of the rescued and masking the struggles Swiss women themselves continue to face in everyday life. Having gained the right to vote on the federal level in 1971 and on the cantonal level in a few cantons as late as the mid-1990s, a number of issues, such as lower pay for similar work, insufficient day-care provision and a preponderance of single mothers among the working poor, continue to face women in Switzerland. The new law on circumcision along with the discussions that surrounded its introduction acts as a cover narrative in which the idealized Swiss woman is positioned in the powerful role of saviour thus deflecting attention away from the these long-standing problems.

Intersections with discourses about the Other

The manoeuvre of self-rescue through the depoliticization of the state is particularly understandable within the context of Switzerland's asylum and immigrant politics of recent years. In 2005, as Roth-Bernasconi was preparing to hand in her motion on FGC, there was a small war waging in Switzerland over the impending revision of the asylum law which was ultimately approved by two-thirds of the population in 2006.[1] This new legislation, so claims Amnesty International, goes against human rights as defined in the Geneva Convention (Information Platform humanrights.ch, 2007) mainly because it requires asylum seekers to produce official papers within 48 hours of their application. Following closely on the heels of the revision of the asylum law, came the so-called *Initiative für die Ausschaffung krimineller Ausländer*, or the initiative for the expulsion of criminal foreigners, initiated in 2007 by the populist party, the so-called Schweizerische Volkspartei (SVP) or Swiss People's Party, and the initiative on the ban on minarets which came to a vote in 2009, also courtesy of the populist party. These initiatives were highly controversial and highly visible in Switzerland both before they came to a popular vote and after, and both were accepted by a majority: 52.9 per cent in the case of the expulsion initiative in November 2010 and 57.5 per cent in the case of the ban on minarets in November 2009.

These two initiatives in particular were accompanied by propaganda that became widely notorious for its racist content, not only in Switzerland but beyond. The so-called sheep poster, used as propaganda in the expulsion

---

1 The new asylum law included longer prison sentences for asylum seekers who resist being sent away, the reduction of social help to the absolute minimum for asylum seekers who were denied asylum but had not yet left the country, and the demand that applicants for asylum must be able to present papers within 48 hours of application. This last condition in particular was considered to go against the Geneva Convention on human rights because asylum seekers from war-torn countries cannot always be expected to have their papers in order.

initiative features three white sheep pictured against a backdrop of the Swiss flag kicking a fourth, black, sheep off the Swiss map. The slogan says 'For more security'.[2] The poster for the ban on minarets showed the Swiss map on which seven black minarets stand like rockets next to the black figure of a woman clad in a burka and the text 'Stop. Yes to the minaret ban'.[3] These posters split the country in two, with cities such as Lausanne, Fribourg and Basel refusing to allow their display in public while Zurich, Geneva and Lucerne decided to allow them in deference to freedom of speech. It also split the country in two in terms of the vote, and it put Switzerland on the global map as a place to watch for breaches in human rights and displays of blatant xenophobia.

All three initiatives, each requiring the active participation of the voting public, while being simultaneously under the attentive scrutiny of the rest of the world, formed the background against which the discussion about the new legislation and the trial on FGC was played out. Together they provided a matrix in which a number of subject positions – the victim, the helper, the extremist, the criminal, the survivor, the foreigner – are constructed and mutually re-enforced so that each becomes exponentially more significant in the public imaginary. There is not only the black African woman constituted as the victim of FGC, the patriarchy and primitive cultures, but also the oppressed Muslim woman threatened by fundamentalist Islam as pictured on the minaret posters, and the wife of the criminal foreigner, always male, who needs to be expelled: each of these figures superimposed on one another. Likewise, the criminal foreigner is at once the extremist Muslim and a member of the oppressing patriarchy. What results is a matrix of positions which magnify each other through a system of cross-referencing that helps to carve out polarized opposites such as them and us, civilized and barbaric, foreigners and national majority. For immigrant men and women, escaping these positions from within such overdetermined categories of otherness and representing themselves as autonomous subjects is almost impossible in a country that relies on the Other to constitute its own exceedingly fractured self as a homogenous whole.

Conclusion

I have argued that the many stories told about the Other in the process of the shaping of a more focused law on FGC in Switzerland and against a backdrop of further negotiations about foreigners constitute a mainstream public discourse in which Switzerland is confirmed in its nationhood and

---

2 www.dailymail.co.uk/news/article-480493/Proposed-Swiss-immigration-laws-rise-new-racism-xenophobia.html (last accessed 25 April 2012)
3 http://news.bbc.co.uk/2/hi/8297826.stm (last accessed 25 April 2012)

its standing in the global order while effectively maintaining a steep social hierarchy that sustains a latent xenophobia. In this reading, the immigrant women from areas in which FGC is practised further serve as the 'abject Other' (Kristeva, 1982) by which emancipated Swiss womanhood is at once constituted and confirmed. Hence, the new legislation on FGC has less to do with the avowed protection of immigrant women and children than with the protection of the Western normalized notion of the female body and its sexual agency. The mainstream imaginary of the black mutilated body, shaped by the interlocking mechanisms of the media and the law, constitutes the background against which the Swiss body politic can appear whole. It is a hard-won appearance, of course, and one that comes at a price: as long as issues such as harsh asylum practices and women's inequality are hidden by discursive sleights of hand and elaborate cover narratives, the real stories of injustice and hardship that mar Switzerland's position as a civilized state cannot be addressed.

References

Abu-Lughod, L (2002) 'Do Muslim Women Really Need Saving? Anthropological Reflections on Cultural Relativism and its Others' **104** *American Anthropologist* 783–90

Ahmadu, L S (2007) 'Ain't I a Woman Too? Challenging Myths of Sexual Dysfunction of Circumcised Women' in Y Hernlund and B Shell-Duncan (eds), *Transcultural Bodies: Female Genital Cutting in Global Context* (New Brunswick, NJ: Rutgers University Press), pp. 278–310

Amsterdam, A and J Bruner (2000) *Minding the Law* (Cambridge, MA: Harvard University Press)

Bell, K (2005) 'Genital Cutting and Western Discourses on Sexuality' **19**(2) *Medical Anthropology Quarterly* 125–48

Boddy, J (1991) 'Body Politics: Continuing the Anti-Circumcision Crusade' **5** *Medical Anthropology Quarterly* 15–17

Boddy, J (2007) *Civilizing Women: British Crusades in Colonial Sudan* (Princeton: Princeton University Press)

Brown, W (2001) *Politics out of History* (Princeton, NJ: Princeton University Press)

Brown, W (2008) *Regulating Aversion: Tolerance in the Age of Identity and Empire* (Princeton, NJ: Princeton University Press)

Bruner, J (2003) *Making Stories: Law, Literature, Life* (Cambridge, MA: Harvard University Press)

Coleman, D L (1998) 'The Seattle Compromise: Multicultural Sensitivity and Americanization' **47** *Duke Law Journal* 717–83

Collins, P L (2003) *The Fattening Hut* (Boston: Houghton Mifflin)

Daly, M (1978) *Gyn/Ecology: The Metaethics of Radical Feminism* (Boston: Beacon Press)
Goldberg, M (2009) *The Means of Reproduction: Sex, Power and the Future of the World* (New York: Penguin)
Gruenbaum, E (2001) *The Female Circumcision Controversy: An Anthropological Perspective* (Philadelphia: University of Pennsylvania Press)
Hosken, F (1979) *The Hosken Report: Genital and Sexual Mutilation of Females* (Lexington, MA: Women's International Network News)
Information Platform humanrights.ch (2007) *Amnesty International Report 2007*, http://www.humanrights.ch/en/Switzerland/Human-Rights-in-Internal-Affairs/National/idart_5263-content.html (last accessed 30 May 2012)
Jacobsen C and D Stenvoll (2010) 'Muslim Women and Foreign Prostitutes: Victim Discourse, Subjectivity, and Governance' **17**(3) *Social Politics: International Studies in Gender, State and Society* 270–94
Kahf, M (1999) *Western Representations of the Muslim Woman: From Termagant to Odalisque* (Austin: University of Texas Press)
Kallenstein, L M (2009) *The Cut* (Phantomfilm)
Kessler, C (2000) *No Condition is Permanent* (New York: Philomel Books)
Kilic, S, S Saharso and B Sauer (eds) (2008) 'The Veil: Debating Citizenship, Gender and Religious Diversity', special issue **16**(4) *Social Politics. International Studies in Gender, State and Society*
Kristeva, J (1982) *Powers of Horror: An Essay on Abjection* (New York: Columbia University Press)
Mohanty, C (2003) *Feminism without Borders: Decolonizing Theory, Practicing Solidarity* (Durham: Duke University Press)
Morison, L (2001) 'The Long-term Reproductive Health Consequences of Female Genital Cutting in Rural Gambia: A Community-based Survey' 6(8) *Tropical Medicine and International Health* 643–53
Narayan, U (1997) 'Cross-Cultural Connections, Border-Crossings, and "Death by Culture"' in *Dislocating Cultures* (New York: Routledge)
Nnaemeka, O (2005) *Female Circumcision and the Politics of Knowledge* (Santa Barbara, CA: Praeger), p. 192
Nussbaum, M (1999) *Sex and Social Justice* (Oxford: Oxford University Press)
Nussbaum, M (2000) *Women and Human Development: The Capabilities Approach* (Cambridge: Cambridge University Press)
Nussbaum, M and J Glover (eds) (1995) *Women, Culture, and Development: A Study of Human Capabilities* (Oxford: Clarendon Press)
Neue Zürcher Zeitung (NZZ) (2008) 'Bedingte Freiheitsstrafe wegen Beschneidung der Tochter. Ehepaar schuldig der Anstiftung zur schweren Körperverletzung', *NZZ Online*, 26 June, www.nzz.ch/nachrichten/zuerich/elternpaar_wegen_beschneidung_seiner_tochter_verurteilt_1.769848.html (last accessed 25 April 2012)

Obermeyer, C M (1999) 'Female Genital Surgeries: The Known, the Unknown, and the Unknowable' **13**(1) *Medical Anthropology Quarterly* 79–106

Obermeyer, CM (2005) 'The Consequences of Female Circumcision for Health and Sexuality: An Update on the Evidence' **7**(5) *Culture, Health and Sexuality* (Themed Symposium: Female Genital Cutting) 443–61

Oxford, C G (2005) 'Protectors and Victims in the Gender Regime of Asylum' **17**(3) *Feminist Formations* 18–38

Rahman, A and N Toubia (2000) *Female Genital Mutilation: A Guide To Laws and Policies Worldwide* (London: Zed Books)

Razack, S (2008) *Casting Out: The Eviction of Muslims from Western Law and Politics* (Toronto: University of Toronto Press)

Robertson, C C (2002) 'Getting Beyond the Ew! Factor: Rethinking US Approaches to African Female Genital Cutting' in S James and C C Robertson (eds), *Genital Cutting and Transnational Sisterhood: Disputing US Polemics* (Urbana: University of Illinois Press), pp. 54–86

Roth-Bernasconi, M (2005) Sexuelle Verstümmelung an Frauen. Sensibilisierungs-und Präventionsmassnahmen. Parlamentarische Motion Die Bundesversammlung. http://www.parlament.ch/d/suche/seiten/geschaefte.aspx?gesch_id=20053235 (last accessed 30 May 2012)

Smith, C (2011) 'Who Defines "Mutilation"? Challenging Imperialism in the Discourse of Female Genital Cutting' **23**(1) (spring) *Feminist Formations* 25–46

Steinem, G (1980) 'The International Crime of Female Genital Mutilation' *Ms Magazine* 65

Shweder, R A (2002) 'What About Female Gential Mutilation? And Why Understanding Culture Matters in the First Place' in R Shweder, M Minow and H Markus (eds), *Engaging Cultural Difference: The Multicultural Challenge in Liberal Democracies* (New York: Russell Sage Foundation Press)

Thomas, L (2000) ' "Ngaitana (I Will Circumcise Myself)": Lessons from Colonial Campaigns to Ban Excision in Meru, Kenya' in B Shell-Duncan and Y Hernlund (eds), *Female 'Circumcision' in Africa: Culture, Controversy, and Change* (Boulder: Lynne Rienner Publishers), pp. 129–50

Trechsel, S and R Schlauri (2004) Weibliche Genitalverstümmelung in der Schweiz: Rechtsgutachten, Schweizerisches Komitee für UNICEF (ed), http://assets.unicef.ch/downloads/UNI_Rechtsgutachten_WGV_de.pdf (last accessed 30 May 2012)

Walker, A (1993) *Possessing the Secret of Joy* (New York: Washington Square Press).

Walker, A and P Parmar (1993a) *Warrior Marks: Female Genital Mutilation and the Sexual Blinding of Women* (New York: Harcourt Brace)

Walker, A and P Parmar (1993b) *Warrior Marks*, documentary directed by P Parmar (New York: Women Make Movies)

Part II
Performing Resistance

5
The Actant Doesn't Speak: Configuring a Law for Research on Humans

Priska Gisler

> I combine the chickens, ducks, rabbits and mice according to my own rules in order to evoke the conditioned reflex in my audience about the absurdity of human rules and the perplexity, which paralyzes our thinking. This is why some viewers associate my stitched-together mice with the rules of marriage or military, my assembled animal groups with social classes... The appearance of emotional symptoms drives people to thinking, but is in itself not deadly. (Kunstmuseum Bern, 2005b)

Introduction

The author of these lines was neither a physicist, nor an alchemist nor even a charlatan. Xiao Yu, a Chinese artist who has gained much attention in Western countries precisely as a consequence of his startling artistic positions, wrote this description of his work. Xiao Yu became the object of a major controversy in Switzerland when a suit referring specifically to his installation was brought against the Kunstmuseum (the museum of fine arts) in Bern. The installation, *Ruan*, was displayed in the museum on the occasion of an exhibit of Chinese contemporary art (entitled Mahjong) in 2005. For this work, the artist had sewn the head of a human foetus onto a pigeon carcass and, thus, created a chimera (see Figure 1). Journalist Adrien De Riedmatten took offence when he visited the exhibit, and subsequently brought criminal charges against the museum based on the portrayal of violence, cruelty to animals and 'for disturbing the peace of the dead'.

Consequently, the entire Xiao Yu display was removed from the exhibit. Some time later, the museum organised a round-table discussion focused on the handling of controversial pieces of art, with the management of the museum declaring that the decision about how to deal with the work, and even whether or not to put it back into place, would depend on the outcome of the discussion.

Ruan, Kunstmuseum Bern (photo: Dominique Uldry)

The controversy took place about midway through a national debate about a new Swiss law aimed at uniting under one legal umbrella several types of human medical experiments, the so-called 'law on research on humans'. For both the debate on the law as well as the art controversy, consideration about what should be allowed in the realm of research became crucial. Should freedom of research be the same for artists as for scientists? How far would this freedom go? As I will show in this chapter, freedom of research consequently became a key term in a double sense. On the one hand, freedom of research was pitted against the concept of human dignity, not only in public discussions about the art piece, but, in particular, in the political debate about the new law. On the other hand, it played a role in serving to reconfigure an established social order.

Biotechnological developments in contemporary society create the backdrop for my argument. These are not limited to Switzerland but are also going on in other democratic states in the Western world. In many nation states, these developments are characterized by similar trends: pressure for the legitimation of increases in national research funds stands in opposition to intense discussions of medical ethics that are highly charged with moralistic connotations. Accordingly, members of the biomedical communities in these countries feel increasingly challenged to defend their manifold scientific activities (Gottweis, 2008), while unwittingly contributing to the configuration of a new ethical understanding (Collier and Lakoff, 2005).

The concrete questions that this article seeks to answer are thus: why have freedom of research and the degrees of liberty to experiment with and explore biological materials and human body parts become such a bone of contention in the artistic as well as the political discourse? How did the enactment of freedom of research coincide with the regulation of research on humans, and how was the concept understood by different actors in relation to different discursive threads? Some of the stories told and the discussions held in different fields about research on humans may reveal some of the politics that are involved in this debate.

In the following sections, I will first propose some theoretical considerations regarding the performativity of public debates, and go on to explore the two separate, yet intersecting, threads of discourse dealing with controversial works of art and the emerging legislation on research on humans. I will then briefly introduce the history of the legislation with respect to research on humans and discuss how freedom of research became a key concept. I will go on to explore the role of this term, discussing the *Ruan* controversy. Following this, the parliamentary negotiations about the emergent legislation at the height of the discussions about freedom of research will be discussed. They help to reveal some of the legal, ethical, economic and social claims that are tied in with experimenting on and with humans. Freedom of research therefore played an inclusive and exclusive role in a social transformation process. I will conclude with some remarks about how different actors rehearsed resistance against these trends.

The debates that will be discussed in this chapter were very much about progress in the biomedical sciences. But, implicitly, they also referred to *who* would be able to generate insight about the human body and *what kind of knowledge* might be acceptable. Furthermore, the debates revealed that nothing short of the significance of values and norms and the changing order of contemporary society were at stake.

An explosion in biomedical legislation

As in many Western countries, the construction of an amended law regulating all research on humans has been preceded in Switzerland by a series of specific laws, such as the stem-cell research law, the transplantation law, the law on medical products and others, as well as by a range of corporate directives[1] and international guidelines.[2] In contrast to this previous regulation

---

1 For example see 'Roche's Ethical Standards' and also the 'Roche Position on Clinical Research', available at www.roche.com/corporate_responsibility/csr_research_and_development/ethical_standards.htm (accessed 27 April 2012).
2 The European Convention for the Protection of Human Rights and Dignity of the Human Being is a perfect example for this trend. For details, see http://conventions.coe.int/Treaty/EN/Treaties/Html/164.htm (last accessed 27 April 2012).

and the so-called soft law, the Swiss draft law is officially based on the idea of an all-encompassing concept of regulating biomedical research. Despite the aforementioned explosion of regulations concerning biomedical topics in contemporary society concernings, the responsible government agency announces on its homepage that '[t]he existing regulation on research in humans is fragmentary and heterogeneous' and the official goal therefore is to deal with this unsatisfactory legal situation by filling an existing void.[3]

As mentioned above, Switzerland hardly stands alone: matters related to the creation of new life-forms, the invention of novel biotechnologies, and the application of assisted medical reproduction have led to increased regulation. In many countries, these types of activity, such as the ability to manipulate, reproduce and transform biological materials or human bodies, have undergone fundamental changes and stirred up debates related to what freedoms should be permitted in respect of experiments on and with humans, animals and biological body parts (Parry, 2004; Mulkay, 1994; 1997; Ong and Collier, 2005; Reubi, 2010). 'Politics of life' themes, as Gottweis (2008) calls them, such as human embryonic stem-cell research, genetic testing, the production of genetically modified crops and the like, are 'highly contested topics that stand at the intersection of society, politics, nature and the human body' (Gottweis, 2008, p. 266). In his view, the emergence of a 'new language of ethics and morality', linked to these politics of life areas (p. 281), is paralleled by the observation 'that "old" definitions [of social order] no longer hold and various groups try to impose new (partial) definitions of a new order on others'. (Gottweis, 2008, p. 283). Thus, the analysis of the role of freedom of research for the artistic as well as the scientific protagonists in the legal discourse on human research may reveal more details about the social configurations inherent in and represented by the threads of debate.

The performativity of 'politics of life' themes

At first glance, one might not see many social or structural parallels between Mahjong (the exhibition of Chinese art) and a Swiss legal amendment relating to research on humans. Without claiming that the exhibition had a direct influence on the public debate of the 'law-in-the-making', I nevertheless propose to consider the two events together here and, hence, make clear some of the transformations of the social order making up the emerging contours of a biotechno-medical world. In both the art scandal and in the public debate on the human research law, concerns were raised by several actors about access to and treatment of biological materials; in both

---

3 'Die geltende Gesetzgebung zur Forschung am Menschen in der Schweiz ist lueckenhaft und uneinheitlich', Federal Office of Public Health homepage, www.bag.admin.ch/aktuell/00718/01220/index.html?lang=de&msg-id=14511.

cases solutions were sought about how to regulate their handling. Moreover, freedom of research as a decisive term was invoked.

Conventionally speaking, art and the legislative can be thought of as representing two different perspectives: art as that which lies in the realm of everyday life; and the legal as belonging to the political sphere. But whereas everyday occurences may be seen rooted and positioned outside the political, the law – as it is laid down in books – seems generated in parliamentarian debates. Certainly, each can be regarded as interacting with the other and constituting that which belongs in the realm of social realities, or better, social worlds. This all the more, since – as Binder and Weisberg claim – the cultural is 'intrinsic to law insofar as law fashions the characters, personas, sensibilities, identities, myths, and traditions that compose our social world' (Binder and Weisberg, 2000, p. 19). And when we look at law-making, that is legislative processes, as well as at discussions of rules and guidelines, we may enter some of the realms, or arenas, that contribute, in their words, to 'generating cultural meaning' (ibid.).

The issue of freedom of research was brought up, then, in such an arena, the public arena in which discussions, among politicians, physicians, artists, museum representatives etc., about research on humans in Switzerland were held. Various participants related different stories about freedom of research and thereby helped shape and transform the agenda for the social groups involved. While the stories were narrated from different points of view – and recorded in news articles, draft law texts, professional and scientific associations' guidelines and transcriptions of the parliamentary debate – Ewick and Silbey specifically mention that 'the structure, the content, and the performance of stories as they are defined and regulated within social settings often articulate and reproduce existing ideologies and hegemonic relations of power and inequality' (Ewick and Silbey, 1995, p. 212). Yet, they also point to a performative function of story-telling: 'the hegemonic gets produced and evolves within individual, seemingly unique, discrete personal narratives' (ibid.). It is therefore worthwhile to take a closer look at how law and the social world are interwoven through the production of cultural meaning. Freedom of research, I will argue, holds a very specific position in this web.

Freedom of research, a term that exists at the intersection of a bundle of legal, economic, and scientific cross-references (Jannidis, 2004, p. 3) is understood in this article as a kind of figure of speech, an actant in the Latourian sense (Latour, 1987; 1999) that took up an active – often translational or intermediary – role in a network constituting the field of biomedicine in contemporary Swiss society. From a perspective of a science and technology studies approach, to focus on freedom of research means trying to understand some of 'the complex and controversial nature of what it is for an actor to come into existence' (Latour, 1999, p. 303). Thus, for the following analysis, I will examine freedom of research as an actant (a term Latour uses to include non-humans) in order to find out more about it through observing what it does, or its performances (Latour, 1999, p. 303). I do not do this under research laboratory conditions as Latour would advocate, but use the very public debates and controversies to analyse its effects.

As stated in the introduction, I will begin my *tour d'horizon* with the history of human research law as it is currently drafted in Switzerland. At first, it may look like just one more ordinary and typically long-winded example of how legislation works in a direct democracy, but it is, in this case, also an example of how political approaches increasingly strive to regulate experimentation with human subjects in Switzerland.

Human research regulation in Switzerland

The participants in the *Ruan* controversy that arose in 2005 were stirred by ethical concerns as well as artistic considerations to defend the artwork under fire. This proved to be a common focal point that linked the controversy, quite unexpectedly, with the debates about the new law regarding research on humans. But we need to look back to about eight years before the 2005 controversy when the demand to formulate a law dedicated to biomedical developments was first raised in the Swiss Parliament.

There was no mention, however, of freedom of research when in 1997 Parliament Member Rosmarie Dormann of the Christian Democratic Party raised a motion to the Swiss Federal Council that a new law be drafted regulating medical research on humans. Such a law would specify ethical and legal principles in order to guarantee 'the protection of human rights', on the one hand, and, on the other, a commitment not to hamper 'reasonable medical research'. Although the Federal Council accepted the motion, for quite a while nothing much really happened. Shortly before the Dormann motion would have been deleted from the agenda, it was repeated by Gian-Reto Plattner in December 1998.[4] The wording was still the same, but Plattner added a time limit to his request. He asked the Federal Council to elaborate a law about medical research on humans by the end of 2001.[5] Now the motion went one step further: the Council of States in 1999 approved the motion and accepted its referral – time had obviously worked in its favour. Since a range of cantonal authorities had started to draft their own laws and the increase in regulation caused some concern about the

---

[4] www.parlament.ch/d/suche/seiten/geschaefte.aspx?gesch_id=19983543 (last accessed 27 April 2012).
[5] www.parlament.ch/afs/data/d/bericht/1998/d_bericht_n_k5_0_19983543_01.htm (last accessed 27 April 2012).

future development of cutting-edge research in Switzerland, the motion was accepted unanimously.

After a break – during which the law on stem-cell research was prioritized and indeed drafted – the work on the regulation of research on humans was resumed (by the Commission on Science, Education and Culture (WBK))[6] in 2003. In the meantime, the motion had been transformed into a constitutional draft law, which meant that the competences concerning the regulation had shifted to the Federal Government. The term 'freedom of research' first appeared in the proposal of the WBK:

> The Federal Council is commissioned to prepare a constitutional amendment on research on humans. Therewith the Federal Government will be assigned an explicit responsibility for the whole field of research on humans. Taking into account the right for freedom of research, important principles concerning the research on humans are to be written down protecting human dignity, personality and health.[7]

In this text, freedom of research appeared for the first time, allocated a most prominent place. Freedom of research had been anchored constitutionally in Switzerland just a few years earlier, in 1999 (Schwander, 2002), and the country followed many others in this regard. A range of democratic nation states – mainly in the EU – devote a paragraph in their constitutions to the protection of freedom of scientific research as well as to the teaching of arts and sciences. In the USA and Canada, this is done under the freedom of thought or expression Acts (Santosuosso et al., 2007). But freedom of research goes back much earlier to the Humboldtian ideal of education, where it also included the financial autonomy of the university. For Switzerland, freedom of research above all meant a call to Parliament to allow and enable scientific research at a national level (see Kley, 2003).

At the same time, Dormann's request concerning the protection of 'human rights' disappeared from the discourse, to be replaced by 'human dignity'. The avoidance of abusive practices, the inclusion of 'voluntary consent' and a respectful treatment of the patient in medical research by due regard for human dignity is, as Ruth Macklin (2003, p. 1419) explains, not much more than treating a person willing to participate in a research project with respect. Thus, the reference to the overarching concept of human rights was replaced by a nearly empty word that was, practically speaking, of mere symbolic value. No controversies emerged from this change, unlike in the debates on freedom of research.

---

6 Kommission für Wissenschaft, Bildung und Kultur.
7 See www.parlament.ch/d/suche/Seiten/geschaefte.aspx?gesch_id=20033007 (last accessed 27 April 2012).

The wording of the law, penned by the Federal Council as a preliminary suggestion, still had to pass the official consultation procedure. This, however, was not due to take place before the beginning of 2006. It was precisely during this gap year, in 2005, the art–science controversy emerged revolving around the use and manipulation of biological materials, an aspect that the law on research on humans was striving to regulate. Freedom of research was explicitly questioned in a newspaper article after the Mahjong exhibition had finished. I now propose to discuss this moment in the debate when the negotiations and the 'boundary-work' (Gieryn, 1983) related to freedom of research gained contours and became visible. They signify a very specific use of the term. In the next section, I will discuss the attributes that were associated with freedom of research in order to include or exclude certain social groups.

Access and right to experiment with biological materials: negotiating the places of art and science

In 2005, under the title 'Constraints of Displaying. Is Art Allowed Rights that are Denied to Science?', Ewald Weibel, a former director of an anatomical institute and ex-president of the influential Swiss Academy of the Medical Sciences (SAMW), wrote an article in the widely respected Swiss newspaper, the *Neue Zürcher Zeitung* (*NZZ*), reacting to the Mahjong exhibition that he had visited in Bern (Weibel, 2005). Weibel took offence to *Ruan* and the discourse surrounding the work. In the article, he asked in a more general sense what artists should be allowed to do and whether they should be able to realize their projects by all possible means, even if this included dead body parts. In the second paragraph, he referred to a curatorial statement about the artist's work that to him seemed revealing: Xiao Yu had been described as a 'creator of new beings whose existence he is researching'. Taking up this comment, Weibel felt entitled to situate the artist in the realm of scientific research. Consequently, he drew a line around this definition by referring to the law: freedom of art as well as freedom of science were already codified constitutionally (Articles 20 and 21), he stated. Freedom of research, Weibel went on, was important for both science and art since both domains explored visions and the unthinkable. Yet, such freedom was to be restricted, and legal rulings should draw boundaries. Since he had identified the artist as a researcher, he felt entitled to refer to the guidelines on biobanking established by the SAMW, which had been drafted in response to the increase in biobanks anticipating official regulation. Thus, the guidelines were introduced earlier than the law itself.

SAMW has an important role within the landscape of Swiss biomedical politics. Traditionally, the medical field (including SAMW as one of its most important players) had been highly successful in formulating and conceptualizing its own rules and regulations (Sprumont and Roduit, 2008). SAMW guidelines function as non-governmental soft law, but, interestingly, they often anticipate subsequent official regulation and, thus, foreclose in certain ways the legal set-ups.[8] They are not legally binding, but are compulsory for the members of the Swiss Medical Association, the accrediting body and federation of Swiss physicians.

A sub-commission of the SAMW on 'human preparations' formulated the medical–ethical guidelines on biobanking to which Weibel referred. This group consisted largely of medical scientists, with a few theologians and lawyers. Following the standard SAMW procedure – a kind of imitation of the Swiss legislative process – the draft guidelines had been published in the summer of 2005 (SAMW, 2005).

In the preamble to the final document, footnote 4 (SAMW, 2006, p. 3) referred to 'Wissenschaftsfreiheit'. The text recalled the right to personal freedom and protection of the private sphere with regard to the donor of human tissue. This right contrasted – according to the guidelines – directly with the interest of the person concerned (the patient) or society at large, in whose names scientific progress – and here the footnote referred to the law on freedom of science in the constitution – ought not to be hampered by overregulation. Thus, the donor was played off against concerned patients or society at large: the right to personal freedom was opposed to freedom of research.

Returning to Ewald Weibel and his application of the SAMW guidelines to an artist such as Xiao Yu, we note the following: since, according to the author the artist's work could be described as research, he felt entitled to apply, at least by way of the newspaper article, the regulations concerning biobanks and anatomical collections. Amongst the basic principles making up the guidelines, three stood out:

1 Preparation activities have the aim of visualizing the normal or pathological anatomical structures.
2 It is forbidden to produce, store or publicly present artistically alienated (or distorted) objects of human tissue.
3 The origin of the objects must be clarified.

The exhibit clearly violated these irrevocable rules. In order to make this explicit, Weibel pointed to Gunter von Hagens 'Körperwelten'/'body worlds' exhibition, which had been based on a former teaching tool created for medical students and later transformed into a successful public show. In

---

8 For more information about when the different SAMW guidelines have found their way into existing regulation or by-laws, see www.samw.ch/de/Ethik/Richtlinien/Archiv.html (last accessed 27 April 2012).

Weibel's eyes, von Hagen's exhibition was dismissible albeit from only one perspective: he had overstepped a boundary when he added an artistic notion to some rare pieces within the exhibition. Yet, most pieces in the show were acceptable for orienting and educating a broad public on purely physiological facts to explain, as Weibel wrote, 'the wonders of nature by explicating the construction of our own bodies'. Thus, as long as the displays were mounted in a so-called realistic manner, they were fine. But, as soon as they departed from this realism or were put in a different perspective by the addition of some novel elements – as *Ruan* was – the displays were placed in an artistic context and were seen as illegitimate. Furthermore, although the fetus that was used for *Ruan* had originally been prepared for a natural history museum, as Weibel wrote, it had been 'alienated', distorted ('verfremdet') by the artist later, before it appeared in the exhibition. According to the guidelines, such activities were not allowed.

In his conclusions, Weibel questioned whether art should be allowed wider latitude of choice than science, and whether different value measures were applicable to art than to medical research, already subjected to austere proscriptions. With this argumentation, he made an implicit point: art, according to Weibel, until this day had been free in a different sense, and it could escape ethical arguments. At first glance, this seemed to stand in sharp contrast to current medical research. Weibel stated that, already at that time, medical research was following guidelines, and that its freedom of research was thus restricted. However, strictly speaking, this was not yet the case. In October 2005, when the article was written, the guidelines of the SAMW still awaited approval by the SAMW Senate. Therefore, the ethical behaviour that they proclaimed was not yet binding for the medical community.

To conclude, while Weibel, in the first move of his argumentation, drew the activities of the artist into the sphere of research, he extended the SAMW guidelines to these artistic activities, so that he was able to rule out the presentation of artistically transformed, or, better, artistically alienated objects. Since he could be sure that freedom of research would be written down constitutionally in the research on humans legislation later, the author felt entitled to apply the professional–corporate guidelines, at least symbolically. He thus made clear what rights other professional fields should be allowed. Manipulation and experimentation with humans lies within the realms of medicine and hence rules out the same activities by others. This is decisive. Although the SAMW guidelines were not yet officially binding, the considerations examined in this newspaper article possessed the power to bestow 'cultural meaning' (Binder and Weissberg, 2000) on a work of art.

The actant freedom of research as applied by the SAMW guidelines and discussed in the *NZZ* article (Weibel, 2005) enabled a boundary to be drawn between those who are allowed to do research with biological materials (i.e. biomedical researchers) and those (in this case an artist) who are not. The message of the writer, himself a key figure in biomedical sciences in Switzerland, conveys what this kind of freedom may allow and enable, while outlining what may be restricted. Freedom of research, it seems, is enacted to generate exclusive effects. Because they are not biomedical professionals or scientists, artists are restricted from inhabiting the world of research on humans.

Freedom of research: integration

Yet, the actant freedom of research also works inclusively because it draws a boundary around the ethical behaviour of physicists and biomedical researchers in Switzerland. Moving from the media back to the political articulations that continued the debate on the regulation of research on humans in 2006, we find the notion of freedom of research deeply contested. The parliamentary discussions dedicated to the legislation allow some insight into further negotiations over what kind of research would be legitimate and whether it is necessary to set limits.

As a result of the official consultation procedure that ran from 2006 into 2007, the Federal Council had to come up with a revised formula representing the concerns expressed. In this decree of September 2007, freedom of research had been ousted from its prominent place because a range of organizations and participants in the consultation process had raised their voices and argued that human dignity had to take precedence over freedom of research. Nevertheless, freedom of research retained an important position in the legal article: 'The government decrees directives concerning research in humans according to demands for the protection of dignity and personality. It protects freedom of research and is mindful the significance of research for health and society.'[9] Consequently, in late 2008 and during 2009, consensus over the individual paragraphs of the constitutional law on research on humans was nearly reached and the proposal moved towards the public vote. Freedom of research, however, remained controversial, proving indeed to be an actant in the Latourian sense, with its own existence, that kept the debate going. Going back and forth during the navette procedure between the two chambers of the Swiss Parliament, it became the ultimate bone of contention. Only after three rounds of heated debate did the smaller chamber, the Council of States (Ständerat), agree upon the inscription of freedom of research in the draft constitutional law.

The Council of States had pleaded and indeed voted for an omission of the clause concerning freedom of research in December 2008, arguing that

---

9 See www.admin.ch/ch/d/ff/2007/6713.pdf (last accessed 27 April 2012).

it was already written down in Article 20 of the constitution. Yet, the larger chamber, the Nationalrat, did not agree to this omission and subsequently brought it back. Indeed, on reading that the councillors stressed the importance of mentioning the norm, it becomes clear that freedom of research was thought to be crucial (Nationalrat, 2009). The notion was defended by many: according to some parliamentarians, it should absolutely be made visible, asserted, written down. A closer look reveals our actant as a trump card played to win the hand.

The symbolic use of the wording had a strategic reason: the researchers had to be kept on board. Hans Widmer, a member of the Social Democrats, made this very clear: 'We also want to have the research communities on board and pass a good constitutional paragraph that is strong not only in terms of form but also in terms of its content.' (Nationalrat, 2009) Thus, he pointed out the danger of losing the researchers and the influential scientific associations if freedom of research were to be omitted. Ruedi Noser of the Liberal Party – usually not at all on the same line as the Social Democrats – supported the request: 'In our view it would be the wrong political signal towards research in Switzerland, to scrap the information concerning freedom of research in this context.' (ibid.) The efforts necessary to keep medical researchers on board might also point to the fact that medical activities, practice and also research have come to be debated more publicly in recent years and, consequently, have moved more squarely into the public eye (Sprumont and Roduit, 2008, p. 415).

Although freedom of research had already been written into the law, the symbolic meaning of repeating the wording cannot be underestimated. The reasons for the inclusion were clear: in order to appease the medical research communities, the mere mentioning of their freedom of research in the constitutional law – living up to a kind of promise – was essential. It was necessary that the powerful scientific and professional medical associations, the biomedical research institutes, as well as the entire medical profession should agree on the legislation. They would all need to be able to live with the new constitutional Bill.

On 17 September 2009, the Council of States accepted the draft constitutional Bill; six months later, in March 2010, the electorate agreed with a 77.2 per cent yes vote. One day after that the constitution included the paragraph regarding research on humans.

Finding the 'right balance': resistances

However, we find the performative function of political debate instantly applied in the reinterpretation that followed the decision. In his final statement that gave the green light for approval, the head of the commission (WBK), Hermann Bürgi, declared that the wording would have to be interpreted in the future: 'The dignity of the human has priority, and freedom of research is secondary. I would like to say what is at stake: Dignity of the human, when competing with freedom of research, always has priority.' (Amtliches Bulletin, 2009)

Under these circumstances, it may not come as a surprise that the goal to achieve a balance between human dignity and freedom of research again became a topic of debate when the National Councillors reassessed the text of the implementation law in March 2011, although the commission was certain that it had found the 'right balance' by then (Nationalrat, 2011). Freedom of research was no longer mentioned in elaborated detail of the text of the law. Yet, it did now contain a clause asking for the generation of 'suitable research conditions'.[10] However, a minority proposal asked for the reiteration and reintegration of freedom of research. Part of the concern may have mirrored the professional field's angst. This popped up in the statement of one of the representatives of the minority proposal. Peter Malama, a Liberal Party member spoke to the protective as well as the facilitating function of the legislation: '[concerned are] at first hand the protection and dignity of the human in research projects, but as well the strengthening of our research standing in Switzerland in an increasingly tough and highly competitive global research environment'(ibid.).

But in the process of the parliamentarian debates this perspective was resisted. Maja Graf, for example, a Green Party member made this clear: 'The goal of the new federal law on research on humans is oriented along a protective law for the humans participating in research – and it is not a law in support of research.' (ibid.) Others, such as Yvonne Gilli from the Green Party, repeated the claim, that the law was not directed at the protection of research but at the patients who 'represented the weakest link in the chain of research' (ibid.). And she also mentioned ethical conflicts that might emerge in relation to research on people in need of protection, on fatally ill or dying persons, disabled persons, children, prisoners.

The parliamentary debate revealed that there were high stakes for including the medical profession – traditionally bound by self-imposed rules and guidelines and rarely controlled by others – in the political process. Freedom of research was thus attributed inclusive connotations. Its implementation in the law allowed for the participation of the biomedical field. From this perspective, we could also say that the wording of the law itself represented a pact. Where partial definitions of a new order were negotiated, freedom of research served as a pledge to win the loyalties of the biomedical field. But it was also resisted time and again by those who articulated their ethical concerns. The final vote on the implementation law made clear that

---

10 Draft: Bundesgesetz über die Forschung am Menschen (Humanforschungsgesetz, HFG), see www.bag.admin.ch/themen/medizin/00701/00702/07558/index.html (last accessed 27 April 2012).

not only was there a balance that kept shifting between freedom of research and human dignity, but also that the winning margin of the majority who did not want the reiteration of freedom of research was only one vote.

Freedom for art and science: performing a new order?

I set out to inquire how the concept of freedom of research could emerge in this discursive setting as an actant stirring up the debate about regulation of research on humans. In the process, I have shown that freedom of research was enacted in the political and public debate as a harbinger of the reproduction of inclusion and exclusion of professional–scientific fields. Yet, when we look at the two interconnected storylines that inform us about different ways to do research on humans, another narrative comes to the fore. We find that the actant, the very notion of freedom of research, was upheld against a range of resistances. In the first place, Xiao Yu seemed to resist rules made by scientific-interest organizations, although later his activities were examined and declared illegal.

Furthermore, when the museum finally held a kind of para-parliament, by convening a roundtable discussion, it acutally formed, albeit tentatively, a kind of new world order: although it discussed the manipulation and treatment of biological materials, biomedical professionals were not invited to share their opinions. Neither the collector nor the artist had to speak for themselves and, thus, were not held responsible. Finally, the museum decided, together with the roundtable experts, what to do with the artwork. When the charge against the museum was dropped by the public prosecutor's office in accordance with the roundtable's advice, *Ruan* was shown again in the museum, albeit now in a separate room with a sign warning visitors before they entered of what to expect.[11] Definitely, this was a solution that stood in opposition to the biomedical field's position that called for restriction of the handling of biological materials to medical professionals and scientists. But in some ways, the artistic perspective acted also in their favour. Art as well as science insisted on freedom as a basic requirement for discussing and probing societal concerns.

Concluding remarks

> ...storytelling instructs us about what is expected and warns us of the consequences of nonconformity' (Ewick and Silbey, 1995, p. 213).

---

11 www.kunstmuseumbern.ch/index.cfm?nav=567,1250,1298,1574&DID=9&SID=1(last accessed 27 April 2012).

Why did the debates regarding this new law focus so consistently on freedom of research? The different actors' positions reveal that a notion such as freedom is seen as an important commodity in relation to the production of biomedical knowledge. Nothing less than the exalted position of the medical research community seems to be threatened by the regulation. Some of the voices raised in the name of freedom seek to secure and stabilise their position. In an increasingly tough research environment, research freedoms need to be bestowed if scientific standing is to be secured. Yet, other voices insist on their own use of freedom. The emerging 'new social order' (Gottweis, 2008) is something to be negotiated.

It might be supposed that, despite further regulation, new and unregulated 'politics of life' themes will not cease to appear. What can be learned from the stories recorded in this chapter might be that these themes do not merely reflect ethical problems. Looking at how and why regulation is drafted and implemented makes visible the range of actors generating different concerns as well as the historical circumstances configuring them. Accordingly, the debate on research on humans as fought out through the actant freedom of research not only contributes to the closure of a legal gap but also to the repositioning of some social groups. Concretely, this means that the biomedical field now has to seek new sparring partners if it wants to do its research, while the political field has successfully won over the medical researchers.

In conclusion, it may not be entirely coincidental that the controversy over what should be allowed in experimenting with humans and with human material at the Kunstmuseum took place first and foremost in Bern. This is, literally, the place where politics are made in Switzerland, since as the capital it serves also as the seat of the national government. The controversy enriched in multiple ways the stage where the debates on the new legislation on research on humans took place. The discourses on art as well as on science co-constituted the arena for the generation of cultural meaning. The cultural agreement, approved by the voting majority, found its way into and constituted the new law. Transformed by a new biomedical understanding, it indicated the dawning of an emerging social order while simultaneously contributing to it.

References

Amtliches Bulletin (2009) Die Wortprotokolle von Nationalrat und Ständerat. Herbstsession 2009. Ständerat, autumn session, 7th meeting (Herbstsession 2009, Siebente Sitzung), available at www.parlament.ch/ab/frameset/d/s/4811/309186/d_s_4811_309186_309237.htm

Binder, G and R Weisberg (2000) *Literary Criticisms of Law* (Princeton: Princeton University Press)

Ewick, P and S Silbey (1995) 'Subversive Stories and Hegemonic Tales: Toward a Sociology of Narrative' **29**(2) *Law and Society Review* 197–226

Jannidis, F (2004) *Figur und Person. Beitrag zu einer historischen Narratologie* (Berlin: De Gruyter)

Gieryn, T (1983) 'Boundary-work and the Demarcation of Science from Non-science: Strains and Interests in Professional Ideologies of Scientists' **48** (December) *American Sociological Review* 781–95

Gottweis, H (2008) 'Participation and the New Governance of Life' (3) *Biosocieties* 265–86

Kley, A (2003), 'Die Wissenschaftsfreiheit (Art. 20 BV)' in P Mauron (ed.), *Schweizerische juristische Kartothek: fortlaufend ergänzte Kartothek der eidgenössischen und kantonalen Recht's- und Wirtschafts-, Sozial- und Steuerpraxis nach dem neuesten Stand der Gesetzgebung und der Rechtsprechung* (Geneva: Schweizerische Juristiche Kartothek), pp. 1–11

Kunstmuseum Bern (2005a) 'Pressemitteilung' in *Einladung zur Podiumsdiskussion im Kunstmuseum Bern*, 16 August 2005

Kunstmuseum Bern (2005b) 'Podiumsdiskussion 22.8.2008: Die Grenzen des Darstellbaren' in Transkription der Diskussion

Latour, B (1987) *Science in Action. How to Follow Scientists and Engineers through Society* (Cambridge, MA: Harvard University Press)

Latour, B (1999) *Pandora's Hope. Essays on the Reality of Science Studies* (Cambridge, MA: Harvard University Press)

Macklin, R (2003) 'Dignity is a Useless Concept' **327** *British Medical Journal* 1419, 18 December 2003, available at www.ncbi.nlm.nih.gov/pmc/articles/PMC300789/ (last accessed 27 April 2012).

Mulkay, M (1994) 'The Triumph of the Pre-embryo: Interpretations of the Human Embryo in Parliamentary Debate over Embryo Research' **24**(4) (November) *Social Studies of Science* 611–39

Mulkay, M (1997) *The Embryo Research Debate: Science and the Politics of Reproduction* (Cambridge: Cambridge University Press)

Nationalrat (2009) summer session, 14th meeting (Sommersession 2009, Vierzehnte Sitzung), available at www.parlament.ch/ab/frameset/d/n/4809/303880/d_n_4809_303880_303934.htm

Nationalrat (2011) spring session, 9th meeting (Frühjahrssession 2011, Neunte Sitzung) www.parlament.ch/ab/frameset/d/n/4817/348384/d_n_4817_348384_348580.htm

Ong, A and S J Collier (2005) *Global Assemblages. Technology, Politics, and Ethics as Anthropological Problems* (Malden/Oxford/Victoria: Blackwell Publishing)

Parry, B (2004) 'The New Human Tissue Bill Categorizations and their Implications' *Genomics, Society and Policy* 74–85

Reubi, D (2010) 'Blood Donors, Development and Modernization: Configurations of Biological Sociality and Citizenship in Post-colonial Singapore' **14**(5) *Citizenship Studies* 473–93

Santosuosso, A, V Sellaroli and E Fabio (2007) 'What Constitutional Protection for Freedom of Scientific Research?' **33**(6) *Journal for Medical Ethics* 342–4

Schwander, V (2002) *Grundrecht der Wissenschaftsfreiheit im Spannungsfeld rechtlicher und gesellschaftlicher Entwicklung* (Bern: Paul Haupt Verlag)

Schweizerische Akademie der Medizinischen Wissenschaften (SAMW) (2005) 'Medienmitteilung. "Biobanken": SAMW setzt Leitplanken', available at www.samw.ch/de/Medien/Medienmitteilungen/2005.html (accessed 27 April 2012)

Schweizerische Akademie der Medizinischen Wissenschaften (SAMW) (2006) 'Biobanken: Gewinnung, Aufbewahrung und Nutzung von menschlichem biologischem Material. Medizinisch-ethische Richtlinien und Empfehlungen', vom Senat der SAMW genehmigt am 23 May 2006, pp. 1–20

Sprumont, D and G Roduit (2008) 'Le corps médical face à droit: l'attitude de la Fédération des médecins suisses et de l'Académie suisse des sciences médicales' *Revue générale de droit médical. Pouvoir, santé et societé* (hors série) 401–29

Weibel, E (2005) 'Grenzen des Ausstellbaren. Darf Kunst etwas, was Wissenschaft nicht darf?', *Neue Zürcher Zeitung*, 25 October 2005, Nr. 249, 44f

6
Giù le mani dalla mia storia:[1] Narrating Regional Identity Politics in Ticino

Sara Steinert Borella

Introduction

Nothing in life rivals a good story. Narrative provides us with paradigms and examples, with structures and clear points of identification that help us make sense of our own selves and the world around us. Storytelling remains intimately linked to identity formation, be it in the quest narratives of the ancient world or on the Facebook page of the latest contemporary social cause: identity evolves from the story we tell of it. As Anthony Amsterdam and Jerome Bruner explain in *Minding the Law*: 'We now understand that stories are not just recipes for stringing together a set of "hard facts"; that, in some profound, often puzzling way, stories construct the facts that comprise them.' (Amsterdam and Bruner, 2000, p. 111) Such is the case in southern Switzerland, where the canton of Ticino, a seemingly inconsequential piece of an already small confederation, may have finally written its own definitive narrative. In March 2008, the workers of the Officine (the machine shop servicing the cargo division of the Swiss railway company) in Bellinzona walked out of their jobs, entering into a month-long strike that pitted the local machine workers against federal and corporate management. The strike proved to be especially effective, both as a narrative and as a legal tool. In this modern-day epic, the workers took on big business and centralized decision-making, fighting for their jobs and drawing on the vigorous support of most of the local population. This chapter examines this tale of unexpected solidarity, one that builds on the heart-warming triumph of the underdog as it deftly weaves together history, culture, language and the law. First, we will look at the construction of narrative, and how, by playing on the power of the strike in Swiss judicial practices and popular memory, the *Giù le*

---

1 *Giù le mani*, or hands-off, is an expression often associated with political or personal causes in Italian. *Giù le mani dalle officine* [Hands-off the machine shop] became the operative slogan of the 2008 machine workers' strike protesting against the dismantling of their machine shop in Bellinzona.

mani dalle officine movement has become the operative one for regional and identity politics in twenty-first century Ticino. By applying narrative theory to the strike itself, we will see how the legal narrative competes with the popular one. To conclude, this chapter will consider how these competing discourses take us beyond the confines of Switzerland, and help us to map Swiss identity, including its very gendered nature, in its national, European and transnational contexts.

The construction of narrative

The construction of this budding narrative builds on several elements that need some explanation here. First, a few words about the canton of Ticino for readers who may not be familiar with this region of Switzerland. Ticino exists in the geographical margins of the confederation, the only canton lying completely to the south of the famed Gotthard pass, cut off from the rest of Switzerland by the Alps. Practically speaking, the distance separating Ticino from nearby Italy is negligible, yet in 1803 the region chose to align itself politically with its northern neighbours and has never looked back.[2] The only all-Italian-speaking canton in the Swiss confederation, Ticino continues to suffer from a minority complex related to its linguistic and cultural status in a country where the majority of the population speaks Swiss-German and where a second, larger minority speaks French. There is little room for Italian language and culture on the national scene, despite the fact that French, German and Italian all represent official languages in confederation politics and daily life. If Switzerland as a nation sometimes suffers from the plight of inferiority, existing in the shadows of its larger neighbours and the European Union, Ticino understands itself as a marginalized minority, one in which such sentiments are only magnified.[3]

From the larger Swiss perspective, Ticino remains a canton inextricably attached to this minority status. Ticino quietly benefits from generous federal subsidies to its media industry, education and cultural offices in the name of support for Italian-language initiatives. At the same time, in the minds of many Swiss from the north, Ticino signifies a sought-after vacation destination, one that boasts of lakes and palm trees in the southern sun. Rarely do the Swiss-Germans or the Swiss-French associate Ticino with labour disputes. Unlike the other linguistic factions, Ticino currently has no federal representative in the Swiss federal council and has not had one in

---

2 For a thorough discussion in English of the development of the Swiss Confederation, see Steinberg (1996).
3 For a detailed discussion of identity politics in twenty-first century Ticino, see Mazzoleni and Ratti (2009).

the recent past.⁴ The impression that Ticino has a weak voice that can easily be manipulated by the governing majority has its roots in everyday political reality.

Hardly surprising then that the Ticinese latched onto a story that cast them as the underdogs and the Swiss Confederation and the federal railway as the dominant forces to be reckoned with. The 2008 strike, the first of its kind in over 90 years, pitted the machine workers of the Bellinzona Officine against the national railway itself.⁵ The plan that provoked the strike proposed a centralization of machine operations in Yverdon in western Switzerland, cutting Ticino out entirely (Gschwend, 2008, p. 49) where the Bellinzona machine shop has been in operation since the late nineteenth-century. It would have left 126 workers without jobs and outsourced most others to the perils of private industry. This plan contradicted 2007 talks that named Ticino as an essential point in north–south rail connections (Gschwend, 2008, p. 44). No one at the Swiss national railway headquarters had counted on hitting a cultural nerve in Italian-speaking Switzerland, despite a history of somewhat fraught relations between Ticino and the capital city of Bern. As Nelly Valsangiacomo explains:

> la Svizzera italiana, zona periferica e di frontiera, ha storicamente un rapporto contrastato con il governo centrale di Berna, il Consiglio federale, che è alla testa delle FFS.' (Valsangiacomo, 2009, p. 138)
>
> [Italian-speaking Switzerland, a peripheral and border region, has historically been at odds with the central government in Bern, the federal council, and those who are at the head of the Swiss railway company.]

The federal government's failure to anticipate local reaction might thus seem unsurprising given a long history of minor misunderstandings. This time, however, something had changed. Anyone born and raised in the southern canton had family or friends employed, or once employed, by the Officine. In fact, since the late nineteenth-century, the railway and the machinists who serviced it had been part of the local landscape. Hence, the lay-offs spoke not just to those affected, but to anyone ever employed by or associated with the Officine. At 7.25 am on 7 March 2008, the 430 workers of the Officine

---

4 The last federal councillor to serve from Ticino was Flavio Cotti (1987–1999) (*Dictionnaire historique de la Suisse*). For a more in-depth discussion of the lack of representation from Ticino in the twenty-first century, see Kunz (2009).

5 The Swiss railway, known for its efficiency and reliability, traverses the country with nearly 3000 km of tracks (*Dictionnaire historique de la Suisse*). It links not only the major urban areas, but small towns and more remote regions as well. For years, the railway once provided the only reliable way to go from the north of Switzerland to the south. It continues to provide a key public service today.

officially went on strike with the popular support of most of the 340,000 inhabitants of Ticino.

The legal implications of the strike: popular culture versus the Civil Code

Before continuing with the storm brewing in Bellinzona, we should consider the role of the strike in Switzerland. According to popular myth, strikes are simply illegal in Switzerland. While a look at the 1999 revisions to the Swiss constitution shows that this is not, in fact, the case, the multiple and complex conditions necessary to make striking legal explain this popular misunderstanding. While the 1874 constitution makes no mention of strikes, the 1999 Federal Constitution explicitly mentions the right to strike in Article 28, in the section devoted to fundamental rights. Article 28, Liberté syndicale, reads as follows:

> La grève et le lock-out sont licites quand ils se rapportent aux relations de travail et sont conformes aux obligations de préserver la paix du travail ou de recourir à une conciliation. [It continues as follows:] La loi peut interdire le recours à la grève à certaines catégories de personnes. (Constitution fédérale de la Confédération suisse)
>
> [Strikes and lock-outs are legal when they involve work relations and conform to the obligations of keeping harmony in the workplace or look toward mediation. The law may prohibit striking to certain categories of persons.]

Hence, strikes are legal in relation to specific working conditions and when they faithfully intend to preserve harmony in the workplace.[6] Note that the right to strike is by no means guaranteed and legitimate only when certain conditions are fulfilled. As Federica Sanna explains in 'La garantie du droit de grève en Suisse et dans L'Union européenne':

> Pour le TF, quatre conditions doivent être cumulativement remplies pour qu'une grève soit licite: tout d'abord, la grève doit être formée par une organisation apte à négocier un tarif salarial; deuxièmement, elle doit poursuivre des buts susceptibles d'être réglementés dans une convention collective de travail; ensuite, elle doit respecter l'obligation de maintien de la paix du travail, et enfin elle doit être proportionnée *ultima ratio*. Pour que la grève soit licite, il faut encore regarder une cinquième condition, qui est de caractère négatif, à savoir l'absence de restrictions légales concernant des

---

6 The notion of harmony in the workplace dates back to the 1937 signing of an agreement between unions and owners in the metal-working industry.

groupes de travailleurs: il s'agit en particulier de la question de la grève dans la fonction publique. (Sanna, 2004, p. 33)

[For the Federal Supreme Court, four conditions must be fulfilled in order for a strike to be legal: first, the strike must be arranged by an organization with the power to negotiate salaries; secondly, the strike must pursue goals that can be regulated by a collective bargaining agreement; in addition, the strike must respect the obligation to maintain a peaceful working atmosphere; and, finally, the strike must be proportionate with the *ultima ratio*. For a strike to be legal, there is a fifth negative condition that needs to be met: there can be no restrictions on strikes in the current bargaining agreement. This is especially relevant for strikes in the public sphere.]

Ariane Miéville points out that the law implies that political strikes and strikes in the name of solidarity are excluded. Likewise, the judiciary only considers strikes organized by recognized unions as potentially legal whereas wildcat strikes are prohibited (Miéville, 2004, pp. 1–2). It is therefore hardly surprising that, considering the numerous complications associated with their legal status and the danger of retribution against those embarking on a strike outside of the legal parameters, strikes are few and far between in Switzerland. In a country that prides itself on harmony in the workplace in order to assure economic prosperity, strikes play a very minor role. Sanna notes in the introduction to her article that there were only 35 strikes between 1975 and 1997, each lasting on average less than 24 hours (Sanna, 2004, p. 1). Unlike in neighbouring France or Italy, where strikes are frequent and even expected as part of the national landscape, strikes have only played minor roles in post-war labour politics in Switzerland.

The strike thus figures as a potentially potent but improbable weapon in the Swiss legal landscape, making its symbolic value particularly great. In March 2008, the workers of the Officine embarked on a strike that served as a catalyst to galvanize an entire population, providing a rallying point for Ticinesi from all points of the political spectrum. In an impressive display of regional identity, the inhabitants of Ticino turned out en masse to support the striking workers. As Alan Del Don and Simone Berti explain in their journalistic account, 'I trentatré giorni che hanno unito Ticino'[7] ['The Thirty-three Days that United Ticino']:

Ben 8 mila persone provenienti da ogni angolo del Cantone e dal Grigion italiano sfilano lungo Viale Stazione per dimostrare la loro

---

7   Alan Del Son and Simone Berti are journalists in Ticino. Their article appears in *Giù le mani dalle Officine*, a book that combines journalistic accounts of the strike with more scholarly articles.

solidarietà agli operai entrati in sciopero...La masiccia adesione alla manifestazione messa in piedi in meno di ventiquattr'ore sorprende gli stessi organizzatori. (Del Don and Berti, 2008, p. 65)

[A good eight thousand people from every corner of the canton and from the Italian-speaking Graubunden paraded along the main avenue to demonstrate their solidarity with the workers who had gone on strike...The massive participation in the event that had been organized in less than twenty-four hours surprised even the event organizers.]

So began a narrative tale that had real popular appeal. The machinists had garnered the regional support needed to propel them to the national arena. As for the legality of the matter, that point seemed secondary as the strike drew support from Bellinzona and the mayor's office as well as from all the cantonal authorities. The legality of the strike took a backseat to the David versus Goliath narrative in the making.

Narrative agency and trouble

The story at hand provided all the elements necessary to achieve its goals, as Amsterdam and Bruner remind us: 'Story, then, specializes in human agency, purposiveness, Trouble, and coping. It is also (usually covertly) normative, enlisting us to root for some agents to achieve some goals and overcome some Troubles, while...we root against others.' (Amsterdam and Bruner, 2000, p. 30) Indeed, the story developing in Bellinzona adhered to a time-honoured formula. The people from Ticino rallied in favour of singular, well-defined goals in the face of trouble, casting the national railways and in particular, the new railway director, as the enemy. But what about the implications of intertwining the popular narrative with the legal one? How does the tale of solidarity in the face of encroaching federalism impinge on the taboo of the strike in the public consciousness? How do we as readers, the representative of this public consciousness, determine which narrative takes precedence? Are there particular identifiable elements that may guarantee the success or failure of the final story? Again, Amsterdam and Bruner provide us with a useful formula against which to measure the success or failure of the narrative:

> The essential elements of narrative are Agents who Act to achieve Goals in a recognizable Setting by the use of certain Means and who run into Trouble...Their story typically moves from an anterior steady state (the prevalence or promise of a usual, expected legitimate state of affairs) through some setback, reversal, or disruption (the Trouble) through strivings to correct

or cope with the Trouble (which may succeed or fail) to either a restoration of the old steady state or the establishment of a new one. (Amsterdam and Bruner, 2000, p. 46)

I would argue that an identity narrative functions along just these lines. In fact, an identity narrative that can adhere to this classical formula with which we are familiar has the greatest potential for success. In this case, the local strike took on the qualities of an epic quest, complete with a valiant hero in pursuit of justice pitted against an evil villain placing countless obstacles (Trouble) in the way of the hero's success. As we see the story unfold, the operative quest narrative will eventually supplant and envelop the legal one.

A successful strike

What made this particular strike so successful? More specifically, what allowed this strike to galvanize support both within the machine workers union and from the outside? Marco Marcacci, in his article 'L'Officina del popolo: Simboli, riti e immaginazione sociale intorno allo sciopero' ['The People's Officine: Symbols, Rites and the Social Imagination around the Strike'] points to three especially original elements that characterized the strike, including its distance from the traditional worker and socialist movements (Marcacci, 2008). Because the strike did not locate itself in leftist discourse, it cut across both class and party lines. This first point seems paramount since it may, in fact, be the key to avoiding the minefields of local politics. Within Ticino, the local socialist and green parties carry little weight. Allying the cause of the striking workers uniquely with the left would have disenfranchised the majority voters in the central (PLR) and central-right (PPD) parties. Instead, the discourses allowed for support from a broad political cross-section.

The second point – that the workers themselves played a major role in the direction and the organization of their cause – assured unanimous buy-in on the part of the machine workers. This unanimous buy-in guaranteed the integrity of the strike and gave leverage to the workers. The local union, UNIA (Switzerland's international trade union),[8] represented the machine workers with a single voice, lending authority and a legal buttress (as noted above, only strikes sponsored by recognized unions may be organized) to their cause. Again, the importance of a campaign that distanced itself from any specific political stance facilitated unanimous support from the machine workers.

---

8 Switzerland's international trade union: www.unia.ch/Home.575.0.html. For a detailed description of union activity related to the strike, see www.officine.unia.ch/ (accessed 30 April 2012).

Finally, Marcacci highlights the regional character of the strike and its function as an identity narrative, one that 'represented the discontent and protests of an entire canton and the Italian-speaking Grigioni against a politic of dismantling public services and the tendency to concentrate north of the Alps both jobs and decision-making' (Marcacci, 2008, p. 130). Thus, the canton found a common voice in this very timely regional identity narrative, one that speaks out against the imminent dangers of globalization in the twenty-first century. The Officine and its striking workers became, as Marcacci suggests, a metaphor for all the inhabitants of the Italian-speaking canton, for the disenfranchised who felt their way of life threatened by this move away from the Swiss model of federalism in favour of a globalized market paradigm.

A successful identity narrative

Let us return briefly to our formula for a successful identity narrative: we see that the 'agents' (the workers) run into 'trouble' when their jobs are threatened, hence the anterior, stable state has been disrupted. They call on the strike as a way in which to cope with the trouble in an effort to restore the old steady state, thus defining their quest. The desire to return to an old steady state depends, at least in part, on a common and nostalgic understanding of this constructed, collective past, of this regional identity narrative. At this point, as with all great quest narratives, the story depends on a hero to articulate and lead the agents in their common cause.

The person responsible for capitalizing on these elements and assuring the success of our quest narrative is, of course, our story's hero. Gianni Frizzo, a machine worker and an insider in every sense, eloquently rose to the challenge, becoming the face of the strike for the machine workers, the union, the media and government authorities. As a union member, he could legally represent the striking workers and did so brilliantly: dressed in an olive green jacket and jeans, he never strayed from his proletarian roots, nor did he become mired in cantonal politics. His grassroots position cast him as a valiant David, the unassuming blue-collar worker going to battle on behalf of an entire canton.

On the one hand, then, we have Italian-speaking Gianni Frizzo, and on the other, German-speaking Andreas Meyer, whose position as general director of the Swiss federal railway placed him at the apex of managerial and fiscal power. Although originally from Basel, Andreas Meyer spent nine years working for the Deutsche Bahn: his ties to the German national railway seemed to give weight to the notion that the closing of the Officine in Bellinzona figured as part of a larger conspiracy to sell the Swiss federal railway to the Germans. The linguistic and cultural divide between the two sides was further exacerbated by the fact that Meyer, like all of his directors, could speak no Italian and could only carry out negotiations and speak with the press in German.

With our hero and his adversary firmly established, the narrative can work to fulfil its quest: discursively, it remained for Frizzo to triumph over Meyer, to restore jobs to the machinists and the canton, and to assure the safe continuation of machinist operations in Bellinzona. The legal narrative might have overtaken the popular one and impeded the successful resolution of our hero's quest if public support had not been combined with unprecedented unity on the part of elected officials in the canton, from municipalities to the legislature. The cantonal leaders sent repeated request to Bern requesting face-to-face meetings with members of the federal council (Mazzoleni, 2008, p. 143). These same officials demonstrated side-by-side with machinists in gestures of solidarity, both locally and in Bern. No one, at least in Ticino, questioned the legality of their actions. The strike, the incarnation of the heroic quest narrative, seemed to take on a life of its own.

Entwining the legal narrative with the popular one

The legal narrative told, however, a somewhat different tale. Even a naive reader of the situation and of the Swiss Constitution can see that the strike was ultimately incompatible with the mandate to maintain harmony in the workplace: the machine workers stopped production for an entire month, soldered tracks together to prevent locomotives from leaving or entering the Officine, and threatened the smooth running of the Swiss railway, tantamount to heresy in a country where one can set one's watch by the trains. As the striking machine workers gained momentum and support throughout the canton, the identity narrative effectively supplanted the legal one.

Even federal councillors Moritz Leuenberger (then responsible for the railways) and Doris Leuthard (at that time in charge of the economic sector) could do nothing to stem the momentum of the *Giù le mani* movement. They tried to point to the illegality of the strike, but to no avail. The local press accused Leuenberger of assuming a position akin to that of Meyer, criticizing him for not making the strike (and the workers' jobs) his priority (Marcacci, 2008, p. 135). As Marcacci writes, Doris Leuthard enraged thousands of Ticinesi for publicly declaring that giving in to the demands of the strikers would have sent out the wrong signal (Marcacci, 2008, p. 136). Both Leuenberger and Leuthard fed fuel to the fire of the minority cause. With striking workers and an irate canton complaining of being excluded from the national discourse, patronizing rhetoric from northern officials only served to aggravate an already tense situation. The federal councillors had no real bargaining power in their role as Goliath. What alternatives remained for the confederation north of the Alps? Certainly, bringing in the army to crush the strike or perhaps finding other machine workers to take over remained a possibility, but even those cast as villains did not see violence or scab workers as a viable option in the Swiss political landscape. Ultimately, Andreas Meyer and the federal government had played all their cards with the original restructuring plan: simply put, they had never expected organized opposition and so had no alternative plan. The Officine, in choosing to strike, opted for a response that trumped restructuring and corporate decisions made unilaterally. The strike narrative proved both compelling and effective, at least in part because of the symbolic social and legal capital invested in it.

On Monday 7 April 2008 at 11.13 am the striking workers voted to return to work. On the previous Saturday, the federal railway company had recalled its restructuring plan, thus acceding to the demands of the strikers and securing, at least for the time-being, the future of the Officine in Bellinzona. Andreas Meyer had been forced to capitulate and Gianni Frizzo as David had metaphorically slain his Goliath. In achieving its quest, the *Giù le mani* movement did not break any new ground, but rather confirmed the status quo: the men returned to their jobs at the Officine, Ticino maintained its favoured minority status within the Confederation, and Switzerland did not sully its image as a state immersed in multilingualism and multiculturalism. Nonetheless, the workers' movement gave rise to an identity narrative that will continue to define the canton's minority position vis-à-vis its northern neighbours for years to come.

Conclusions

As the quintessential quest narrative, the *Giù le mani* movement would not be much of a story if its only audience lay south of the Alps and north of Milan. As readers and theorists will readily acknowledge, reception matters. The reception of the story of the workers from Bellinzona helped transform a regional tale into one with national ramifications. For if, on the one hand, a very explicitly Ticinese tale painted the German-speaking northerners as wrong-doers, another reading allows for an alternative interpretation of the story. In his article, 'Sul concetto d'identità collettiva' ['On the Concept of a Collective Identity',] Marco Marcacci acknowledges that we cannot yet be sure if the strike movement signals a new regional consciousness on the part of the southern canton or simply a rehashing of age-old complaints against neighbours to the north (Marcacci, 2009, p. 53). Marcacci emphasizes, however, that the *Giù le mani* movement spoke specifically to Swiss national ideals, and in particular, to the concept of federalism:

> E parso però chiaro a tutti che, in una questione così sensibile
> e di grande impatto politico e ideologico, i ticinesi sembrano

confidare più nel federalismo elvetico e nelle sue concrete manifestazione sul territorio—in questo caso un'istitutione dalle forti componenti identitarie e integratrici come le Ferrovie federali—che nelle potenzialità transfrontaliere e nell'economia globalizzata. (Marcacci, 2009, p. 53)

[It appeared clear to all, however, that when it came to this very significant issue, one of great political and ideological impact, the Ticinesi seemed to have more confidence in Swiss federalism and its concrete, local manifestations – in this case, an institution like the federal railway that played on strong identity and integrative factors – over transnational potentiality and the global economy.]

This notion of federalism, one that depends on the strength of its individual cantons, coupled with a strong belief in the national institutions that serve the public, in particular the railways, holds an appeal that extends well beyond the confines of Ticino. Here then, was a story that mattered, that spoke of the fundamental features associated with Swiss identity (Kriesi 1995; Mottier 2002).

I would argue that the gendered nature of the strike created a second point of affinity for the national consciousness, one that effectively crossed cantonal borders. The Officine, an institution dating back to the nineteenth century, embodied a wholly masculine work place, a tradition easily reinforced by the male-dominated machine workers profession. The majority of images of the striking workers in union meetings feature men. Women played an explicitly supporting role: 'le moglie e le compagne degli operai si sono organizzate in un gruppo culturale e di mobilitazione (Officina donna. L'altra parte della resistenza)' (Valsangiacomo, 2009, p. 140). ['The wives and partners of the workers organized in a cultural group ready for action (Women's Officine. The other part of the resistance)'.] The movement led by Frizzo told a story that threatened men's livelihoods, and then by extension those of their wives and families. Women turned out faithfully in support of the strike and its aims. The strike thus recalls and reinforces the Swiss bourgeois family ideals dating back to Jean-Jacques Rousseau and the eighteenth century, where the woman, charged with the responsibility for the family, remains in the domestic sphere (Gisler et al., 2009). In this example, the woman ventures out of the domestic space into a public one, but clearly in support of her husband or partner rather than as a worker. Such notions of work and family resonated beyond Ticino: hence, when children and their parents carried banners in Bern with the slogan 'Giù le mani dai nostri papà' ['Hands off our dads'], the reference was clear. The lay-offs in Ticino could be read as a threat to the Swiss family and to the broader notion of

Swiss identity itself. As Véronique Mottier reminds us, 'political...narratives of Swiss national identity are thus embedded in gendered and de-gendered hierarchies of power' (Mottier, 2002, p. 8). So, the story that propelled the workers of the Officine movement toward local fame resonated, or had the potential to resonate, in a broader Swiss context.

The final point that helped catapult the strike into the national arena relates to the legal understanding of the strike itself, thus bringing us full circle. The gravity of an endeavour that involved something as emblematic as the Swiss railway was apparent to all involved. I would contend that the legal understanding of the strike, the reception of the strike as an *ultima ratio*, and the eventual acceptance of the strike as a legal bargaining tool within Switzerland had everything to do with a broader Swiss identity narrative. The successful resolution of the strike and the return to a stable, recognizable Swiss narrative – one of hard-working fathers who support their families by helping to maintain the national railway – assured the legality of the otherwise illegal acts. Ultimately, the success of the quest narrative has thus secured the success of the legal one.[9] The strike itself embodied resistance to the legal status quo and to the national narrative: its resolution, however, assured a safe return of the rogue canton to its cherished place in the tale of the Swiss confederation.

To conclude, let us consider what this national narrative can tell us about Switzerland in a European or transnational context. This becomes especially significant if we read the Ticino movement as representative of any number of smaller, identity-based national or regional movements in Europe in the twenty-first century. We have seen that the story that resounded so strongly in Ticino contained the necessary elements to propel and transform this tale from a local one to a national one. By playing on notions of federalism, gender and the law, this narrative tells a very specific story of Swiss nationhood, one that is, in fact, at odds with a larger Europe. For by highlighting Swiss allegiances to the federal state, family and harmony in the workplace, we have effectively articulated much of what has separated and will continue to separate Switzerland from the larger concept of Europe. Why does Switzerland not belong to the European Union? One might cite lack of economic incentives and the role of the Swiss banks in the world economy as compelling reasons. Or, we might look to the stories we tell about identity. The Swiss have a convincing national narrative: one that features multilingualism and direct democracy, federalism alongside cantonal initiatives, a belief in the

---

9 The Bellinzona cantonal library has compiled an excellent website that includes links to all aspects of the strike, including the legislation that pertains to it at the cantonal and federal levels. See www.sbt.ti.ch/bcb/home/drt/dossier/officine/completo.html (accessed 30 April 2012).

sanctity of public services and a clear, legal framework in which to process any threats to these ideals. For now at least, the predominantly economic narrative in support of the European Union does not cause enough trouble to disrupt the tale of an independent Switzerland. Or, as Paul Schiff Berman reminds us, 'the narrative we tell is not truth; it is a choice' (Schiff Berman, 2003, p. 140). The Ticinesi and the Swiss have chosen their own identity narrative rather than a European one, thus fulfilling the epic quest: *giù le mani dalla mia storia*, or hands off my story.

References

Amsterdam, A and J Bruner (2000) *Minding the Law* (Cambridge, MA: Harvard University Press)

Constitution fédérale de la Confédération suisse, Article 28, www.admin.ch/ch/f/rs/101/a28.html (accessed 30 April 2011).

Del Don, A and S Berti (2008) 'I trentatré giorni che hanno unito il Ticino' in *Giù le mani dalle Officine* (Bellinzona: Salvioni)

Gisler, P, S Steinert Borella and C Wiedmer (2009) 'Double Narratives, Double Lives: Tracing the Story of the Family in Rousseau, the Swiss Civil Code and the Fathers' Rights Debate' 17(2) (August) *Feminist Legal Studies* 185–204

Gschwend, H (2008) *Sciopero a Bellinzona: Il Cantone si rivolta* (Locarno: Rezzonico)

Kriesi, H (1995) *Le système politique suisse* (Paris: Economica)

Kunz, J (2009) 'Sulla passionale indifferenza fra il Ticino e la Svizzera' in O Mazzoleni and R Ratti (eds), *Identità nella globalità: Le sfide della Svizzera italiana* (Bellinzona: Giampiero Casagrande)

Marcacci, M (2008) 'L'Officina del popolo' in *Giù le mani dalle Officine* (Bellinzona: Salvioni)

Marcacci, M (2009) 'Sul Concetto d'identità collectiva' in O Mazzoleni and R Ratti (eds), *Identità nella globalità: Le sfide della Svizzera italiana* (Bellinzona: Giampiero Casagrande)

Mazzoleni, O (2008) 'Un'eccezione e le sue radici: la mobilitazione politica per le Officine di Bellinzona' in *Giù le mani dalle Officine* (Bellinzona: Salvioni)

Mazzoleni O and R Ratti (2009) *Identità nella globalità: Le sfide della Svizzera italiana* (Bellinzona: Giampiero Casagrande)

Miéville, A (2004) 'Suisse. Un droit théorique dans une "paix du travail" bien réelle' 1 *La Question sociale*, available at www.laquestionsociale.org/LQS/LQS_1/QS1_sommaire.htm (accessed 30 April 2012)

Mottier, V (2002) 'Narratives of National Identity: Sexuality, Race and the Swiss "Dream of Order"' *Revue Suisse de Sociologie* 2–22

Sanna, F (2004) 'La garantie du droit de grève en Suisse et dans L'Union européenne' *Basler Schriften zur europäischen Integration* 70 (Basel: Europainstitut der Universität Basel)

Schiff Berman, P (2003) 'Telling a Less Suspicious Story: Notes Towards a Non-Skeptical Approach to Legal/Cultural Analysis' in A Sarat and D Simon (eds), *Cultural Studies and the Law: Beyond Legal Realism?* (Winston Salem: Duke University Press)

Steinberg, J (1996) *Why Switzerland?* (Cambridge: Cambridge University Press)

Valsangiacomo, N (2009) 'Materiali d'Officina. Un Progetto Archivistico e Soriografico su uno Sciopero in un Paese dove non si Sciopera' *Historia Magistra*

7
'That's Life': Actualizing the *Non-Lieu* as an Empty Space
Fabio Ferrari

A closet by any other name

In 2008, when I wrote the essay that follows, I was just embarking on the process of becoming a first-time parent: a supposedly natural *rite de passage* rendered, in my case, a bit more challenging because of my identity as a gay man who resides in a country where adoption is tacitly denied if you are gay and single, and explicitly denied by law if you are gay and have entered into a registered partnership. In my country of residence, surrogacy – the option my partner and I chose to pursue in 2008 – is illegal, indiscriminately and across the board: gay or straight; registered, married, or single.

Illegal is not a pretty word to contend with, especially in the normally joyful context of family planning. Perhaps for this reason, the word illegal was never mentioned in any of the many communications I have had with my lawyers over the past three years. Rather than questioning the rationale behind laws designed, above all, to safeguard conventional definitions of procreation (that deny the assistance of a third-party egg donor, or a gestational carrier) and traditional notions of what constitutes a family, the attorneys from whom I have sought advice searched, in much more pragmatic terms, for immediate solutions to the various legal dilemmas that my partner and I have encountered since the birth of my son. They searched for these solutions in the gaps left open by an absence of prior jurisprudence or in loopholes created by vague or poorly written legislation. They worked conservatively within the existing system, leaving me to wonder what I could do, if anything, to help to modify the system and challenge the cultural preconceptions that would rob me, as a gay parent, of expected rights and privileges, as a direct result of the fact that my son was not conceived 'naturally' through heterosexual intercourse.

In the quick-fix legal strategy of seeking out gaps and loopholes, my lawyers have superficially upgraded my status in the eyes of the law from illegal to irregular. *En cherchant de bénéficier d'un non-lieu*, my illegality found an acceptable but tentative justification in a 'non-space' which temporarily accommodated my dilemma by, paradoxically, denying its very existence.¹ Indeed, there is no law in my country of residence that states in clear terms that a man, national or foreign resident, cannot enter into a financial contract with a woman to carry his child if said contractual agreement is legally recognized in the country where the surrogacy is to take place. Further, there is no law in my country of residence that denies residency rights, or a passport, to said child, once he or she is born.

Because my son was born in the United States, in a state where surrogacy is legal, my team of attorneys on two continents have always expressed confidence that my family can hope to live undisturbed in Europe for years to come, thanks to the generous ambivalence of a *non-lieu*. What, then, is the only condition for the luxury of family life in limbo? Never to disclose the irregularity of our situation: not to consular authorities, not to immigration, not to school authorities, social workers, journalists, employers and never to the press.

As I suggest in my essay, after decades of experience of 'benefitting' from the ambiguity of non-spaces, the lesbian, gay, bisexual, transgender and queer (LGBTQ) community knows full well both the temptation and ultimate danger of accepting closets in the form of compromises. Because societal acceptance is what many of us desire, silence seems initially to be a fair price to pay for the courtesy of just being left alone. According to a logic stripped of any sense of social justice, it may be considered sound legal advice to suggest that LGBTQ families in Europe accept the conditions and confines of a *non-lieu*. But, of course, both philosophically and practically speaking, the burden of living on these terms does not prove sustainable over time.

As my essay suggests, the lessons learned by the LGBTQ community have much to contribute to contemporary debates about prejudiced societal codes that inform and corrupt the current culture of the law, especially with regard

---

1 I use the term *non-lieu* in a philosophical sense: for its resonance as a place of legal limbo; a non-space, or site of ambiguity, which I seek to empower by linking it to the Brookian concept of a transformative empty space (2008). The ambiguity of a non-space that negates difference thus becomes a vestibule, or entry point of potentiality, for staging acts of authentic human creativity. As a non-native speaker of French, I first heard the legal term *non-lieu* pronounced by Caroline Mécary in the context of a conference on international surrogacy (as recounted in my essay). To my recollection, Counsel Mécary used the term in reference to a case of twins, born to a heterosexual French couple with the aid of a surrogate mother in the United States. Because the parents of the twins were suspected, in 2007, of having violated French surrogacy laws (Article 16-7 of the French Civil Code and Article 227-12 of the French Criminal Code), there had been an initial refusal on the part of the French authorities to recognize the validity of the American birth certificates. The French Cour de Cassation overturned this decision and allowed for the births to be registered in France, without, however, making any pronouncements for or against the issue of surrogacy in general. As Counsel Mécary explained, the specific case had been positively resolved for the parents in question but only on the grounds of a *non-lieu*, by clever legal navigation through a bureaucratic loophole.

to the personal/social costs of closeted LGBTQ families: parents and children alike (Antier and Gross, 2007; Cadoret, 2008; Huber and Leemann, 2008; Lalli, 2009). There is still much left to be written about this engaging topic which, in some ways, here still remains incomplete, partly because of the intentional immediacy of my approach and, also, due to the open metaphor of non-living non-space, which I borrowed in 2008 from Peter Brook, one of my favourite dramatic theorists, as a conceptual platform for launching an initial reflection on surrogacy, current cultural and legal obstacles to LGBTQ procreation, and LGBTQ family rights.

Admittedly, the present discussion raises more questions than it answers.

What is most clear to me now is that a subject's maternity or paternity – gay or straight, registered, married, or single – can never ethically be confined to a non-space of passive resignation or silent consent. To use the Brookian metaphor, an actor must counteract the *non-lieu* by engaging it: he or she must actualize the static ambivalence of non-space by challenging it, redefining it, making it vital: thereby transforming an ambiguous gap between words into an experimental stage for emerging new traditions.

As it turns out, 'irregular' is hardly an improvement over 'illegal'; and this fact rings especially true for an LGBTQ community that seeks recognition for its families on terms that, yes, do wish to respect the authority of a just law while, however, militantly advancing a politically informed concept of culture that has no further use for retrograde and injurious parameters of normalcy where issues of sexuality and procreation (in its various assisted and alternative forms) are concerned.

The queer father to be, or would-be 'actor'

In *The Empty Space*, Peter Brook encourages actors to shift from the traditional paradigm of what he calls the 'deadly theatre', where reality is approximated and conventionally performed, to the 'immediate theatre', which is compellingly alive due to a more genuine and creative relationship between player, subject and audience (Brook, 2008). The success of this shift is provisional on the players' determination to accept the risks of their experimentation and will to possess the bare stage, declaring their humanity without reserve or compromise. The capacity to claim the empty space as a stage allows for the actors' investment of authenticity (into the text and before the public), thereby activating the possibility for true actions of generosity, as opposed to mere acts. If the Brookian experimental actor is considered a life-giving force, the traditional actor, who acquiesces to pre-established forms, denies the value of play and thus undermines the immediate synchronicity which must exist between theatre and life.

Once enabled, the player's generosity 'works both ways', in the interest of both self and other. Because, as Brook sees it, in renouncing the deadly role that established traditions have assigned to the actor as a performative tool, the genuine player becomes an invaluable instrument for the production of new truths, as 'rough' as they are 'living'; as 'sincere' as they may be 'transitory' (Brook, 2008, pp. 11–14).

Midway through his essays, Brook extends his philosophy of the rough, living, sincere and transitory risk of the immediate theatre to the analogous possibility of immediate writing. Brook-essayist occupies and invests the empty page with a self-portrait that 'moves' the reader with the undeniable force of its self-avowed fragility, based in the ontological struggle of the printed word imprinted in time:

> Now, I must become unashamedly personal... This is a picture of the author at the moment of writing—searching with a decaying and evolving theatre. As I continue to work, each experience will make these conclusions inconclusive again. It is impossible to assess the function of a book, but I hope this one may perhaps be of use somewhere, to someone else wrestling with his own problems in relation to another time and place. (Brook, 2008, p. 112)

Inspired by Brook's challenge for genuine immediacy at the risk of roughness, I would like to reflect freely on what fatherhood means to me, today, as a gay man who, after 20 years of figurative rehearsal time, wishes to fully 'play out' his role on the stage of life. I would like, here and now, to claim the empty space of the page as my own and 'give voice' to my most sincere opposition to those established traditions that would direct me to 'play along' with the rules set forth by a deadly theatre. Recalling the urgency I felt, in 2008, in my status as a queer father-to-be and life-giving force, I would like to accept Brook's call for immediate authenticity and claim possession of a constraining, yet-undefined legal space which has been called a *non-lieu*.

In the spirit of claiming freedom from established tradition, I would like to disregard, as best I can, the acquired terms of my formal scholarly training which tend, still, to dictate the structure and style required in academic writing. I would like to offer instead a rough experiment on the theme of queer parenting, hoping, like Brook, to become 'unashamedly personal' and generously share the fragile force of my experience and ideas.

If you will, consider what follows as a stream of consciousness monologue. The only rule governing this monologue is that it will be true to the flux of a single day in the life of a man – a would-be 'actor' and father-to-be – who strives above all to transform the empty space of a *non-lieu* into a vibrant, living stage.

So here goes: my rough and wandering account of one day in Paris, 18 October 2008.

Parisian flâneries and an immaculate conception

This morning, I woke up early. I had breakfast with old friends on a familiar *terrasse* and enjoyed a leisurely walk along the river before attending a promotional conference on international surrogacy, organized by the Boston law firm with which I am currently working to realize my dream of becoming a parent. Today was a warm, sunny day and I was enjoying catching up with my friends. I was looking forward to the afternoon conference. But, the truth is, I was feeling a little shaken after learning about the death of a young man, a French actor, just about my age, who reportedly died of pneumonia a few days back.

My Parisian friends were quick to tell me that, in 2008, 'pneumonia' was still the media code word of choice for AIDS-related death (Kaim, 2006; Tervonen, 2009). In reaction to my horror at the possible existence of such a code, I was told 'mais bien sûr,' which translates from French into contemporary English as 'Hello. Get a grip.'

After a few more shots of espresso, it was explained to me that the French press, 'out of honour and respect for the privacy of the deceased', was probably attempting to be discreet, because the true cause of the young man's untimely death was, 'bien sûr', ultimately a private family matter. My friends looked at me and waited, as if preparing to pounce.

OK, I thought, here it comes. Having 20 years of experience of conversation with Parisians, I braced myself for the inevitable forthcoming lecture on the immeasurable superiority and sophistication of European discretion compared to the tell-all Oprah-Winfrey-style blab associated with American culture. 'Whatever,' said I, regressing, as I am sometimes known to do, indulging in my preferred adolescent 'X-gen' defence mechanism, 'Whatever.'

But the truth of the matter is that this so-called sophisticated Old World discretion disturbed me more, or almost, than the passing of the beautiful young performer whom I had admired since my days as a student in Paris in the late 1980s. I'm pretty sure that my vulnerability showed, and this, I know by now is 'a no no' in French café society. My feigned indifference to the cultural justification for censorship (in the name of honouring the dead) was no match for the extraordinary capacity of my French entourage to be brutally blasé: 'Qu'est-ce que tu veux, mon cher. C'est la vie.'

'C'est la vie?!' I could hardly believe my ears.

In 20 years of friendly fencing exchanges in French, I don't think I had ever heard one of my friends or contemporaries pronounce this clichéd expression. Its effect, on me, was like the sudden firing of a secret weapon: a deeply disquieting motto of surrender and resignation which persisted in resonating in my head, hours after having bid my friends goodbye.

Later, I took my resonating headache and over-caffeinated body to a park bench and scribbled a few thoughts in my journal. I had intended to prepare some questions for my Boston lawyer, whom I would soon be meeting face to face for the first time after a year of acquaintance via long-distance phone calls and email exchanges. But the apparently trivial phrase, 'C'est la vie', had gotten under my skin and was quickly imposing itself as the philosophical question of the day.

What does the expression 'that's life' evoke for me as a gay man who desires to create new life but can't help thinking about what living life means today, when life is compromised, 'mais bien sûr', by a submission to traditions that honour silence as the only legitimate means for honouring death?

Thinking back 20 years, 'C'est la vie?' was the same question that I had struggled with as a student when I checked in for a doctor's appointment at the American Hospital in Paris and was told by a nurse that my heart rate had accelerated to the point that, if I didn't calm down immediately, I might have to be admitted. I had searched out an English-speaking French doctor after having fainted, believe it or not, for no apparent reason. No apparent reason, I explained to the doctor, except that I was 19 (blablablab, thump-thump-thump) and had just moved to a foreign country where I didn't yet speak the language and, so, was feeling more than just a little bit anxious and alone. And also, at the risk of being unashamedly personal, I confessed to my doctor that my heart was racing because, well (blablablab, thump-thump-thump), I knew Rock Hudson had died recently of pneumonia at the American Hospital and, as a young student (blablablab, thump-thump-thump), I was now asking myself all sorts of difficult existential questions related to my own sexual orientation, my hopes for sexual fulfilment in the era of AIDS, my hopes for emotional fulfilment and a life-long companionship in a future that seemed increasingly uncertain (blablab) and even a little bleak (thump-thump).

Following the public secrecy surrounding Hudson's death, 'C'est la vie?' seemed like one question worth asking as a gay teenager trying to understand what it means to be a man. 'Is this hushed-up tragedy part of what defines life as a gay adult?' I wanted to know. Is that life? Is the honour of discretion really the key to a satisfactory existence according to the rules of the game?

I was far too shy to have been mistaken for a provocateur but, that said, I could see plainly that I had made a mistake, committed a grave cultural faux pas, thinking that my tell-all, Oprah-Winfrey-style, blab-it-all-out technique would help liberate me from my teenage anxieties. Naively, perhaps, I had thought that a doctor might reassure me that my fainting spell was merely stress related. Instead, I faced a reply from the doctor that shocked me as much then as it continues to shock me today, 20 years later. 'Monsieur,' the forthright French doctor said to me, in a stern voice of cold, scientific authority, 'might you happen to be hiding any lesions under that newspaper-boy *casquette* of yours? Please, be so polite as to remove your cap in the presence of your doctor, young man.'

'C'est la vie?' I repeat today, embittered by two decades of French lessons on Old World superior etiquette.

And I repeat this too: that maybe the sense of urgency in finding the answer to this question, now, is because, soon, I hope to participate in the creation of a new life; because I hope to act as an instrument in guiding that new life to an authentic and meaningful existence. Can my (gay) pride ever become articulated as a father's life lesson about the immeasurable value of never cowering, never conforming? I hope that in becoming a parental authority I will not neglect to teach the wisdom I learned when I was much younger: of always standing up to authority when it puts you down; especially when it seeks to humiliate while claiming all the while to educate or protect you.

What I have been jokingly calling my 'immaculate conception' is scheduled to take place in early December of this year (2008), and, yet, call me crazy, but I can't help but continue to question what meaning can be attributed to life in a world in which I, father-to-be, like it or not, belong to a marginalized minority sub-culture based on my sexual orientation. I guess the prospect of becoming a father renders my concern all the more active in the Brookian sense, as both actor and activist. My idealism has never been so vocal or exigent as it is now, in my new state of paternal expectancy.

The day progresses and, after the conference on international surrogacy, I scribbled some more questions in my journal. Am I being a good father if I demand respect for my difference and pledge an unswerving faith in the value of my difference? Or, perhaps, am I just being a 'drama queen'?

This evening, before making my way home to write this essay, I chatted with some American colleagues about the 'impasse of difference' within the gay rights movement, about how some things have changed and some things haven't budged an inch. The tone of my American colleagues was encouraging and hopeful but, also, I felt, prematurely self-congratulatory.

Privately, of course, I do feel 'free' to be open and honest about who I am and what I think. I know that who I am and what I think is strongly conditioned by my identity as a gay man and this, thank goodness, rarely causes me reason for anything but immense pride. In public contexts, however, such as at work – with fellow faculty, administrators and students – I have too often felt the tacit obligation to keep my true self to myself. 'C'est la vie?'

I asked my American colleagues as we talked about the nexus of identity in the separate realms of career and family.

And the answer I got to my, perhaps obsessive, question *du jour* was a reasonable objection: 'But, straight or gay, what does your sexual orientation ultimately have to do with doing your job well? What does it matter who you choose to sleep with when you go home at night? That's nobody's business but your own, right?'

'Well,' I thought (but didn't have the courage to say then), 'sorry to be difficult, but I don't believe my queer identity can at all be limited to the gender of the person I go home to sleep with at night. I believe my sexual orientation – my queer identity – is denied any broader social purpose if it is considered an *affair privée*. I don't care for discretion on principle and, more importantly, I don't think discretion favours the fundamental purpose and aims of education as I see it. To my mind, education is a public extension of parenting. For me, being a professor is not about passing down tradition or professing to be an authority of a tradition, but about nurturing the individual and preparing the student intellectually to create new traditions, true to the student's own unique voice.'

To my mind, this is my mission as an educator, and as a father to be. My life is about claiming wholeness, shifting my wholeness from margin to centre, and queering the space of traditions which silence the open expression and public value of difference and, worse still, accept the defeat of difference with a shrug of the shoulders, as if to say, again and again in so many different but interrelated contexts, 'Mais bien sûr. C'est la vie.'

Self-effacement and compromise have nothing to do with the heritage I wish to pass on to either my students or my children. There is no success story I can remember in life or in literature that has taught me to believe otherwise. Not even skewed readings of *The Gospels* can convince me that martyrdom is the proposed Christian model for a successful life. That just demonstrates poor reading skills.

And yet, other people, gay and straight, with other definitions of success, repeatedly tell me differently. On numerous occasions I have been reminded, for instance, that compromise and sacrifice are burdens that everyone (especially parents) contends with in life (especially at work) and that, as a working father-to-be, my queer idealism is more than just slightly 'over the top'.

Again, as a gay man, I become a drama queen if I complain about how social discrimination has personally affected my life. I am an ingenuous idealist because I want to reconcile public and private personae, and live a life unfractured by spatial and performative concepts such as 'out' and 'in'. Does this make any sense?

Perhaps, to some extent, the drama queen label fits in my particular case. To some degree, my entourage of French and American friends is right. They – the voices of so-called reason and common sense – may have a point when they remind me, for example, that, as a gay white man, I have little right to consider my struggle for respect and authenticity as, in any way, exceptional. 'Don't flatter yourself, your highness,' my friends remind me, 'you're far more normal than you may like to think.'

Now, don't get me wrong, I do appreciate the humour and truth in such friendly criticism but, beneath the wisecracks, I do believe there is a dangerous tendency nowadays to underplay the ethical necessity to persevere in the struggle for gay rights. Oppression is not imaginary just because it is 'felt'. Oppression is not irrelevant just because of a gay man's apparent and apparently successful assimilation.

If I am writing this essay tonight it is because I feel the burden of the Establishment even though, for all intents and purposes, I have been successfully assimilated within it. In a sense, I agree with those who tell me that my feelings of discomfort are not 'exceptional', but, unlike them, I insist that this apparent normalcy should be cause for action, not resignation. The Establishment and I are far from reconciled; and that's the way I want it. Referring, again, to Brook's incitation to occupy the stage with rough humanity as opposed to deadening tradition, 'Her Majesty', otherwise known as me, is determined to exist fully as an instrument, and never again to content myself with passing as a tool.

Why does this basic human request for authenticity seem to upset so many people? I am still too shy to be mistaken for a provocateur, but, then again, here I am tonight, apparently still committing a cultural faux pas by demanding the respect I know I deserve and have deserved for 20 years, since I was brave enough to come out and play.

I break for dinner, a long long-distance telephone call, and now I'm back at the computer with a new question: is asking for the opportunity to fully affirm one's difference simply asking too much?

According to some within the LGBTQ community, the answer is yes. The reason?

'Well, my dear, let's start with the fact that you are a white, upper-middle-class man with a good job, a nice house in a beautiful part of the world, and a handsome, loving, long-time companion: how can you not realize how good you "have it" compared to the "real" challenges faced by "real" minorities (Blacks, Asians, Hispanics, Jews) or women (heterosexual, transsexual, or lesbian), who continue to be discriminated against with far more serious consequences than you may ever be able to even fathom: white upper-middle-class drama queen that you are.'

Having for many years bought in to the notion of 'how very lucky I am' to be an invisible minority, my rebuttal to these reassuring advocates of reactionary relativism is now tinged with royal irony: 'Okay, got it. Thanks for clarifying. I guess I will just shut up now and be grateful that I have the special ability as a Caucasian homosexual man to vanish into the oppressive Establishment if I so choose. Self-denial. Self-effacement. The option to wear a performative mask for the rest of my days. What a luxury! How could I have taken such a gift for granted? I'm really so glad you pointed out the veritable "non-existence" of my emotional and moral predicament.'

Right. There you have it. I'm glad I got that off my chest.

Now, to dutifully redirect the focus of my essay towards the subject of queer parenting, the reader should be reminded that I am not a father yet, nor am I exactly a father-to-be though I do prefer to think of myself in those terms. I am, according to my contractual agreements, an 'intended parent' working from a European country (which I choose to remain nameless) with a lovely egg donor in California and a wonderful surrogate mother-to-be in Texas. While I'm on the subject of my hypothetical hyper-globalized future paternity, I should also mention my patronage of a state-of-the-art fertility clinic in Connecticut and Food and Drug Administration-approved laboratory in Minnesota: all arranged by my Boston lawyer's fine team of facilitators and savvy advisors.

As the reader already knows, I am writing this essay in Paris, France, on the evening (now night) following a promotional conference arranged by the Boston agency in the basement of a luxury hotel off the Place Vendôme. It was a very nice basement (as far as basements go) and everyone on the panel was also very nice. No complaints here.

The conference was attended by two dozen or so mostly French gay (mostly male, all apparently wealthy) couples pursuing their (expensive hence elite) dream of becoming parents through international surrogacy options which, of course, are absolutely legal in certain states in America, though not technically legal in France: as I was reminded, repeatedly, at several points throughout the afternoon Q&A session. This was the point of the day when the legal term *non-lieu* started to get my adrenaline pumping; and the term *non-lieu*, in turn, is probably what drove me into an American bookstore in search of Brook's teachings and 'militant allegory' of emptiness; the heritage of a decaying theatre in which actors perpetuate rituals of creative inertia, like puppets, in a 'non space' instead of actualizing that space through vital renewal (Brook, 2008, p. 11).

Confused? Yes, well, so was I, sort of. So let me keep this simple, catch my breath, and start over again.

What 'technically legal' or 'technically illegal' truly means in French jurisprudence is not for me, as professor of literature and culture, to judge.[2] What

---

2 An intended parent can get around French laws by contracting a surrogate in another country, such as the United States or the Ukraine. This is technically illegal but, also, a reality that the law, in 2008, had only once sought to address (see n. 1 above).

I can say, is that, as an intended parent, the fact that today's conference was held in the basement of a five-star hotel off the Place Vendôme amounts to a very telling metaphor which, sadly, confirms the effective reality, in Europe, of my non-existent predicament as a gay upper-middle-class man who hopes, one day soon, to become a father. Allow me to clarify.

The promotional message underlying this afternoon's speeches was loud and clear, even for a queer idealist and member of the (g)literati such as myself. To sum up, this was the bottom line: 'We live in fortunate times when science and technology can help couples realize dreams that, only years ago, would have been considered impossible. If fatherhood is one of your dreams, send us US$125,000 and our expert team of lawyers and social workers and medical professionals will help you create the family you have always desired and, perhaps, never imagined that – very soon – could really be yours. Operators are standing by to take your order. It's just so easy, so long as you have the money to pay for it. We do not discriminate against gays or lesbians: your gay personal cheques, lesbian international wire transfers, Visa, MasterCard, or American Express are all accepted and equally valued.'

Now, I have already told you that I am a satisfied client of this agency and that, with the help of my companion (whom I have been told not to name), our cheques have been cashed by our nice Boston lawyer and, I guess, by anyone else's definition of success, today I should have considered myself among the most fortunate in the fancy five-star hotel basement. Had I given heed to the so-called voices of reason and common sense that, over the years, have tried to convince me of how good I have it, I probably would have kept my drama queen comments to myself during the Q&A. But, having said that, and as lucky as I am, I can't help but feel very real distress knowing that the custody of my child (I've been instructed not to say 'our' child) depends not on a law which positively affirms my rights as a biological father but, rather, on a single past judgment of *non-lieu*: a French precedent which somehow may be called on in order to protect me on the proviso, 'bien sûr', that I maintain the utmost discretion vis-à-vis the authorities.[3]

The utmost discretion? At 39 years of age, as I face the prospect of parenthood as a minority which continues to cower under the privilege of its acquired wealth and option for invisibility, I think it has to be asked one last time: 'C'est la vie?'

'What are we doing in this fancy basement?'

'What are we doing, congratulating ourselves as the fathers-to-be of children whose precarious legal status in most European countries depends

---

3 See n. 1 above and Tervonen, 2009, p. 26.

on fitting oneself tightly into a legal loophole which requires us to be discreet (i.e. lie) in order to guarantee our rights?'

Drama queen jokes aside, what I would like to share with you tonight, 18 October 2008, is the grave concern and real anxiety I experience due to the larger ethical and social questions connected to the current legal climate under which queer parenting in Europe continues to operate. These concerns are deeply significant to me because, quite simply, I would very much like one day to be proud of and open about my difference as a gay father; and not just pay the price to be like everybody else who, perhaps, may be more content than I to count themselves among an invisible elite, eating puff pastries and drinking wine in a basement while socially and legally constrained by an unethical expectation to keep one's mouth firmly shut.

Before I take the important step towards fatherhood, the urgency of my desire to get out of that metaphorical fancy basement feels more pressing by the day. As I draw closer to my December 'appointment with destiny', I quickly lose my patience with friends, colleagues and acquaintances who tell me to count my blessings – and hush.

I typed the preceding words and promised myself to conclude here. It's very late. So what the hell am I getting ready to complain about now?

Well, let's start with the fact that in most countries in Europe, including the country in which I reside, gay couples in registered unions are denied the legal right to procreate.[4] Sorry to make a fuss at the last minute, but I find that simply disgusting.

As far as the federal and local laws of my country of residence are concerned, civil unions for same-sex couples explicitly forbid the custody of children, unless the children are born prior to said union. Surrogacy, for gays and heterosexuals alike, is also forbidden by law in most European countries. Again, I find that rather revolting.

Revolted or not, I can't help recalling how today, among all those nice people at the conference, I was informed, in very politicized and strangely aggressive terms by a French legal gay rights advocate, that there is 'no reason at all' for gay parents to feel they ought to tell the authorities the truth about how one's child was conceived.

'The state has no right to ask,' I was told (reassuringly?), 'and gay parents have no interest in telling. Until more progressive laws are extended to same-sex couples, a gay European really has no choice but to keep quiet and wait for the laws to change.' In other words, don't go blabbing your business to the world like a dumb American. If you are able and willing to keep quiet,

---

4 Surrogacy Laws are changing quickly, becoming more liberal in some US states or more conservative, depending on many political factors and social forces. The same holds true in the international context. For more information on US laws on surrogacy and international surrogacy (see Markens, 2007).

a hypothetical custody case can be successfully defended and, most probably, dismissed in a European court as a *non-lieu*.[5]

'OK, got it,' I replied, '*Non-lieu*. Very reassuring concept, thank you. Very discreet. Very clever. But my question, madame, was not strictly a legal question. So please listen carefully. If my unnameable partner and I, who live in an unnameable country, also accept the moral necessity of lying to an unjust state in the interest of maintaining custody of my biological child or children, what conditions – on an ethical and psychological and sociological level – are we creating for a culture and tradition of dishonesty within the family itself?'

Admittedly, my French language skills got a little overheated at this stage of debate with my passionate Parisian interlocutor but, in short, I think I made my point. And my point, of course, was merely a reformulation of the same question I've been asking myself for 20 years (you know the one).

The various books I've read so far on gay parenting repeatedly stress the vital importance of being honest and transparent with children born into alternative families (Strah and Margolis, 2004; Gross and Peyceré, 2007; for a more theoretical approach to the subject of queering childhood, see Stockton, 2009). It is clear, from my own experience as a gay man who has struggled with the social value placed on secrecy and discretion, that no success story can come from lies or even half-truths. So, to me, these books simply reaffirm the golden rule of honesty being the best policy. Call it a categorical imperative, if you prefer. Call it what you will.

Fact is, once a child is old enough to understand the complexity of his or her origins, it makes sense to me that the child must be told that he or she was conceptualized by a loving same-sex couple (in my case, two fathers) but that this beautiful idea also required the aid of an egg donor and a surrogate mother in order to lead from conceptualization to conception.

What I heard this afternoon in the basement of a fancy Parisian hotel teaches me that this type of honesty simply 'cannot be' and 'has no reason

---

5 The pressure to conform to models rooted in hegemonic, heterosexist power relations can be visible or invisible, explicit or implicit. An example of invisible oppression that is unstated but deeply felt could be the following: in order to apply for my son's passport I was advised, by my lawyer, to misrepresent myself to consular officials – 'for the sake of expediency, and to guarantee a successful outcome'. The absence of a maternal figure, normally required to sign off on a passport application, needed to be 'explained away' with a convincing narrative that 'made sense' in the dominant heterosexual cultural context in which I live. My lawyer was only trying to help me achieve my practical ends with his advice, that is clear. Between the lines, and in the gap of my lawyer's efficient but oppressive logic, I (the authentic I, the enabled I) needed to disappear, and be 'explained away'. In short, I was being asked to fictionalize myself as a hetero man who had had meaningless sex with a casual female partner (wink, wink) and now required a passport because (wink, wink) the so-called mother abandoned her son at birth and I was left with the sole responsibility of raising 'my poor child'. What man, or woman for that matter, at the consulate, would condemn me for such a seamless performance? Drama is a deadly theatre, as Brook might have said himself.

for being'. There is no point in telling a child the truth; or, at least, not until the child is mature enough to understand the necessity of hiding his/her origins from authority figures, such as teachers, who may feel impelled, out of duty to the law, to request the intervention of family services.

Now, I don't know if my Parisian interlocutor somehow misunderstood my political leanings but, when I retorted that, to me, defining the maturity of a child in accordance with his/her capacity for complicity in perpetuating a lie about his/her origins and identity was a pretty foul prospect, I was personally attacked. At this point, *Madame* dared to question my allegiance to the cause of gay rights and implied that I seemed more sympathetic to those right-wing institutions that champion the rights of children as a means of defending family values and, thus, maintaining the status quo by acquiescing to the appeal of a Christian heritage which deifies the child and considers his or her rights as sacrosanct, while vilifying any individual who deviates from the parameters of the traditional male–female bond.

Uh-huh.

Well, all I could think to say to that was 'Whatever.' Welcome to Paris, where queer militants, sipping wine and eating puff pastries in a five-star hotel, justify their pose of radicalism by reducing the very real moral concerns of a gay father-to-be to an intellectual debate rooted in age-old political hostilities between church and state.

Is there a conclusion on the horizon or am I going to just have to force myself to quit in order to get some rest?

I don't honestly know how best to conclude these rambling diaries of a day in the life of an intended parent/flâneur. Perhaps I should sum up my wandering monologue by saying that, at almost 40 years of age, I have finally 'had it' with any rhetoric, gay or straight, that seeks to convince me, in countless ways, that I already 'have it all'.

I do beg to differ.

As long as a life-to-be can only be justified on the compromise and conditions of a *non-lieu*, I cannot dismiss the feeling that this legal loophole I am being handed stands as a coil of compliance with the same heterosexist Establishment that I must oppose in order to evolve beyond mere performance and claim the space necessary to assert myself as a vocal and generous protagonist of life.

The *non-lieu* is not primarily a French legal term for me. Thanks to Brook's teachings, I can choose to reinterpret the term freely as a metaphor for a queer journey. As an actor might play with an expression or infuse life into a meaningful pause, I too can risk this as a man, as a father-to-be, and as a scholar. I can be in Paris. I can be in a basement. I can be in a non place. I can be a father-to-be. I can be 'whatever'.

'I can take any empty space and call it a bare stage. A man walks across this empty space whilst someone is watching him, and this is all that is needed for an act of theatre to begin.' (Brook, 2008, p. 11)

↑ (Look no further.)
C'est la vie!

References

Antier, E and M Gross (2007) *2 papas, 2 mamans, qu'en penser? Débat sur l'homoparentalité* (Paris: Calmann-Lévy)
Bond Stockton, K (2009) *The Queer Child: Or Growing Sideways in the Twentieth Century*, M Aina Barale, J Goldberg, M Moon and E Kosofsky (eds) (Sedgwick, Durham: Duke University Press)
Brook, P (2008) *The Empty Space* (London: Penguin Modern Classics)
Cadoret, A (2008) *Genitori come gli altri. Omosessualià e genitorialità*, F Leoni (trans.) (Milan: Feltrinelli)
Gross, M and M Peyceré (2007) *Fonder une famille homoparentale* (Paris: Éditions Ramsay)
Huber, F and U Leemann (2008) *Lesbiche con figli*, Associazione gay lesbica (trans. from German) (Ticino, Bellinzona: Edizioni Imbarco Immediato)
Kaim, S (2006) *Nous, enfants d'homos. Homoparentalité, une generation témoigne* (Paris: Éditions de la Martinière).
Lalli, C (2009) *Buoni genitori* (Milan: il Saggiatore)
Markens, S (2007) *Surrogate Motherhood and the Politics of Reproduction* (Berkley: University of California Press)
Strah, D and S Margolis (2004) *Gay Dads: A Celebration of Fatherhood* (New York: Tarcher/Penguin)
Tervonen, T (2009) 'Ces gays qui optent pour un mère porteuse' 2(143) (April) *Têtu News*

Part III
Shifting Epistemologies

8
'On the Study Methods of our Time': Methodologies of Law and Literature in the Context of Interdisciplinary Studies

Jeanne Gaakeer

Law and literature

The interconnection of the various forms of disciplinary co-operation that can be discerned in the field of law and literature, and the methodologies involved, is a topic that is of increasing concern to me. I say so as a scholar combining literary–legal scholarship with legal practice and as a judge working in the field of criminal law. My central concern is that, in the field of law and literature, it is more important now than ever before for us to address the issue of the form of interdisciplinarity that we espouse, whether we start from the law side of things or come to the field from literary theory, and that, subsequently, we need to pay more attention to the ways in which we aim to show the importance of our literary–legal negotiations for legal practice.

Both elements of my thesis originate from, first, what I have begun to perceive in the field as a lack of reflection upon the significance of law and literature in the combined term 'law and literature'. What do we mean when we speak of law or literature? A second root of my thesis lies in my observation that much of what law and literature hoped for has not yet materialized. I suggest that we need to be more outspoken about law and literature methodologies and, at the same time, reflect on how our methodological choices affect the meta-level of (the application of) interdisciplinary studies generally. On the premise that in law theory and practice are always interconnected, I suggest in this chapter that the perspective offered by Giambattisto Vico is still of interest today, not only because of his views on a general humanist education, but more specifically for his advice to strive for cultural knowledge as a whole and to unify our cognitive and creative capacities by connecting our critical reflections on the human condition to contextual understanding and the imagination. To me, this makes Vico admirably suited as a source of inspiration for a discussion on literary–legal methodologies, considering the emphasis placed in law and literature on the (legal) imagination. Hence also the title of this chapter, which refers to Vico's 1708 oration *On the Study Methods of our Time* that serves as a metaphor for the view I propose and elaborate on below (Vico, 1990).

Why the question matters

If we recapture the historical background of the revival of interest in the humanistic study of law that led to the genesis of what is now called law and literature, it is important to note that, in the 1960s and 1970s, an increase of statutes necessitated American lawyers to address issues of interpretation in a way different from traditional common law methodology, and they looked to the humanities for help. They rediscovered literature as a source for the legal professional. As John Wigmore had already suggested, lawyers at the start of the twentieth century would do well to remember that the portrayal of law *in* literature offers valuable lessons to lawyers (Wigmore, 1908). Shortly thereafter, American lawyers began to take an interest in what literary theory had to offer. Furthermore, they reverted to the seminal work of Justice Benjamin Cardozo on the bond between law and literature in both form and style, and the usage of their common instrument, language; the view, in short, that law can be seen *as* literature (Cardozo, 1925).

This development was supported by the fact that the social sciences too were in the process of turning to interpretation (Geertz, 1973; 1983). Economics and statistics had by that time already shown their importance as auxiliary disciplines in the study of law, as the development of both common law and legal theory since the days of Oliver Wendell Holmes Jr showed. Sociological jurisprudence and legal realism had found worthy successors in the law and society movement and law and economics. In short, lawyers had to face the fact that, in order to find answers to questions that they had before considered as belonging to the exclusive domain of law as an autonomous discipline, it was necessary to open the door to other disciplines. From then on, as disciplines complementary to law expanded their territory, the 'law and...' movements were on the rise. Law had lost that tranquil quality of being 'a subject properly entrusted to persons trained in law and in nothing else', as Richard Posner succinctly defined law's autonomy (Posner, 1987, p. 762; and Posner, 1990).

Posner's definition is important when dealing with conceptual issues in law and literature, not least because his view on the importance of literature for law is rather restricted in that his answer to the question 'What can lawyers learn from literature?' would be 'Not much.' To him, literary works and literary theory are of use only when they highlight technical, doctrinal aspects of law. When literary works deal with questions of justice, lawyers are advised to stick to their own trade. Posner's book on the subject, now in its third edition, is on practically every reading list for students of law and literature (Posner, 1988; 1998; 2009): rather paradoxical since Posner restricts the possible value of research on law and literature to an instrumental one. According to Posner, interdisciplinarity is the mere importation of a technique or methodology from one field to another, for the purpose of solving a specific problem, if the solution cannot be found in the original field itself. This too is a restricted view on disciplinary co-operation, one that is better defined as transdisciplinary, for it is a method of merely finding the exact point at which opportunities for co-operation exist, after which, disciplines go their own way; rather than true interdisciplinarity which, in my view and following James Boyd White's view (White, 1990), involves an integrative approach by means of which something new comes into being.

The above is important to note because, both in the Anglo-American common law tradition and the continental civil law tradition, hence inside and outside of legal positivism so to speak, the substantive question of legal theory – 'What is law?' – has always been and remains on the agenda. Legal theorists habitually ask whether reconciliation is possible between law's normative claims to authority and law's workings as an institution in society, and in doing so they cannot escape bringing forth a concept of law as they see it. The controversy between natural law and a positivist concept of law is another case in point. There are good reasons, of course, to insist on making explicit one's concept of law. One is for purposes of legal scholarship, as Ronald Dworkin made clear when he disagreed with H L A Hart's definition of law as descriptive (1961) (rather than morally or ethically evaluative), because, or so Dworkin claims, 'a legal theory itself rests on moral and ethical judgments and convictions' (Dworkin, 2004, p. 2). In legal theory, it is de rigueur to examine the relationship between metaphysical issues of the type Dworkin raises and the implicit or explicit philosophical assumptions underlying them. A second reason is that it is necessary for semantic clarity when it comes to the distinction between law and justice, between the just as a regulative idea and ideal and, as Paul Ricoeur put it, the legal as the predicate of the domain of positive law(s) (Ricoeur, 2005, p. 15).

The latter distinction is important for law and literature when it offers the humanities as a repository of values and proposes to incorporate what literature knows into the discipline of law, because all too often in literary–legal analyses a semantic collapse of law and justice can be perceived. The discussion of Shakespeare's *The Merchant of Venice* in literay–legal studies serves as a case in point when historical notions of positive law in Shakespeare's day, philosophical aspects of equity and justice, and contemporary legal theories dealing with the differences between natural law and legal positivism are often happily lumped together. I would suggest that a clarification of our usage of the concepts of law and literature is necessary. What is it that we bring to law and literature as lawyers, as literary theorists or as scholars in the humanities? We need to show our conceptual colours, for the outcome of our interdisciplinary meeting depends on what we bring to it.

What struck me first is that even though another, more pragmatic reason for the rise of law and literature is said to lie in the fact that a constricted job market for graduate students in the humanities in the 1970s in the USA led many to seek refuge from unemployment by entering law school (Minow, 1987), this does not seem to have had a great impact as far as their bringing a concept of literature to the field. This also goes for the influx of philosophical and philological hermeneutics, from the Yale school of literary criticism centred round Paul de Man to the legal academy in the 1970s, culminating in poststructuralist deconstruction. Once interpretive methods began to be looked upon as strategies in the sense of instruments to justify existing power structures, and the possibility of a single objective meaning of a text was denied in favour of a subjective, reader-based constitution of meaning, law as the subject of literary–legal research became politicized and was held up before us as an ideology. That shifted the focus as far as the concept of law was concerned in that it restricted law to the level of the polity and moved away from the perceived hegemonic.

The 'law in–law as' bifurcation and the road not taken

One of the reasons, I think, that attention to conceptual issues has lagged behind is that almost immediately, from the very start of the reappraisal of the humanities for law, the focus in law and literature scholarship was on the division into 'law in literature' and 'law as literature' and, more generally speaking, on literature's instrumental value for law. On this view, the legacy of Wigmore and Cardozo is that it makes us reaffirm rather than rethink – and, rest assured, I myself plead guilty to this as well – this bifurcation of the ways in which literature can help lawyers reflect on things ethical and help mitigate the disciplinary tendency of legal education and legal practice to insist on an instrumental methodology of reading texts for purposes of analysis and finding the unequivocal right answer.

The division of law and literature is by now exhaustively documented (Ward, 1995; Gaakeer, 1998; Dolin, 2007; Lachenmaier, 2008) so just a few remarks suffice to illustrate my point. When Wigmore defined a legal novel as 'simply a novel in which a lawyer, most of all, ought to be interested', that did not really offer a specific view on either law or literature; furthermore, literature to Wigmore seems to coincide with the genre of the novel since to him this is 'the true work of fiction' (Wigmore, 1908, p. 579). Cardozo's plea for a lawyer's turning to literature focused on the lessons to be drawn for the purpose of establishing the right connection between style and message, form and content. While his plea is no doubt firmly rooted in the common law tradition, Cardozo being a practitioner, this conceptual presupposition lingers in the background and is never specified. In addition to Wigmore and Cardozo is Richard Weisberg who, while crediting Ephraim London for coining the term 'law in/as literature', in fact helped constitute the bifurcation for the contemporary movement (Weisberg, 1999, p. 50; see also 1976; 1979).

Early critics also pay tribute to this bifurcation. When Harold Suretsky, for example, remarked that literature had too long been seen as 'a seasoning or subtle spice for the lawyer's professional cuisine' but that with the coming of age of law and literature, literature had been accepted as 'a source of truth which can help to analyze and criticize the law itself and to define its societal roles more clearly', we are not told what that concept of literature is, could, or should be other than 'socially-conditioned expressions of consciousness' (Suretsky, 1981, pp. 29 and 34). Furthermore, when critics distinguished between the alternative neo-Marxist, Nietzschean and New Critic strands of law and literature scholarship, or spoke in terms of the case of aesthetics versus ideology (Pacher, 1990), the opportunity to address the significance of literature, let alone in relation to law, was usually foregone. As a consequence, literature was time and again offered as an external, auxiliary resource to law. As a result, law and literature cannot truly be called an interdisciplinary movement, but at the most a transdisciplinary one in the definition noted above, or one in which the findings of literature are put to use for law.

Of course, there are notable exceptions, such as James Boyd White's insistence on the homology of law and literature (White, 1984; 1985); Richard Weisberg's own view on the unity of form and content (Weisberg, 1984; 1992; 1996); Robin West's call for the connection of concepts of law and legal theory to a typology adopted from literary theory (West, 1985a); and, ironically perhaps given his view on the merely auxiliary value of literature to law when it comes to interpretative methods (Posner, 1986a), Richard Posner in his debate with West about Kafka (West, 1985b; Posner, 1986b; West, 1986); and, more recently, Maria Aristodemou who advocates an interdisciplinary view in the strongest sense arguing for an approach 'that is sensitive to both the *literary qualities of law and the law-making qualities of literature*' (Aristodemou, 2000, p. 5, emphasis in original).

Of course, one might counter by saying that lack of attention to the concepts of the two foundational disciplines of our venture is, in fact, a thing of the past. Or one might claim that those advocating a literary–legal canon inevitably offer some concept of literature. But when the latter asks us to accept at face value the importance of literature to law as it is traditionally conceived, a discussion of the concept of law and literature is honoured more in the breach than in the observance.

By way of a first, intermediate conclusion, I think it justified to say that the traditional bifurcation of law and literature has proved to be authoritative and formative to such an extent that a tendency can be perceived to simply fit in new scholarly works in either subfield disregarding the need of clarification of what we mean by the terms 'law' and 'literature'. Our focus on the edifying function of literature for law, or humanistic values in general, has caused attention to move away from foundational issues. Our continued talk about the law, and about literature, is indicative of a focus more on the ends to be attained by means of law and literature than on the μετα την όδον (*meta ten hodon*), or the way to these ends. Thus we run the risk of both demeaning literature as no more than a frill or an instrument, and we demean law, regardless of our notion of it, as sorely lacking any insight into the human condition.

To me, Milner Ball's early warning not to create 'an elegant academic ghetto for a few of us' still holds true (Ball, 1989, p. 191; Heilbrun and Resnik, 1990). While I would dismiss the idea of our needing to build a theory of law and literature for the sake of theory, merely to attain the status of a literary–legal science, we should consider the need for our scholarly venture to seek more methodological and conceptual reflection, and that includes, to start with, a clarification of the terms theory, concept and method as used in the co-operating disciplines. I say so also in view of what I think is necessary for the future of law and literature, or any other interdisciplinary field in which law is involved for that matter, and that is to seek the company of, and contribute to practice, rather than remaining at the purely academic level. From my point of view as a legal practitioner, law and literature so far has generated an enormous and valuable scholarly output, but as an academic field it has not sought co-operation with those working in legal practice. That, I think, is to be deplored given the circumstance that lawyers are writers and storytellers by reason of their profession, an aspect on which I elaborate below.

Here too, one may rebut and argue that from the very fact that law and literature is alive and kicking, we may conclude that the theoretical support we have had so far has proven to be quite sufficient. In short, the vitality of our ongoing debate proves that ours is not a transitory movement. We might, on the same view, conclude from our growth that we managed to get where we are without any theory or methodology, so why bother with it now? I would certainly hesitate to recommend writing a book entitled *The Concept of Law and Literature*. Nevertheless, the possible consequence of a lack of attention to methodological aspects may be a lack of coherence at the interdisciplinary plane. If we rest at the traditional bifurcation, or at alternative classifications for that matter, useful for purposes of education, although they both may help us understand the rich complexity of the field and its contributors, we run the risk of missing opportunities to the extent that we keep talking at cross-purposes. For the further development of a European context, the issue is even more acute now when we are still in the habit of paying homage to the Anglo-American roots of law and literature, as recent European anthologies show: the traditional strands of law and literature are reiterated, disregarding the specificity of our different legal systems and cultures (Brogniez, 2007; Jongen and Lemmens, 2007; Garapon and Salas, 2008).

A little learning is a dangerous thing

This brings me to the question of the reciprocity of our disciplinary relationships. Given the institutional and scholarly successes of law and literature and its intellectual diversity as far as the propositions for new jurisprudences are concerned, law has obviously negotiated a relationship to literature. The picture, however, remains the same. The role of literature to law is an important albeit a predominantly auxiliary one, where literature functions as an antidote to help soften the harsher qualities of its host (Fludernik and Olson, 2004, p. xxxi). From this point of view, literature is still the perspective from which to view law, rather than the other way around. Furthermore, there is another debate lingering in the background: is law part of the social sciences, or does it belong to the humanities? The position taken here is obviously important when it comes to the discussion about the future of law and literature as part of the broader field of law and the humanities or law and culture.

So let's, if only for the sake of the argument, turn things the other way around. If literature is supposed to teach lawyers to render their own field less abstract, if literature is thought to be the instrument with which to humanize lawyers, if literature is a storehouse of topics and claims of meaning to law, in short, if literature can serve a variety of utilitarian purposes, then the salient question would be, what is law to literature, or rather what can literature learn from law?

Of course, a literary discourse impregnated by legal issues such as revenge and retribution can be found in classical Greek tragedies as sites of crisis and hence sites of judgment. Furthermore, as far as literary production is concerned, examples abound of the influence of law on the writings of authors as varied as Balzac, Stendhal, Dickens, Tolstoy, Dreiser, Kafka, Musil and Gide. Additionally, one might argue that, as far as the genre of the crime novel is concerned, for it to be able to lay a minimal claim of authenticity, it must be realistic in terms of law (Müller-Dietz, 1990). I think it is fair to say, nevertheless, that when literary scholars turn to law in order to learn, they often do so in order to gain a better understanding of the socio-legal and socio-historical context of literary production, including issues of ideology and gender (Schramm, 1999).

To me, the question of how literature can benefit from law and the question of reciprocity force us to address the issue of what follows from the similarities and dissimilarities between literary production and legal production as we engage in practice. This means that we would do well to shift our focus to the comparative aspects of literary–legal research in the European context, not least because of the original symbiosis of law and literature in practice, with medieval France and the German oral tradition of *Dichtung und Recht* as cases in point (Bloch, 1977; Kaufmann, 1984). In other words, given the relatively recent, nineteenth-century *Ausdifferenzierung* (the process of the differentiation of knowledge into separate disciplines) of law and literature as distinct fields and disciplines, as well as the comparable process of differentiation within law itself (law being the mother discipline of economics, sociology and anthropology), research into the history of ideas of the interrelation of law and literature might serve to investigate the reciprocity of law and literature at the concrete level of practice(s). It is therefore remarkable that in contemporary interdisciplinary literary–legal work, the value of its contribution to the day-to-day work of those in legal practice is usually disregarded, although there are notable exceptions (Watt, 2009). It is also remarkable when we think of the analogies in the construction of a jurisprudential canon and a literary canon. Given that on the normative plane both enterprises are based on precedent in the sense of a pre-given source of authority, interest in practice would seem called for. And although law's aim is generally thought of in terms of normativity and the realization of societal goals, and literature's normative claims are often referred to as aesthetic (lawyers often regard literature's self-referential quality as a disadvantage since law resists an unbounded form of pluralism), this need not preclude literary–legal research of the type I advocate here. The comparative perspective is called for exactly because of the similarities and dissimilarities of law and literature as far as hermeneutic methodologies are concerned (Sharpe, 1999; Malaurie, 2008).

From yet another angle, the lack of attention to practice is even more remarkable: in the past decades, we have witnessed a tendency to move away from the notion of high culture, or in other words, we have moved from Dostoevsky and Shakespeare to *Crime Scene Investigation* and *Boston Legal*. As far as I am concerned, when it comes to upholding the values we care for in law, the influence of popular literature and popular culture from tabloids to television series calls for a counter-reaction to popular culture's law-bashing or farcical, perverse portrayal of law. On the subjects of the interrelation of law and popular culture and the incorporation of the visual in legal practice, Richard Sherwin has already made important contributions from an Anglo-American point of view. Here, too, exists the possibility to discuss differences and similarities between the various legal cultures and systems and their representations in cultural artefacts. Again, this also teaches us to focus on what is it that we do and bring to our enterprise. Especially now that, paradoxically, the gist of so many products of popular culture is, at the same time, that law is the great redeemer and that in the end law and justice will prevail. Such notions exist in sharp contrast to everyday legal reality that includes plea-bargaining, miscarriages of justice, biased jury selections in common law legal systems, the law's delay, or the consequences of assigning heavy tasks to relatively inexperienced judges (Garapon and Salas, 2006; Lehmann, 2006). The further study of this very contrast is called for, or so I would argue, by means of discussing the various insights from the humanities on how both textual and visual representation in and of law make their claims for meaning. As already noted above, those in legal practice are writers and storytellers. By means of language they claim meaning and are themselves influenced by what others – be it opponents in a court of law, judicial opinions, or legal codes – have to offer. That is why, as a legal practitioner, I now turn to the subject of the relation of facts and interpretation in law, and to Vico's view on the importance of the humanities for law.

Without wonder, what knowledge?

In view of the distinction between law and justice made above, awareness of the circumstance that in law, theory and practice are interrelated in the sense of their being mutually dependant, is of the utmost importance for interdisciplinary studies. The development of law and literature as a scholarly endeavour has made us forget that the impetus for the legal turning to literature was originally found in the observation that the legal profession was in need of a broader cultural foundation in the humanities. In my view, it is necessary to redirect our scholarly attention to this starting point. Why? Because essential to the methodology of the legal perception of the case at hand is what the German jurist Larenz called the 'Hin-und Herwandern des Blickes' (Larenz, 1960), letting both the mind's eye and our literal gaze go to and fro, from the facts of the case and back to the legal norm. Hence, not only are both the facts and the law subject to our interpretations, but also what we call the facts are themselves the products of our selection processes with respect to *other people's acts* and of our imposing narrative coherence upon them. Here we see a crucial difference between the legal and the literary scholar in that the literary scholar does not have to deal with unmediated brute facts in the sense of concrete human action. Thus, legal methodology is always doubly directed in that it necessarily focuses on the combination of norms and the perception of the facts, both of which demand interpretation. That process, in turn, is guided by our 'pre-judices', not in the usual negative sense of biases, but in the sense of our *Vorverständnisse* as Gadamer called them in *Truth and Method* (Gadamer, 1975). *Vorverständnisse* refer to our present understandings of the world prior to any new judgment, and they too are guided by our theoretical knowledge and our practical experience. In short, the primary object of legal interpretation is never the (legal) text in and of itself.

As a consequence, law is by definition open to change, to refinement and improvement: new situations and new cases constantly force the lawyer to rethink legal doctrine and act on the demands for changes (im)posed by them. This process is constantly at work as we move from perception to the level of ordering, both in the sense of the outcome of the case and our view of what the law is. Thus the combination of facticity and normativity is implied in the ordering process of law itself. For the relation of law to legal theory, the consequence is that theoretical knowledge and legal interpretation are intertwined. Legal practice provides theoreticians with actual cases and questions of law that often go beyond the doctrinal imaginable.

Here too is an opportunity for a humanist jurisprudence of the type offered by law and literature. Law and literature share the methodology of hermeneutics, both in the sense of the interpretation of texts and as a method to speak meaningfully of human action. This methodology is necessarily differentiated according to object and purpose. The application of interpretive efforts is the aim of legal theory in that it generates solutions in the service of practical questions of law. Literary theory obviously has more hermeneutic freedom than legal theory. Given the rise of cultural studies, we have even more reason to think of matters conceptual and comparative when we engage in interdisciplinary learning.

That both literary and legal theory have as their starting point a methodologically educated *Vorverständnis* leads me to the question: what exactly is our *Vorverständnis* in law and literature? While law and literature obviously share the methodology of moving from text to meaning or interpretive result via the method of hermeneutics in the sense of claiming meaning after a process of interpretation, law necessarily moves beyond this phase when the institutional power of its word directly and radically affects the lives of people in society. Furthermore, the fact that law is always institutionally embedded works as a corrective on what can and may be said under specific circumstances. So the interaction of text and action, of theory and practice is central to law and legal theory. As a consequence, law as a discipline comprises both doctrinal law and a methodology of hermeneutics, making any interdisciplinary venture a language problem inescapably connected to conceptual presuppositions. This also speaks for comparative research in law and literature.

To me, therefore, the humanistic study of law should be a *praxis*, one that seeks to reconnect legal and literary theory to the practice of law. I am inspired here by Giambattisto Vico's *De Nostri Temporis Studiorum Ratione* (*On the Study Methods of our Time*), the seventh of a series of inaugural orations, delivered at the start of the academic year in Naples in 1708 as part of what was required of Vico as a professor of Latin eloquence whose duties among others involved helping students achieve the necessary qualifications for the practice of law (Vico, 1990). It is an early example of Vico's works on a methodology for a humanist education and I think it is admirably suited to serve as a reminder if we are serious about dropping our disciplinary methodological camouflage and aim at having law and literature make an indispensable contribution to both scholarship and practice.

In general, we accept the claim that, 'law's narratives may help create truth' and that 'Judgment is not, then, a search for "the" truth, but involves choices among competing truths. To understand the legal situation of parties, a decision maker must learn to grasp their "self-understandings"' (Baron, 1991, pp. 88 and 104), and the claim for interpretation and the (results of the) application of practical wisdom that the situation demands to attain knowledge should gain in prominence. It is not incidentally that Gadamer refers precisely to this oration when he connects practical wisdom and eloquence (in law) via the idea of common sense as a form of probability. Note also that the Latin root of the term jurisprudence is *iuris prudentia*, insightful knowledge of law, prudence in and of matters legal. All this is even more topical in view of the traditional concept of legal doctrine in the sense of the categorization of what may count as knowledge in law. In order, therefore, to speak meaningfully to and with one another in our disciplines, we will do well to return to Vico's thoughts and more specifically to his methodology on the basis of his thesis that the true and the made are convertible.

Remembrance of things past

Vico is important, first, because, in *On the Study Methods of our Time*, he takes the 'happy opportunity to devise an argument that should bring some new and profitable discovery to the world of letters' (Vico, 1963, p. 146), and this promotion of the value of the *litterae humaniores* is one that interdisciplinary fields, especially those that share language as their basic tool, need to cherish (Gaakeer, 2010). Vico laments the analytical methodology that Descartes developed in *Discours de la Méthode*, in which clarity and certainty in human knowledge collapse, because it insists on its own monistic character. That is to say that the fact that '[M]odern philosophical "critique" is the common instrument of all our sciences and arts' and that it claims to supply us, 'with a fundamental verity of which we can be certain even when assailed by doubt' (Vico, 1990, pp. 6 and 9) is a direct reference to Descartes' *cogito*. Or, as Mootz puts it succinctly, *Study Methods* is 'one of the most concise and incisive articulations of the peril of wholesale surrender to Cartesian methodologism' (Mootz, 2008, p. 1097). Descartes obviously held the world of language and letters in contempt. Vico's emphasis is on the combined human capacity for rational thought and for expressing emotion, and the image immediately introduced to personify Vichean man is the lawyer: 'The anti-thesis Vico–Descartes is…the contrast between the mentality of the jurist and that of the mathematician, between the spirit of erudition, and that fostered by the "exact" sciences.' (Vico, 1990, p. xxviii) To Vico, what matters most here is our human *fantasia*, our imagination as the capacity to give form to what experience offers us, and that requires an act of consciousness as well as our awareness of it. This characteristic, or precondition, is what makes a good lawyer, and it can serve as the linchpin when it comes to combining the disciplines of law and literature in the interdiscipline law and literature: the imagination is what matters in and to the humanities. It is important to note that, throughout his work, Vico therefore warns against a one-sided approach to education, or one favouring the natural sciences above the humanities, as can be seen from his remark that:

> the greatest drawback of our educational methods is that we pay an excessive amount of attention to the natural sciences and not enough to ethics. Our chief fault is that we disregard that part of ethics which treats of human character, of its dispositions, its passions, and the manner of adjusting these factors to public life and eloquence. (Vico, 1990, p. 33)

That has an uncanny contemporary ring to it. In October 2009, for example, Dutch captains of industry complained that young employees with a masters degree fell short when it came to ethical behaviour, and they strongly suggested that the universities do something about that. It would seem, then, that there is nothing new under the sun.

Vico is important as well for the epistemological debate on types of inquiry because, long before Dilthey and later thinkers such as Weber, he already spoke in terms of *Verstehen*, the method of understanding, as a way of knowing that is essential to history and other disciplines in the humanities, and in contrast to the explanatory method of the natural sciences, *Erklären* (Berlin, 1976, pp. 27–30 and 106–8). The origin of the struggle to promote the methodology and unitary model of knowledge of the natural sciences for all disciplines can already be found in the development of rationalism and empiricism since the late sixteenth and seventeenth centuries (Toulmin, 1990; 2001). The debate rages on in law and legal theory, given another interdisciplinary development, namely the influx of the empirical sciences such as sociology, statistics and economics in law. That is yet another reason why a reflection on Vico's starting points may help to enlighten our conceptual premises in interdisciplinary investigations.

In scientific inquiries, Vico starts from the thesis that the true and the made are convertible: *verum et factum convertuntur*. The root for this *verum–factum* principle can be found in *Study Methods* where Vico challenges the presumed certitudes of the exact sciences by saying: 'the principles of physics which are put forward as truths on the strength of the geometrical method are not really truths, but wear a semblance of probability' and 'We are able to demonstrate geometrical propositions because we create them; were it possible for us to supply demonstrations of propositions of physics, we would be capable of creating them *ex nihilo* as well.' (Vico, 1990, p. 23) To Vico, any scientific endeavour is equivalent to knowledge of the way in which things came into being. Knowledge, in short, is genetic knowledge. If we have a strong belief in and through acquaintance with a *factum* – and it should at once be emphasized that *factum* refers to things man-made – then on this precondition and presupposition we are able to reach a *verum*, cognition of a truth. In all this, Vico's focus is on the humanities, *factum* as man-made leading us to man's creations such as literature and languages as well as poetic literary creations and, not surprisingly, the habits and customs of man, the latter leading directly to the inclusion of law as *factum*.

With Vico, we may then also ask ourselves what the genesis and subsequent development of law and literature have been so far. What is it that we have made with and of law and literature? If with Vico, and later thinkers on the subject of hermeneutics such as Heidegger and Gadamer, we agree that there is no place outside language from which we can observe human beings and their *facta*, then we can bring our attention to the products of our human action rather than keep trying to claim scientific certitude for the humanities, and thus move beyond the object–subject dichotomy of scientific inquiries. In other words, we must accept the contingency of our inescapable intersubjectivity. Here is another argument for incorporating legal practice into our attempt to develop a literary–legal jurisprudence, especially now that Vico promotes the value of literature and points to universities as centres of learning. The demands of practice in the sense of being able to do what is necessary under the circumstances needs the input of what theory may provide in order to move beyond the individual case, while at the same time each new case may be the start of an argument that innovates theory, one that changes doctrine. The ultimate aim of the whole endeavour, of course, is to arrive at the (best possible) truth.

To take this line of thought one step further: if the *verum–factum* principle has any validity, then any construction depends on the circumstances of the case, in principle infinite in possibilities. Exit the positivist insistence on the separation of law and morals. Enter the claim that law and ethics meet in the professional demand for practical wisdom that combines the head and the heart, exercising prudence while being knowledgeable about things legal. Enter law and literature and the realization that we are the agents in the construction of this *factum*.

If by way of conclusion we return to our earlier question, we may ask how law and literature grounds itself, or rather how it authorizes itself through the (hi)story it tells. If we want to bridge the chasm between the reality of what we call our world and our understanding of it, we will do well to realize that what we posit as reality is a *factum* too, one open to debate. That means that we need an interactionist perspective, from its early form in Vico to its contemporary form in philosophical and legal hermeneutics, in legal theory and practice, and in interdisciplinary studies, in order to understand reality as a *factum* that tolerates a range of meaningful interpretations but does not accept a nihilist, or ultimate deconstructionist 'anything goes' type of argument. That is what a further *rapprochement* to practice can also teach the academy, and the academy in turn can contribute by bringing coherence to a body of learning, not in the Cartesian way, by imposing a single system on all disciplines, but by following Vico's advice, 'to be well versed in all fields of knowledge' (Vico, 1990, p. 78). In doing so, we need to reflect on the variety of ways in which we construct narrative coherence, and to probe the reciprocal relation between law and literature on this plane, for, as Maria Aristodemou argued, 'narratives are not neutral: they investigate but also suggest, create, and legislate meanings' (Aristodemou, 2000, p. 3). Whether or not I have fully succeeded in doing so in this chapter, mine also being the internal perspective of law and law and literature with its corresponding prejudices, remains to be decided. But here it is, and so I end on a sobering note – or a disclaimer typical of the jurist? – for did not Vico write:

> It is a common experience to see an individual who has concentrated all of his efforts on a single branch of study, and who has spent all his life on it, think that his field is, by far, more important than all others, and to see him inclined to make application of its specialty to matters wholly foreign to it? (Vico, 1990, p. 80)

References

Aristodemou, M (2000) *Law and Literature: Journeys from Her to Eternity* (Oxford: Oxford University Press)

Ball, M (1989) 'Confessions' **1** *Cardozo Studies in Law and Literature* 185–97
Baron, J B (1991) 'The Many Promises of Storytelling in Law' **23** *Rutgers Law Journal* 79–105
Berlin, I (1976) *Vico and Herder: Two Studies in the History of Ideas* (London: Hogarth Press)
Bloch, R H (1977) *Medieval French Literature and Law* (Berkeley: University of California Press)
Brogniez, L (ed.) (2007) *Textyles: Droit et Littérature* (Brussels: Le Cri Edition)
Cardozo, B N (1925) 'Law and Literature' *Yale Review* 489–507
Dolin, K (2007) *A Critical Introduction to Law and Literature* (Cambridge: Cambridge University Press)
Dworkin, R (2004) 'Hart's Postscript and the Character of Political Philosophy' **24** *Oxford Journal of Legal Studies* 1–37
Fludernik, M and G Olson (2004) *In the Grip of Law: Trials, Prisons and the Space Between* (Frankfurt: Peter Lang)
Gaakeer, J (1998) *Hope Springs Eternal: An Introduction to the Work of James Boyd White* (Amsterdam: Amsterdam University Press)
Gaakeer, J (2010) 'Law and Literature in Europe: A First Pragmatic Inquiry' in B Pozzo (ed.), *Teaching Law through the Looking Glass of Literature* (Bern: Staempfli Publishers), pp. 59–75 and 121–32
Gadamer, H-G (1975) *Truth and Method*, G Barden and J Cumming (eds) (New York: Seabury Press)
Garapon, A and D Salas (eds) (2008) *Imaginer la loi: le droit dans la littérature* (Paris: Éditions Michalon)
Garapon, A and D Salas (2006) *Les nouvelles sorcières de Salem: Leçons d'Outreau* (Paris: Seuil)
Geertz, C (1973) *The Interpretation of Cultures* (New York: Basic Books)
Geertz, C (1983) *Local Knowledge* (New York: Basic Books)
Hart, H L A (1961) *The Concept of Law* (Oxford: Clarendon Press)
Heilbrun, C and J Resnik (1990) 'Convergences: Law, Literature, and Feminism' **99** *Yale Law Journal* 1913–56
Jongen, F and K Lemmens (eds) (2007) *Recht en Literatuur – Droit et Littérature*, (Louvain-la-Neuve: Anthemis, Die Keure/La Charte)
Kaufmann, E (1984) *Deutsches Recht* (Berlin: E Schmidt)
Lachenmaier, B M (2008) *Die Law as Literature-Bewegung* (Berlin: Wissenschaftlicher Verlag Berlin)
Larenz, K F (1960) *Methodenlehre der Rechtswissenschaft* (Berlin: Springer)
Lehmann, C (2006) 'Legal Fictions' *California Lawyer* 38–41 and 70–1
Malaurie, Ph. (2008) 'Les exigences contraires de la littérature et du droit' in A Garapon and D Salas (eds), *Imaginer la loi: le droit dans la littérature* (Paris: Éditions Michalon)

Minow, M (1987) 'Law Turning Outward' **73** *Telos* 79–100

Mootz, F J (2008) 'Introduction to Recalling Vico's Lament: The Role of Prudence and Rhetoric in Law and Legal Education' **83** *Chicago-Kent Law Review* 1097–105

Müller-Dietz, H (1990) 'Die Kreise der Dichter und der Juristen. Zur historischen Beziehung zwischen literarischem und juristischem Diskurs' *Diskussion Deutsch* 243–63

Pacher, D K (1990) 'Aesthetics vs. Ideology: The Motives behind "Law and Literature"' **14** *Columbia–VLA Journal of Law and the Arts* 587–614

Posner, R A (1986a) 'Law and Literature: A Relation Reargued' **72** *Virginia Law Review* 1351–92

Posner, R A (1986b) 'The Ethical Significance of Free Choice' **99** *Harvard Law Review* 1431–48

Posner, R A (1987) 'The Decline of Law as an Autonomous Discipline: 1962–1987' **100** *Harvard Law Review* 761–80

Posner, R A (1988) *Law and Literature: A Misunderstood Relation* (Cambridge, MA: Harvard University Press); 2nd revised and enlarged edn (1998) and 3rd edn (2009) are entitled *Law and Literature* (both Cambridge, MA: Harvard University Press)

Posner, R A (1990) *The Problems of Jurisprudence* (Cambridge, MA: Harvard University Press)

Ricoeur, P (2005) *Le juste, la justice et son échec* (Paris: L'Herme)

Schramm, J-M (1999) 'Is Literature More Ethical than Law? Fitzjames Stephen and Literary Responses to the Advent of Full Legal Representation for Felons' in M A Freeman and A D E Lewis (eds), *Law and Literature: Current Legal Issues* (Oxford: Oxford University Press), pp. 417–35

Sharpe, T (1999) '(Per)versions of Law in Literature' in M A Freeman and A D E Lewis (eds), *Law and Literature: Current Legal Issues* (Oxford: Oxford University Press), pp. 91–115

Suretsky, H (1981) 'The Concept of Ideology and its Application to Law and Literature Studies' **5** *ALSA Forum* 29–39

Toulmin, S (1990) *Cosmopolis* (Chicago: University of Chicago Press)

Toulmin, S (2001) *Return to Reason* (Cambridge, MA: Harvard University Press)

Vico, G (1990) *On the Study Methods of Our Time*, E Gianturco (trans.), 'Preface' by D Ph. Verene (Ithaca and London: Cornell University Press)

Vico, G (1963) *The Autobiography of Giambattista Vico*, M H Fisch and Th. G Bergin (trans.) (Ithaca and London: Cornell University Press)

Ward, I (1995) *Law and Literature: Possibilities and Perspectives* (Cambridge: Cambridge University Press)

Watt, G (2009) *Equity Stirring: The Story of Justice beyond Law* (Oxford and Portland, OR: Hart Publishing)

Weisberg, R H (1976) 'Wigmore's "Legal Novels" Revisited: New Resources for the Expanding Lawyer' **71** *Northwestern University Law Review* 17–28

Weisberg, R H (1979) 'Law, Literature and Cardozo's Judicial Poetics' **1** *Cardozo Law Review* 283–342

Weisberg, R H (1984) *The Failure of the Word* (New Haven and London: Yale University Press)

Weisberg, R H (1992) *Poethics* (New York: Columbia University Press)

Weisberg, R H (1996) *Vichy Law and the Holocaust in France* (New York: New York University Press)

Weisberg, R H (1999) 'Literature's Twenty-Year Crossing into the Domain of Law: Continuing Trespass or Right by Adverse Possession?' in M A Freeman and A Lewis (eds), *Law and Literature: Current Legal Issues* (Oxford: Oxford University Press)

West, R (1985a) 'Jurisprudence as Narrative' **60** *New York University Law Review* 145–211

West, R (1985b) 'Authority, Autonomy, and Choice: The Role of Consent in the Moral and Political Visions of Franz Kafka and Richard Posner' **99** *Harvard Law Review* 384–428

West, R (1986) 'Submission, Choice and Ethics: A Rejoinder to Judge Posner' **99** *Harvard Law Review* 1449–56

Wigmore, J H (1908) 'A List of Legal Novels' **2** *Illinois Law Review* 574–93

White, J B (1984) *When Words Lose Their Meaning* (Chicago: University of Chicago Press)

White, J B (1985) *Heracles' Bow* (Madison: University of Wisconsin Press)

White, J B (1990) *Justice as Translation* (Chicago: University of Chicago Press)

9
The Reader as Thought Experiment: Character, Moral Luck and the Contingent

Melanie Williams

Introduction

Though certainty and consistency in law is critical to the maintenance of justice, as the living instrument of humankind's exercise of social regulation, law must be responsive to the normative motivating forces of human agency as they are revealed through scientific, social scientific and philosophical reflection. Whilst the certainties of biblical tenets and taboos, for example, provided firm foundations for the designation of legal principle and continue to provide a proving ground or benchmark against which the development of subsequent principles may be evaluated – for those foundations, after all, arose in response to some fundamental truths concerning human nature – the story of what it is to be human and to exist in the world of events and actions, is still being revealed to us.

Certain revelations are particularly uncomfortable. Over the last one hundred years we have learned that modern civilisation is hardly a bastion against iniquity with the citizen often revealed as less than robust in moral crises. The findings of science may inform this realisation – genetics as well as neuroscience disrupt classical notions of free-willing agency – yet we remain uncertain, sometimes resistant, as to the resultant moral imperative. And just as science, history, law, politics and philosophy can tell us much about ourselves, literature too, often regarded as an entertainment or an indulgence, may engage some of the deepest questions in helping us to understand the challenges of our nature and existence. Suspicious of the motivational, as well as evidential standing of the literary form, some science – and social science – scholars are, and will be, deeply hostile to such a suggestion (for discussion and response to such critics see Williams, 2009a). Nevertheless, one may assert that literary fiction provides a means of testing out the complex drives and human responses as they play out against networks of event, circumstance and consequence. Noting that the thought experiments of philosophy are themselves fictions, often unnaturally divorced from circumstances and human qualities, the thought experiments of literary fiction frequently reveal a percipient understanding of deep human identities and human truths, truths critical to the fundamental mechanisms of justice. Korsgaard (1996) explains that any normative theory must appeal, in a deep sense, to such deep identities; it concerns our conception of who we take ourselves to be. Korsgaard explains that insofar as morality, in its name, demands sacrifices, sometimes even death, a moral theory must account for how moral claims bind themselves to our identities. She explains: 'If moral claims are ever worth dying for, then violating them must be in a similar way, worse than death. And this means that they must issue in a deep way from our sense of who we are.' (1996, p. 18) Where the norms of a society are essentially dystopic, the 'deep identity' available to its citizens may be similarly skewed, the ability to discriminate moral choices correspondingly flawed and the experiments of imagination may help us to interrogate such phenomena.

This essay will consider just such a thought experiment, Bernhard Schlink's *The Reader* (1998), a novel concerned with unpalatable questions of historical truth and event, and of moral and legal questions of culpability, individual and collective. My aim in analysing *The Reader* is to explore the difficult lesson in human nature – and the implications for law – explored by the book and by the film (first screened in 2008 and directed by Stephen Daldry) of the same name. Reflection upon the message, the hypothesis posed by this book makes pertinent consideration of the philosophical concept known as moral luck since the convergence of worlds represented by the bringing together of morality with luck encapsulates the profound reality of conflicted agency engendered by our existence in the world, challenging the sanitised separation of the normative from the contingent, a separation so neatly claimed and promoted by law. Further, consideration of the reception of this message of both the book and the film by a range of scholars, writers and reviewers, is revealing. These responses disclose resistance to Schlink's vision of the ordinary person and of the implications for law of such ordinariness; of the pathos, the impotence of the individual as against ideological, historical tides. Polarised, either by hostility to (a misperceived) advocacy in the novel of wholesale exoneration of the perpetrator, or by over-empathic identification with the same, such glosses for the most part avoid the simple, yet devastating conclusion concerning the normative frailty of classical notions of agency. Whilst Schlink does not offer a solution to the problem this raises for law, his fiction – not always perfect in its construction, but direct and compelling in its sincere concern with the question nonetheless – invites a steady reconsideration of the issues relevant to moral and legal responsibility in times of deep and violent conflict. The accommodation of human frailties by the law is rightly cautious, slow and resistant to the indulgence of individual motivations of doubtful moral standing. Yet, where this resistance virtually requires that individuals exhibit near extraordinary qualities in the darkest moments, where individuals may be fixed with the guilt of the collective, examination of the legal principle and of *its* motivation should be particularly conscientious if justice is to be preserved.

Recent years have seen a number of fictions attempting to engage with the moral conflict posed in times of war and the disturbingly substantial loss of integrity permitting such atrocities. Bernhard Schlink's *The Reader* is a case in point and functions as a work conceived in response to the author's personal observation and experience of a perplexed generation. On one view merely provoking, a self-serving account suggesting that fate rather than choice directs agency, the tale is, alternatively, provocative, assisting in a review of the role of history and of justice when confronted with the impact of the contingent upon human nature. Initially a story of a young man's affair in post-second-world war Germany, with an older woman, Hanna, *The Reader* becomes a moral quest with the disclosure of Hanna's involvement in the machinery of the Holocaust and with her trial forming a significant element of the text.

The title of the text, *The Reader*, highlights an element of the story which adds a symbolic twist to the tale, for Hanna, the woman, later convicted for her part in the deaths of a large group of Jewish civilians, is illiterate. This additional theme of literacy provides an enriching symbolic dimension to the story of the affair and of the tragic history, trial and aftermath, though the potentially glib – and some would say inauthentic – use of illiteracy as handicap has attracted condemnation (though Niven, 2003, p. 396, notes concerns subsist in Germany even today in relation to the record concerning literacy and numeracy skills). Readers and audiences quickly light upon the idea that Hanna learns morality or grows in moral wisdom as she is introduced to the world of literature and, later, learns to read herself. Reading is a trope for the wider interpretative practice that is moral judgment, of our engagement with the complex moral choices and decisions presented to us by the fact of existence. The trope also bears more widespread and profound cultural significance given the widely appreciated fact that Germany, a country of the highest intellectual and cultural achievements in literature, philosophy and the arts, formed the cradle for an appalling humanitarian crime. Literacy alone did not (and does not) guarantee moral probity. Nevertheless, the idea that literature presents a resource for the development of moral sensibility remains tenable however contestable the actual impact of that influence in the individual or collective case.

At the same time, *The Reader* may invite an immediate suspicion of an all too-ready sympathy with perpetrators and failure of compassion for victims.

Certainly, the response to *The Reader* has been polarised and frequently hostile. Yet arguably, meaningful engagement with the dilemmas of the foot soldier, one faced by members of many armies across the world, is a key purpose of this text. That is not to say that the atrocity that was the Holocaust is wholly comparable or analogous to other atrocities, but it may well help us to consider some of the features common to such circumstances, of economic and political turmoil, of an all-encompassing ideology, attractive to the morally or socially impoverished, terrifying to detractors and only now emerging into the light of disinterested enquiry; Cocks (2007), for example, describes the subtle psychological edifice engaging the mindset in Germany during the period, whilst Moorhouse (2010) provides an historical account of the surreal nature of city life. With this context in mind, we may consider that the thought experiment presented by *The Reader* can and should be given serious attention.

The thought experiment for law: a new literary epistemology

It may be suggested that one of the problems with thought experiments is that, in the distillation of a moral dilemma down to a pure, simplistic scenario, they fail to capture the true nature of the dilemma. It must be noted, of course, that a too-ready notion of individuals swept along by events glosses the central issue of free will and responsibility. It must also be acknowledged that any discussion of this interaction between history and the impact upon individual will is wholly overshadowed by the tragedy of being the *absolute* victims, for whom the time did not represent merely the diversion of the realm of choice, but the end of all time, of all choice.

Thought experiments are most frequently referred to within mainstream philosophy as well as in the philosophy of science. Well-known examples are those of the trolley problem (see Edmonds, 2010) and the ticking time bomb – imaginary scenarios created in order to test moral propositions and in which we are asked under what conditions we might sacrifice one life for the sake of many. The trolley problem is a thought experiment in ethics, first introduced by Philippa Foot, which asks thinkers to imagine themselves confronted with a scenario involving a runaway train trolley hurtling towards innocent persons. The thinker must imagine that he or she may intervene in this impending tragedy by throwing a switch but in doing so will change the course of the trolley so that it will instead run towards another victim or victims, smaller in number than the first. The ticking time bomb scenario asks thinkers to consider whether torture of a suspected terrorist or bomber is likely to result in the saving of lives and, in light of this consideration, whether torture may ever be justified. Such thought experiments are designed to 'test' the rational possibilities of scenarios which may be deployed in justification of actions or policies of moral and legal significance. The debate on links between torture and the ticking time bomb scenario is of course polarised (apart from Luban, 2005, see Dershowitz, 2006, and Brecher, 2007, for examples). Indeed, such scenarios may present quite misleading logical progressions, as an analysis of the ticking time bomb (which has attracted a revival of interest in the so-called war against terror) scenario illustrates (Shue, 1978).[1] In law, thought experiments are rarely mentioned (except insofar as such hypotheses help to interrogate arguments about the legality of torture, for example) yet they are, perhaps often quite unconsciously, drawn upon in reasoning through doctrinal issues and putative and actual case scenarios, as well as more consciously drawn upon in the reasoning of the hermeneutics of social science, including legal and political theory (see Shafer, 1986; Lagenbucher, 1998; Hunter, 2001; 2008; see also Lamond, 2006). Whenever a lawyer or judge hypothesises analogous or linked scenarios believed to have a bearing upon the case before them, they are essentially working through the basis of a thought experiment. More prosaically, every time we use precedent in application to the permutations presented by new case scenarios, we are essentially operating in the realm of the thought experiment. Certainly, *The Reader* scenario[2] – where one person must run the risk of losing control and being overwhelmed in order to grasp the opportunity to free a contingent of prisoners in a burning church – could be characterised as a challenging thought experiment given the historical context of the scenario, of the inexorable and terrifying nature and massive scale of the German war machine. Recognising in full the extent of the terrible crimes against the victims of German aggression in the Second World War, the philosophical explanation for this remains contentious. And, as von Kellenbach notes: 'The frequent calls for closure, the *Sclusstrich,* forgiveness, and full rehabilitation have proven futile and deeply flawed.' (von Kellenbach, 2003, p. 316)

The Reader engages in this debate, humanising the German perspective; this of itself is provocative, bearing in mind the brutal profile and record of the regime.

Although the evidence from history appears to point, with chilling strength, to mass voluntary participation, Bernhard Schlink raises the possibility of individuals, motivated by the fact that enlistment promised regular work and thus survival, being themselves largely the creatures, rather than

---

[1] Shue provides strong moral arguments against those who would attempt to justify the use of torture. Luban (2005) elaborates and updates the arguments first posited by Shue, providing cogent practical examples of how the 'thought experiment' that links the idea of torture to the 'ticking time bomb' scenario are not borne out by experience.

[2] Hanna is on trial as one of several female former Nazi guards accused of letting 300 Jewish women die in a burning church on the death marches following the 1944 evacuation of Auschwitz concentration camp.

the creators, of the historical moment. The model is relevant as a thought experiment because, with the deaths in the church forming the central, damning event, Schlink has pieced together significant factors, most of which are brought to light in the trial scene. We learn that Hanna was not conscripted into the army, but elected to join in response to a recruitment drive at the Siemens factory. This layered plot indicates the complexity of motivations to be interpreted in the court of law; volunteering for military service can be made to look like active enthusiasm for the regime, coupled with an appetite for the power bestowed by military status. Yet, perhaps one is meant to understand that any citizen working in private industry, such as the Siemens factory (which was given over to the manufacture of munitions) was already implicated, in so far as they were earning a wage directly linked to the military machine. Not visible to the court is the fact that Hanna also moves from job to job, including the move from the Siemens factory, as a means of evading detection of her illiteracy. We learn that she was charged, along with her comrades, with the task of selecting those to be sent to their deaths. This task was reduced to a mechanical, processing routine – Hanna explains that it was necessary to select some to make room for those coming in, though Hanna gave a temporary and somewhat self-serving reprieve to some prisoners – arranging that they read to her for a brief time. Though this element forms yet another rather unlikely instance of the 'reading trope' imbricated throughout the tale, the reduction of the selection process to an unavoidable mechanism is indicative of the morally reductive nature of the terrible machine of mass murder.

The moral bind or the case for cultural contingency

The court scene is pivotal in demonstrating the dubiety of a jurisprudence built upon pious retrospect, when all those taking part are implicated by the culture giving rise to the event. The judge's silence reflects the moral bind affecting all those present, including himself, not just in terms of his own personal history (what did *he* do in the war) but also in terms of the limitations of moral choice for every individual in such circumstances. Though some scholars (Donahue, 2001) query whether the critical questions posed to the judge in the trial scene are so very defensible, Hanna's question – 'What would you have done?' – arguably reflects the true impasse, the sense which must have prevailed for many foot soldiers at the time, of the impossibility of questioning orders and the sense of their role being simply a functional inevitability in part of a bigger, mechanical process. As McCoubrey notes:

> Both under the classical 'ought to know' doctrine and the claimed Nuremberg doctrine it is clear that a soldier may and should query a *prima facie* unlawful order...At the same time

the extent of both knowledge and capacity to question may vary considerably and this too is a factor to be taken into account. (McCoubrey, 2001, p. 391)

Osiel (2005) gives recognition to the moral bind. He notes that we can accommodate more readily the attribution of responsibility to the very architects of wrongs, but the spectrum is difficult to chart with any accuracy: 'The law's reach is thus...both over inclusive and under inclusive...this creates the "inescapable aura of arbitrariness" hovering over so many trials for mass atrocity.' (Osiel, 2005, p. 1764)

Again, as reader–witnesses of the film and book, we know that *an* explanation for this chain of events is offered in relation to Hanna: simply, illiteracy. As a German citizen from the poorest social stratum, Hanna's choices have been skewed constantly by this handicap to social engagement, just as other, less overt handicaps or personal qualities may direct seemingly perverse choices in life. That this key contributory factor of illiteracy remains obscured from the court contributes to the symbolism of the reading motif, that the readers of a situation may only interpret what is presented to them, whether in the courtroom, or society at large. Presumably, Schlink inserts the 'reprieve' element to underscore the continuing fact of Hanna's illiteracy but also to indicate her own compromised moral standing – a guard, yet a guard (if the sympathetic version is to be believed) who wishes to provide what succour she can, even if only able to do so fleetingly and doing so with every appearance of benefitting herself in at least equal measure. Holocaust survivors such as Primo Levi confirm that the incidence of 'sympathetic' guards was virtually non-existent; note also that using a 'female' guard has semiotic implications (see Alison, 2006). The scenario nevertheless links, more broadly, to the very notion of the moral status of intervention – a complex normative puzzle, as the trolley-bus experiment indicates.

The key act of moral dereliction and criminal significance relates to the deaths of prisoners. The court is told about the appalling death by fire of the group of prisoners for whom Hanna and her co-defendants were responsible. Whilst on a forced march, the prisoners, all women and children, are herded and locked into a church, in order to maintain some order during a bombing raid; the church is, however, hit and catches fire, with all but two of the prisoners burnt to death. Hanna and her co-defendants are challenged with having failed to liberate the prisoners from this death; the official report on the event, signed by Hanna and her co-defendants glosses over their failure to respond, though, being illiterate, Hanna may not or simply does not know this. Whilst Hanna's illiteracy creates a neat trap exploited by her co-defendants, the unfolding tale reveals the skewed logics leading to such deaths. Of such logics, Katz comments: 'the question of performing good or evil deeds becomes irrelevant...Etzionia postulates three different sorts of compliance patterns – alienative, calculative, and normative – that are found in different sorts of social settings' (Katz, 1982, p. 514). Skewed cultures beget skewed choices and whilst the agents of such choices are neither without guilt, nor are they wholly the producers of the vision. In the dystopic world of Nazi reality, order is all, the terrible machinery of death already turning inexorably. And, as Katz (1982) indicates, normative landscapes are much more complex in such circumstances than in everyday life. The thought experiment that is the text may pose the actual, as opposed to the idealised, either/or dilemmas facing soldiers of the Reich. More realistic than the trolley bus or the ticking bomb, it resurrects the sense of numbing inevitability that must have prevailed for guards as well as victims, compromising moments of supposed choice. Few seem to have agonised over their roles, or at least there is little overt evidence of insurrection, but this may reflect the real weakness of the abstracted form of the thought experiment, its artificial, engineered separation from the subtleties and strains working upon the human psyche *in extremis*.

Moral luck

A similar difficulty arises with an additional conception – termed 'moral luck' by Bernard Williams (Williams and Nagel, 1976) – of the collision of the will with the contingent. Philosophers of moral luck discourse upon the feasibility of juxtaposing the moral with the contingent whilst further debating the separability of those influences which determine the constitution, circumstances and consequences of human actions.

Arguably, *The Reader* is a particularly apt illustration of the vision of the relationship between event and agency that is the concept of moral luck. In general, writings about the relevance of moral luck to jurisprudence are particularly one-dimensional, focusing upon culpability as to consequences rather than combining this focus with consideration of circumstances. Yet Schlink maintains a position which is plausible and relevant to any thought experiment and to the notion of moral luck, recognising the fact that different categories combine, that issues of personal history and personal qualities interact with the impact of external contingent events. *The Reader* engages the combination of constitutive and circumstantial luck that puts a certain type of person (one who does not tend to agonise too deeply over the moral fabric of circumstances before them) into a particular type of moral dilemma. Recall here the Milgram experiment (Milgram, 1974), demonstrating that most people will obey in the service of authority. Moral persona is complex and can combine gruff kindness with pragmatism and lack of reflectiveness. 'Deep' identity in terms of unwillingness to admit illiteracy is analogous to the 'permanent characteristic' argument in criminal law – a characteristic so imprinted upon the persona of the subject that their judgment is directed by it. In addition, the conjunction of the factor of illiteracy with contingent developments could well direct one's choices in very particular ways. Illiteracy in this tale is of particular importance for two reasons: it drives the employment choices made by Hanna and it corroborates her account that she was not the main author, or even a signatory, to the false and self-serving account of the death of the prisoners (invisibly to the court, but evidently to us, the witnesses to her story). Yet it also serves a further purpose, being an example of the deep and less explicable characteristics which drive moral identity. Here, the thought experiment is enriched by the concept of moral luck. The thought experiment encourages a rather functional approach to the question: what might I or you have done under such circumstances? Moral luck focuses more intimately upon the *normative* implications of the collision of contingency and agency; *The Reader* certainly presents a good illustration of this perspective. Bernard Williams (Williams and Nagel, 1976) sets out to use the term as a means to *interrogate* the wholly *abstracted* vision of moral choice: choice as generally represented, something which can be asserted as if wholly free of invasive influences.

As with many philosophers on the point, his focus is on the impact of resultant fortune in assessing moral choices made at an earlier time. Zimmerman's (2006) stance reveals how this focus upon consequential luck may contribute to an oversimplification of the actuality of the kinds of dilemma faced *in extremis*:

> Thus, whether one is obligated can be a matter of luck. But this has only to do with the incurring of obligation. It does not follow that whether one fulfils the obligations that one has can be a matter of luck. On the contrary, given that obligation requires regulative control, whether one fulfils one's obligations is *not* a matter of luck. Thus, even if one can be condemned to be obligated, one cannot be condemned to do wrong. (Zimmerman, 2006, p. 606)

If we apply the thought to Hanna, Zimmerman's view still abstracts the dilemma, though she may have been swept into her role as guard. Finding herself 'condemned to be obligated', she still, according to Zimmerman, had a choice to do right at the key moment. Strictly, this must be the case, but is it realistic in this context? Is there truly a realm of choice, bearing in mind the circumstances and mindset necessary to such an existence at such a moment in history? Hanna is charged with being a signatory to a sanitized account of the deaths in the church. Yet even without such a signature, she is still implicated by her own inaction, the inaction for which the judge himself has no answer.

Where we may be dealing with omitting to act, the law does have a model for behaviour; models most discussed relate to the duty to rescue where the subjects are strangers. Where there is a *relationship* creating a *duty* to act, then failure to act will only be tolerated where the omission is in the best interests of the subject of the omission. There are similarities with the trolley experiment in that inaction will lead to a greater harm where action produces a different kind of harm, though with the burning church example, the harm avoided by inaction is, at most, physical risk to the agent and the loss of control of the prisoners, a small risk compared to that of inevitable deaths. The trolley, like the church example, is interesting in part because it is a reminder of the fact of the contingent world: an agent may 'find themselves' in a situation not willed by them or created by their particular act, which is already rolling, of itself, towards an awful conclusion. Intervention will alter that conclusion but perhaps only in a different problematic way; the paralysing fact of the rolling contingent is powerful. The difference though is that in the trolley experiment there is no suggestion of a relationship of duty; it is a model meant to interrogate the duty of strangers, if it is meant for any case at all. But *The Reader* is also a dystopic world where the regime in which the agent is engaged means to kill all the prisoners.

Of course, it may be said that participation in such a corrupt regime, even as a minor player, implicates all parties, albeit that they have been acculturated into a world which suggests that their actions are compliant with the law (for an analysis of the status of Nazi laws, see Miller, 1995). It may also be said that the relationship of guard to prisoner suggests a special relationship of duty of care towards the prisoners such that *this* death, somewhat within one's control and permitting appalling suffering, imposes a duty to act in avoidance, even in the context of the unavoidable death to be delivered further on. Nevertheless, the duty of care rationale, when applied to a special relationship which must inevitably result in the violent and unnecessary death of the subjects of care, is skewed indeed. It might be argued that this toxic duty of care is more estranged than the stranger encountering an imperilled subject and thus occupies a peculiar position in the spectrum between stranger and relationship. The Geneva Convention[3] attempts to assert the parameters of such a duty of care and the continued assertion of such a duty must remain crucial to our dealings with such situations. Yet, from Guantanamo to Gaza, we continue to learn how the toxicity of the relationship blights rational life. Indeed, empirical research, such as the

---

3 See Convention (III) Relative to the Treatment of Prisoners of War, Geneva, 12 August 1949, available at http://icrc.org/ihl.nsf/7c4d08d9b287a42141256739003e636b/6fef854a3517b75a c125641e004a9e68 (accessed 2 May 2012).

Stanford Prison Experiment,[4] demonstrates that dehumanizing tendencies are commonplace in the general population.

The essential charge against Hanna is, for the most part, one of attenuated agency (in the counting out of prisoners, so participating in the selection process) and inaction, rather than action, or even sadistic action. Schlink tries to convey the reality of the challenge presented by a dystopic world. It is not as historical revisionists that we should think of the issues raised in *The Reader*, but as conscientious moral historiographers, wishing to explore the possible explanations for individual and collective behaviour beyond the too-easy reliance on the soldiers-as-monsters perspective. In jurisprudence, as in philosophy generally, there is a need to engage with the full implications of history. Those who denounce the text or film as part of a glib glamorization of the past, a past where, it is claimed, the Holocaust implicates the mass of the German people as signatories, as readers of the unfolding holocaust story, cannot explain the mystery lodged between orthodox jurisprudential accounts of individual responsibility and this seemingly anomalous complicity of a whole nation.

Reception of *The Reader*

There have been several strong, scholarly responses to *The Reader* demonstrating a wide range of views.[5] Many are sensitive to the perspective that Schlink is attempting to absolve those whom Hanna represents. McKinnon accuses Schlink of attempting to 'erode distinctions between the guilty and innocent, between perpetrators and victims' (McKinnon, 2003, p. 16).[6] Weisberg resolves the conflicts presented by the novel by absolving you, that other reader, asserting the character Michael, within the text may be 'genuinely happy (as we need not be) that, within an otherwise failed life, (Hanna) has found the energy and the skill to learn to read and write' (Weisberg, 2004, p. 233). This otherwise harmonizing analysis fails to recognize the moral challenge posed to all of us: what of the compromised nature of judgment, even in the face of such facts, and of the moral challenge posed to us all and implicit in the dilemma? For literary scholars Tabensky and Liu, the reality

---

4 The Stanford Prison Experiment revealed the extent to which apparently normal citizens may rapidly exhibit gratuitously cruel and sadistic behaviour. See www.stanford.edu/dept/news/pr/97/970108prisonexp.html (accessed 2 May 2012).
5 For Niven: 'A hallmark of post-unification discourse on the Nazi past is this ongoing search for a balance between public and private memory work. Schlink's novel is a part of this discourse.' (Niven, 2003, p. 396) Metz presents a strong hypothesis about the semiotic influence of the key trope ('Nazism-as-Woman') (Metz, 2004, pp. 301–5).
6 Later, McKinnon (2004, p. 182) argues that Schlink is 'preoccupied' with the idea that 'justice would be better served if the law were able more deftly and generously to accommodate emotion' (McKinnon, 2004, p. 195). For McKinnon, this would subvert 'the very nature and role of judgment, the psychological thesis mistakes the committed work of justice for mere detached action' (McKinnon, 2004, p. 195).

of this challenge is profound indeed. Tabensky (2004, p. 207) believes that judgment is so compromised that we may consider disavowing the concept of desert. Tabensky's analysis is most penetrating in recognizing the fact of interaction between psyche and agency, concluding that 'Hanna...was, as we all are, destined to go on as we do by the circumstances surrounding our tragic or blessed lives and also by the unique and irreducible "mental circumstances" that define us as agents.' (Tabensky, 2004, p. 226)

Thus, Tabensky shrinks from the very idea of judgment as condemnation. For Sarah Liu, the focus of the book remains concerned with the metaphor of illiteracy, which, she asserts, holds for all society (Liu, 2009, p. 328) with atrocity rendering us all illiterate. Though such perspectives may seem to engender a betrayal of true and ultimate victims, they are nevertheless an attempt to give expression to the truly complex and collective nature of moral agency.

Whilst literary critique presents such subtle debates, responses to the film have been more markedly hostile and in being so, fly in the face of the philosophical nuances that Bernhard Schlink invites us to consider. Philosophy frequently remains comfortable because, in the abstract, it can avoid the truly hard case, or, if dealing with the hard case, can orchestrate the circumstantial context. Factors likely to be considered significant by those writing on *The Reader* frequently reflect a concentration upon Hanna's presumed moral baseness, signified by her affair with an adolescent, her voluntary transition into the Nazi regime. Commentators either try to link to some profound finding about the power of love or the power of literacy or the incontrovertible presence of evil. In particular, those who have studied the context of the Holocaust provide extensive evidence of the lack of remorse, of the high incidence of sadism and of mass compliance, frequently amounting to enthusiasm, of members of the German public and the German army in facilitating the crime. Rosenbaum (2009), Dargis (2008) and Bower (2009) all express strong antipathy to the attempted redemptive stance sought by the film: Bower likening Hanna to a 'sadistic thug'. The problem with the vision might lie, as Bower indicates, with the potential mismatch between the evidence available to us of actual attitudes and behavioural patterns and those Schlink advances. The tensions, reflected in the responses to the book, and more markedly to the film of *The Reader,* are illustrative of those between the historians Christopher Browning and Daniel Goldhagen and echo the concerns raised by Bower. Browning's 1992 book, *Ordinary Men*, argued, as this chapter inclines, that the scale of Nazi atrocities could only be made intelligible via the explanations offered by the cultural and psychological work of theorists such as Stanley Milgram.

This would confirm that persons perpetrate horrors as part of a culture of compliance and that this should not be regarded as a bizarre mitigation of the crimes (that they simply couldn't help themselves) but rather as a reorientation of our understanding of human nature. In contrast, the book *Hitler's Willing Executioners,* by Daniel Goldhagen (1996), set out strenuously to refute the compliance model and amassed a great deal of evidence to support his assertion that the perpetrators were not simply compliant, but willing executioners who, given opportunities to absent themselves from such violence had, in the vast majority of cases, chosen to remain and take part. In addition, his research into female concentration camp guards found not only a willing *compliance* with the cruelties of the regime, but a routinely cruel and sadistic culture, apparently endorsed and actively supported by those involved. For Goldhagen, the evidence also required one to conclude that a cultural or mass psychology explanation risked wholesale moral failure in terms of historical and philosophical record; *individuals* had perpetrated the horrors and individuals should be held fully accountable.

Implications of moral luck and cultural contingency for jurisprudence

The rich insights offered by literary reflection inform our relative worldviews. Interdisciplinary scholarship, thinking across the boundaries between the sciences, social sciences and humanities, gives access to a kind of disinterested anthropology of agency, gleaning clues from the meeting places between science and imagination. Where the truth lies in this debate goes to the very heart of the conceptions of human nature underpinning jurisprudence and flagged by the notion of moral luck. For, if human beings are largely compliant creatures who, given the optimum circumstances for wrongful acts, demonstrate what we might call a mass psychopathy, free will as the ultimate trump card of the contingent world – the world of opportunity as well as chance – is, for the most part, a somewhat misleading concept. If, on the other hand, individuals largely *choose* to align themselves with certain forms of agency, the conclusion is, in a sense, even darker: on an *individual* basis, a much higher proportion of the population will exhibit homicidal tendencies *as of will,* given the opportunity.

One of the questions raised by the example of the Holocaust is that of whether the pattern reflects upon the cultural profile of a particular nation: in other words, does this tell us something about belonging to a particular group, or being human? Goldhagen argues that German culture had, for centuries, fomented a poisonous anti-Semitism, of which the Holocaust was the ultimate expression and that German culture thereby produced a wholly unique mindset. Goldhagen's critics point to the fates of their non-Jewish prisoners and of the myriad examples of similar atrocities perpetrated around the world. Recent events, from Eastern Europe, to Rwanda, Cambodia or Guantanamo, add to this vision of shared capability.

The example of Hanna in *The Reader* offers a profound contribution to the conceptual engagement of understanding moral agency, an engagement sometimes simply polarized by the Browning–Goldhagen debate and by scholarship examining the book and the film *The Reader*. If, as an apparently passive onlooker who, despite her gruff persona, tries to bestow acts of humanity where she can and does not exhibit any particular antipathy towards her charges, she is thereby wholly unrepresentative of the reality of such guards, then the links between moral character, contingency and individual and collective perpetration that Schlink has built arguably are insupportable: the thought experiment that is *The Reader* presents yet another abstracted imaginary, our sympathies fraudulently invoked. If, on the other hand, she is illustrative of even a small, yet significant and representative portion of similar agents, the example of Hanna remains relevant to debate. Though historical accounts do not reveal significant examples of such passive, neutral agency, Hanna's identity – as someone capable of isolated acts of kindness, but already alienated from her own feelings, gruff, pragmatic and largely willing to exist within, and contribute to, the dominant regime – is plausible.

Illiteracy works both as a metaphor for individual moral myopia in the face of desperate conditions and the larger, cultural failure: of the rise of atavistic values, of the failure to distinguish, critically, between one published information source and another. Of course, those influences and stimuli may amount to a similarly fateful emotional illiteracy as dehumanizing norms gain the ascendant. *The Reader* suggests that, however we may aspire to being free-thinking, critical individuals, the attitudes and beliefs informing our actions must draw upon the wellspring of available collective ideas, whether or not in literary form.

Thought experiments, moral luck and the law might therefore take account, not just of the interactions between the contingent and the determined, but also of the process shaping individual beliefs from which actions spring. In civil law, allowance is made for the eccentric belief or choice which may run counter to all common sense even where the resultant decision affects the well-being of the subject. In practical terms, the provision of some accommodation of eccentric beliefs driving actions in criminal law must be reined in, given the potential harm to others. Yet the truth of the perpetrator may be that, genuinely, they had reached a psychological place alienated from the immediate horrors confronting them. Again and again, the perpetrators on trial during the 1960s in Germany – as Hannah Arendt so carefully observed – exhibited no remorse, reporting dispassionately upon the terrible cruelties visited by themselves and others, whilst yet maintaining solicitous affections within their families. In psychological, psychiatric and neuroscientific terms, uncertainty remains as to what this reveals about the operation of free will and moral choice (see further Williams, 2009b). Philosophically, if we are not to conclude that a far greater proportion of the population than believed are nascent psychopaths, then we must conclude that free will and moral character is much more subject to local influence than understood hitherto, that our individual realities are vulnerable to more dramatic reformulations than generally believed.

Conclusion

Schlink's contribution of *The Reader* to hypotheses of human nature *in extremis* is valuable, not least in making accessible the subtleties of the case. It may well be that, for a feasible individual – imagined or real – whom we might call Hanna, a seemingly irrelevant but core characteristic such as being – literally or figuratively/emotionally – illiterate may form the central driver of deep identity, the sense of selfhood to which we must cling if we are to maintain any identity. As moral philosopher Christine Korsgaard (1996) has argued, such deep identity may prove more compelling, as a motivating force than the threat of death itself. Even without the issue, trope or metaphor of illiteracy, such characteristics are arguably relevant to any realistic reading of moral character, an issue which must be understood to stand at a conceptual and phenomenological crossroads between a range of fields, with philosophy, jurisprudence, psychology, psychoanalysis and cultural studies each providing their own narrative gloss. As Stanovsky comments:

> Freud notes that the ethical demands made by society on the individual seem to have little regard for 'whether it is possible for people to obey' them. For Freud, unlike Kant, 'ought' in no way implies 'can'... It may be that instances of moral luck are best understood as yet another place where ethics makes demands that individuals cannot carry out... (Stanovsky, 2006, p. 459).

Such a view points to the gap between legal theory and legal purpose. For though the law surely sets out to interrogate and punish the true mindsets and motivations of accused persons, it seems likely that the classical notion of the free-willing individual is a great fiction, borne of a wholly abstracted notion of the self.

The film *The Reader* provides a graphic contribution to the view that culturally determined characteristics, such as an obsession with order, combined with the repression of empathy, can strongly determine agency and moral judgment, especially in moments of cultural failure. If this is so, then constitutive moral luck is key. And literacy, as one's access to the normative wisdom discoverable in the written word or access to reading empathic relations, becomes a culturally complex instrument in the plethora of resources drawn upon in the making of a human agent. Nagel specifically uses the example of Nazi experience in his essay:

> The third category to consider is luck in one's circumstances... the things we are called upon to do, the moral tests we face, are importantly determined by factors beyond our control. It may be true of someone that in a dangerous situation he would behave in a cowardly or heroic fashion, but if the situation never arises, he will never have the chance to distinguish or disgrace himself in this way and his moral record will be different... A conspicuous example of this is political. Ordinary citizens of Nazi Germany had an opportunity to behave heroically by opposing the regime. They also had an opportunity to behave badly, and most of them are culpable for having failed this test. But it is a test to which the citizens of other countries were not subjected. (Williams and Nagel, 1976, p. 145)

Despite this concession, however, Nagel concludes that we are condemned to condemn ourselves:

> even when we have seen that we are not responsible for our own existence, or our nature, or the choices we have to make, or the circumstances that give our acts the consequences they have. Those acts remain ours and we remain ourselves, despite the persuasiveness of the reasons that seem to argue us out of existence.
>
> It is this internal view that we extend to others in moral judgment – when we judge *them* rather than their desirability or utility. We extend to others the refusal to limit ourselves to external evaluation and we accord to themselves, like our own. (Williams and Nagel, 1976, p. 149)

Nagel's view seems to both deny and recognize the illogicality of such condemnation. As a personification of the issue, Hanna, we find, simply lacks an internal view and so cannot engage with the complex internal/external milieu in the way Nagel suggests. She has learnt to get by and is no more sentimental about *herself* than others. A complex moral character, demonstrating good impulses, yet largely inscrutable in her quiet pragmatism, she is a survivor who has put away, or simply never experienced, the life of feeling, which is why reading is so illuminating for her. What her very schematic background – with no family, poor circumstances, moving from job to job to survive – may corroborate, is the need to develop the very pragmatic, unsentimental and slightly harsh persona that Hanna seems to present, with virtually no sentiment accorded to herself. Hers is a life experience which has not provided opportunities for reflective moral endorsement. It may also be to her moral credit, although undoubtedly to her practical disadvantage, that we learn that Hanna is not capable of presenting a vulnerable persona engendering sympathy in others.

Schlink here remains true to the dogged persona he has created, a blinkered, stolid individual. He does not attempt to elaborate a rationale derived from living in fear of one's comrades, and indeed, evidence suggests that the reality provided an unforced culture of complicity (see, for example, Goldhagen, 1996, p. 383). Nevertheless, her quandary remains in the air, discomfiting and unanswered by the judge: perhaps only exceptional, rather than ordinary or reasonable persons could pledge they would have acted otherwise. Twice, the judge has no answer, reflecting the morally compromised position of all those present. And any 'ought' which lies so much in doubt carries dubious normative standing. The text provides several examples of Hanna failing to arrogate opportunities to mitigate provided at trial. Where she can provide an accurate answer, she does so, but at other times remains silent. This portrayal has attracted some criticism since this same Hanna has demonstrated her ability to perpetrate a long-standing fraud in disguising her illiteracy. Niven notes that, in debate within Germany upon *The Reader,* 'one reader pointed out in a letter to a leading daily that awkward questions, such as how an illiterate could have signed up to become a concentration-camp guard, had been asked of Schlink in Germany at a reception given by the Federal President in December 2000' (Niven, 2003, p. 381). Furthermore, the implication of virtuous motivation driving Hanna's blinding honesty in the court of *The Reader* is not found so typically in the real courts of such cases. Yet, one may argue, the elements of this persona are wholly credible and therefore possible. She is a purveyor of facts, distanced from her emotional self, yet capable of pragmatic acts of sympathy for those with whom she comes into contact. Against this background, the literacy/illiteracy issue may be deployed not just as a trope for moral insight but as a means to explain how a seemingly quite random factor or characteristic can form the invisible, yet driving force behind an action, series of actions or life vision. The title *The Reader* may also act as a kind of moral mirror, implicating the moral challenge for another reader: you (or the collective we). Moral luck as to circumstances, made tangible in the thought experiment of *The Reader*, emphasises the intimate interaction between internal characteristics and qualities and external, material and contingent influences, a profound message for those who would claim certainty as to the attribution of moral responsibility.

References

Alison, J (2006) 'The Third Victim in Bernhard Schlink's *Der Vorleser*' *The Germanic Review,* March 22

Bower, T (2009) 'My Clash with death-camp Hanna' *Times Online*, available at http://entertainment.timesonline.co.uk/tol/arts_and_entertainment/film/article-5733408.ece (accessed 2 May 2012)

Brecher, B (2007) *Torture and the Ticking Bomb* (Oxford: Blackwell Publishing)

Browning, C (1992) *Ordinary Men: Reserve Police Battalion 101 and the Final Solution in Poland* (London: Harper Collins)

Cocks, G (2007) 'Sick Heil: Self and Illness in Nazi Germany' **22**(1) *Osiris* 93–115

Dargis, M (2008) 'Innocence is Lost in Postwar Germany' *New York Times*, available at http://movies.nytimes.com/2008/12/10/movies/10read.html (accessed 2 May 2012)

Dershowitz, A (2006) 'Should We Fight Terror with Torture?' *The Independent*, 3 July 2006

Donahue, W (2001) 'Illusions of Subtlety: Bernhard Schlink's *Der Vorleser* and the Moral Limits of Holocaust Fiction' **54**(1) *German Life and Letters* 60–81

Edmonds, D (2010) 'Matters of Life and Death' *Prospect Magazine*, available at www.prospectmagazine.co.uk/2010/10/ethics-trolley-problem/ (accessed 2 May 2012)

Goldhagen, D (1996) *Hitler's Willing Executioners* (London: Little Brown)

Hunter, D (2001) 'Reason is Too Large: Analogy and Precedent in Law' **50** *Emory Law Journal* 1197

Hunter, D (2008) 'Teaching and Using Analogy in Law' *Journal of the Association of Legal Writing Directors* 2, available at SSRN: http://ssrn.com/abstract=1089669 (accessed 2 May 2012)

Katz, L (1982) 'Implementation of the Holocaust: The Behavior of Nazi Officials' **24**(3) (July) *Comparative Studies in Society and History* 510–29

Kearns, M (2002) 'Ethos, Morality and Narrative Structure: Theory and Response' **56**(2) *Rocky Mountain Review of Language and Literature* 61–78

Korsgaard, C (1996) *The Sources of Normativity* (Cambridge: Cambridge University Press)

Lagenbucher, K (1998) 'Argument by Analogy in European Law' **57** *Cambridge Law Journal* 481–521

Lamond, G (2006) 'Precedent and Analogy in Legal Reasoning' in *Stanford Encyclopedia of Philosophy* (Stanford, CA: Center for the Study of Language and Information) http://plato.stanford.edu/

Liu, S (2009) 'The Illiterate Reader: Aphasia after Auschwitz' **7**(2) *Partial Answers* 319–42

Luban, D (2005) 'Liberalism, Torture and the Ticking Bomb' **91**(6) *Virginia Law Review* 1425–61

McCoubrey, H (2001) 'From Nuremberg to Rome: Restoring the Defence of Superior Orders' **50**(2) *International and Comparative Law Quarterly* 386–94

McKinnon, J E (2003) 'Crime, Compassion and *The Reader*' **27** *Philosophy and Literature* 1–20

Mckinnon, J E (2004) 'Law and Tenderness in Bernhard Schlink's *The Reader*' **16**(2) *Law and Literature* 179–201

Metz, J (2004) ' "Truth is a Woman": Post-Holocaust Narrative, Postmodernism and the Gender of Fascism in Bernhard Schlink's *Der Vorleser*' **77**(3) *German Quarterly* 300–23

Milgram, S (1974) *Obedience to Authority: An Experimental View* (New York: Tavistock Publications)

Miller, R L (1995) *Nazi Justiz: Law of the Holocaust* (Westport, CT: Praeger Publishers)

Moorhouse, R (2010) *Berlin at War* (London: Bodley Head)

Niven, B (2003) 'Bernhard Schlink's *Der Vorleser* and the Problem of Shame' **98**(2) *Modern Language Review* 381–96

Osiel, M (2005) 'The Banality of Good: Aligning Incentives against Mass Atrocity' **105**(6) *Columbia Law Review* 1751–862

Rosenbaum, R (2009) 'Don't Give an Oscar to *The Reader*' *Slate*, www.slate.com/id/2210804/ (accessed 2 May 2012)

Schlink, B (1998) *The Reader* (New York: Vintage Books), first published (1995) *Der Vorleser* (Zurich: Diogenes Verlag AG)

Shafer, G (1986) 'Construction of Probability Arguments' **66** *Buffalo Law Review* 799

Shue, H (1978) 'Torture' **7** *Philosophy and Public Affairs* 124–43

Stanovsky, D (2006) 'Stealing Guilt: Freud, Twain, Augustine and the Question of Moral Luck' **63**(4) *American Imago* 445–61

Tabensky, P (2004) 'Judging and Understanding' **16**(2) *Law and Literature* 207–28

von Kellenbach, K (2003) 'Vanishing Acts: Perpetrators in Postwar Germany' **17**(2) *Holocaust and Genocide Studies* 305–29

Weisberg, R H (2004) 'A Sympathy that Does not Condone: Notes in Summation on Schlink's *The Reader*' **16**(2) *Law and Literature* 229–35

Williams, B and T Nagel (1976) 'Moral Luck' **50** *Proceedings of the Aristotelian Society* 115–35 and 137–51

Williams, M (2009a) 'Law and the Humanities: A Question of Integrity' (5) *International Journal of Law in Context* 243–61

Williams, M (2009b) 'A Normal Man...Hardly Exists' **62**(1) *Current Legal Problems* 168–201 (C O'Cinneide (ed.))

Zimmerman, M (2006) 'Moral Luck: A Partial Map' **36**(4) *Canadian Journal of Philosophy*, 585–608

10
Between the Rational and the Marvellous: Edgar Allan Poe and the Counter-Enlightenment Origins of the Modern Detective Story
Neil Sargent

Introduction

This chapter examines a seminal text in the emergence of detective fiction as a new popular literary genre, Poe's *The Murders in the Rue Morgue*. Published in 1841, and occupying an ambiguous epistemic stance between the rational and the marvellous, as with much of Poe's writing, the narrative explicitly confronts the reader with the philosophical question: how can we know? Not just the practical question of 'whodunnit?'; but what is the basis of our knowledge claims when confronted with a mystery that appears to defy the laws of nature? How can two persons be cruelly murdered in such a horrific fashion inside a closed and locked room to which no other person had access without relying on metaphysical explanations such as witchcraft? The authorial use of a non-human perpetrator of the gross deed only adds to the epistemic tension between witchcraft and science that the text implicitly confronts.

At the same time, the setting of the mystery in Paris also sets up a narrative tension between the Cartesian rationalism of the prefect (who is described by Dupin as being 'all head and no body', Poe, 1975a, p. 168), and the empiricist investigative method employed by Dupin, who is able to imaginatively reconstruct the events of the mystery from the available forensic evidence and witness testimony, and thus deduce the existence of a murderer who is all body and no mind. Consequently, the conventional notion of motive (which depends on 'reason', in both senses of the term) that the prefect relies on to justify the arrest of the suspect LeBon can no longer be called upon to provide a satisfactory explanation of the mystery, especially in the absence of any forensic evidence to link the suspect to the murder. In much the same way, the inchoate capacity for language use on the part of the perpetrator not only adds to the evidentiary confusion surrounding the case, but also precludes the police from obtaining sufficient proof of guilt through confessional testimony on the part of the murderer.

In establishing the literary conventions governing the production and consumption of this new literary genre, the text thus also confronts many of the operative assumptions concerning the relationship between 'proof' and 'truth', and the reliability of confessional testimony that are implicit in the criminal trial process. By setting the mystery in Paris and constructing the narrative in the form of a contest between detective and prefect over methods of evidence-gathering, the text aligns itself philosophically with the empiricist assumptions underpinning the adversarial criminal trial process familiar to Poe's American readers. As such, the text provides an interesting comparative point of departure from which to examine the ways in which both law and the detective story genre share a common epistemological commitment to what Ian Watt, in *The Rise of the Novel*, has called 'the circumstantial view of life' (Watt, 2000, p. 31).

The literary detective as historian

In a 1946 essay on the philosophy of history, the English historian R G Collingwood remarks that the task of the detective in literature is in many respects akin to that of the historian (Collingwood, 1946, pp. 243, 266–8; Sargent, 2010, p. 291). Both are confronted by the methodological problems inherent in trying to reconstruct a reliable narrative of events which have occurred in the past, to which we only have access through selective traces of that past that still remain available to us in the present. For the historian, there is never any guarantee that the available historical sources will be complete, or that the evidence will prove to be reliable when subjected to critical examination. How, then, can we gain reliable knowledge of the course of events that have taken place in the past when the only sources of evidence we have with regard to the events we are investigating are in all likelihood incomplete, or else compromised by biases of perception, or inadequate information, or even by the conscious intention to influence the perception of those who come afterwards, by selectively arranging the evidence, leaving things out of the testimony, even fabricating events or destroying documents?

Readers of detective fiction will be very familiar with the evidentiary problems of trying to construct a historical narrative of a series of events that have occurred in the past, to which the investigator was not a direct witness, and thus has to rely on traces of evidence found at the scene of the crime, or the testimonies of witnesses to the events in question. Collingwood observes that the best literary detectives, like the best historians, have to adopt an explicitly critical stance towards their sources and never take anything at face value, unless it can be verified or corroborated with other evidence, which itself can be reliably verified (1946, pp. 266–8; Sargent, 2010, p. 292). Most especially, witness testimony cannot be taken at face value, since witnesses may lie, they may be mistaken, they may reach faulty conclusions from inadequate premises, or any of a whole host of other problems may arise that are familiar to television viewers and connoisseurs of detective fiction from Poe to Borges.

The natural scientist does not confront this kind of problem, according to Collingwood, (1946, p. 201), since the experimental method stipulates that the natural scientist should draw inferences only from data of the senses directly accessible to the researcher. No hearsay evidence is allowed. The scientist is expected to rely on sense data derived from direct observation; and from that seeks to draw inferences and to formulate hypotheses, which can then be tested under experimental conditions. Any theoretical inference which lacks empirical data to support it presents a problem for the natural scientist because it cannot be experimentally verified. It remains in the realm of speculative or theoretical knowledge.

But for the historian, as with the literary detective, it may be that the best evidence the investigator has to go on is hearsay evidence. The very nature of the object of inquiry – events which have taken place in the past to which the investigator was not directly present as a witness – means that the security provided by the model of experimentally testing inferences drawn from directly observed sense data is rarely available.[1] Sometimes the historian or the detective has to make inferences or formulate hypotheses in the absence of sufficient reliable evidence – to leap out into the unknown, in order to bridge the chasm between what is known, or what can be verified according to the sense data, and what cannot. Where was the victim between the hours of 8 pm on Monday night when seen in the company of Y, and 6.12 am on Tuesday when his body was found by C? And what was C doing in that particular vicinity at that particular time in the morning in order to stumble across the body in the first place?

Collingwood further elaborates on the distinction between the methods of the natural scientist and the methods of the historian in his discussion of human nature and human history. Consistent with the Weberian concept of *verstehen* or 'understanding from within' (Burrell and Morgan, 1979, pp. 82, 229–31), Collingwood argues that the methods of the natural sciences can

---

1 Cassirer (1972, p.174) puts this as follows: 'If a physicist is in doubt about the results of an experiment he can repeat it and correct it. He finds his objects present at every moment, ready to answer his questions. But with the historian the case is different. His facts belong to the past, and the past is gone forever. We cannot reconstruct it; we cannot waken it to a new life in a mere physical, objective sense. All we can do is "remember" it – give it a new ideal existence. Ideal reconstruction, not empirical observation, is the first step in historical knowledge.'

never be fully applicable to the study of historical events. For the natural scientist, the focus of the investigation is on observable processes and material causes. He or she looks at the object of inquiry from without, so to speak, and seeks to relate the phenomenon under investigation to other classes of observable or measurable phenomena by reference to general scientific laws (Collingwood, 1946, p. 214; Cassirer, 1972, p. 174). From this perspective, there is no essential difference between the methods of investigation used to discover the chemical composition of the DNA molecule and the methods of investigation used to examine the internal structure of a complex social organization such as a corporation or a democratic voting system. But the historian is studying actions, not just events or processes, and social action is necessarily the product of human consciousness, of human purposes, and human interpretations of the motives of others. So the historian must always be concerned with the 'inside' of the events in question, and must seek to imaginatively re-enact the events from the historical actors' own point of view (Collingwood, 1946, p. 213; Cassirer, 1972, p. 177; Berlin, 1976, p. 12).

> The historian, in investigating any event in the past, makes a distinction between what may be called the outside and the inside of an event. By the outside of the event I mean everything belonging to it which can be described in terms of bodies and their movements: the passage of Caesar, accompanied by certain men, across a river called the Rubicon at one date, or the spilling of his blood on the floor of the senate-house at another. By the inside of the event I mean that in it which can only be described in terms of thought: Caesar's defiance of Republican law, or the clash of constitutional policy between himself and his assassins. The historian is never concerned with either of these to the exclusion of the other. He is investigating not mere events (where by a mere event I mean one which has only an outside and no inside) but actions, and an action is the unity of the outside and the inside of an event... His work may begin by discovering the outside of an event [such as the discovery of a body in the library on a certain date, in a detective story], but it can never end there; he must always remember that the event was an action, and that his main task is to think himself into this action, to discern the thought of its agent. (Collingwood, 1946, p. 213)

In this short passage, Collingwood captures what might be thought of as the essence of the analytical detective story. The problem confronting the literary detective is invariably one of how to make sense of the mystery being investigated from the standpoint of the actors involved; how to look beyond the physical evidence of the body in the library, or the testimony that the leading suspect was on the train to Baltimore at 4.30 pm on Friday when the murder was committed, in order to understand the 'inside' of the events that culminated in the body being discovered in the library with an ice pick through the neck? (Collingwood, 1946, p. 215; Chesterton, 1974, pp. 11,12)

The real task of the literary detective, as with the historian, only begins where the evidence of the outside of events leaves off. As Collingwood puts it, if the past could be remembered, there would be no need for historians (1946, p. 58). The historian's job, therefore, begins at the frontiers of memory, and always involves a journey or investigation into the unknown. So it is with the literary detective. If the police had sufficient forensic evidence or eye-witness testimony they would not need the intervention of a specialist. The task of the literary detective, to extend the metaphor, begins at the frontiers of forensic memory, or where the leads provided by the witness testimony or forensic data run out. And the real job of the literary detective is to apply his or her reconstructive historical imagination to the 'facts' of the case as revealed by the physical evidence or the testimony of eye-witnesses in order to discover the real meaning behind the curious series of events that so puzzle the police.

Before going on to examine Poe's famous story, it is worth reminding ourselves that law as a form of historically situated institutional practice, with its own associated canons of proof and evidence, necessarily confronts many of the same kinds of epistemological and evidentiary problems faced by historians and literary detectives. Every form of trial represents an institutional attempt to address the problems involved in reconstructing a series of events that have taken place in the past, of which the trier of fact normally has no direct knowledge, in order to assign accountability, or non-accountability, for those events to some person or persons who appear(s) to be implicated in the events under investigation. And this is no less true of the medieval trial by battle or trial by ordeal as it is of the 'modern' adversarial trial process of the Anglo-American legal system or the inquisitorial European criminal trial process (Esmien, 1913; Langbein, 2003).

The medieval forms of trial by ordeal and trial by battle represented modes of responding to the problem of how to construct a reliable narrative of events which had occurred in the past, in the face of conflicting testimony about those events – based on God's revelation. And when the growth of scholarly reason demanded more rational modes of arriving at judgment, the forms of trial also changed accordingly (Langbein, 1974, p. 131; McAuley, 2006). Inquisitors trained in scholarly methods of evidence-gathering, in taking depositions and culling depositions to make judgments about factual events, increasingly replaced the medieval forms of trial, first in ecclesiastical courts and then in secular courts. In this context, trial by jury, or by local knowledge, was seen as less modern and less rational than trial by the new inquisitorial mode of evidence-gathering and proof (Langbein, 1974).

Of course, we know from the historical record that these new forms of evidence-gathering could still coexist with belief in supernatural causality. And this in turn influenced the form of trial and the requirements of proof. If, as an inquisitor, I believe that an evil-intentioned look from a person who has made a compact with the devil can cause illness in cattle and in people, can cause wombs to become infertile, or milk to stop flowing, or other assorted catastrophes, then I do not need evidence placing the accused at the scene of the crime in order to satisfy the demands of proof (Girard, 1986, p. 17). All I need is the testimony of witnesses that a secret compact has been made, or evidence of signs or indicia of witchcraft on the body of the accused, and conviction will assuredly follow. The very secret nature of the crime being enough to obviate the need for evidence of material causality and to suspend doubt (Peters, 1978, p. 154; Shapiro, 1991, p. 209–11; Ginzburg, 1992).

It is only when official belief in witchcraft has been superseded by a new faith in science – that we live in a rational universe, governed by the laws of mechanical causality – that doubts about such evidence are likely to arise. In this new world, it seems highly improbable that a malignant look can cause blindness unless some material link can be established between the action of looking and the advent of blindness (Hobbes, 1968, pp. 657–64; Thomas, 1971, pp. 682, 689–90). In a world of observable material effects, we need proof of material causes to explain them. Consequently, the canons of proof and requirements of evidence-gathering are likely to undergo considerable pressure for change, not only in the natural sciences, but also in the related domains of law, religion and philosophy and in popular fiction (Shapiro, 1991; Welsh, 1992; Shapin, 1994; Schramm, 2000).

It is in the context of just such a shift from the inward-focused consciousness of the Romantic movement, towards the more quotidian, outward-focused orientation of the realist novel, that we encounter the emergence of the detective story as a distinctly new form of literary genre. Many candidates have been proposed as the originator of the detective story, from biblical tales (Murch, 1968), to Voltaire's *Zadig*, Godwin's *Caleb Williams* (Symons, 1985), and to Hoffmann's tale, *Mme Scuderi* (Alewyn, 1983). But the consensus opinion still declares that Poe's tale, *The Murders in the Rue Morgue*, published in 1841, deserves the prize (Haycraft, 1951; Symons, 1985; Rzepka, 2005). Poe's tale is the first in which the four central elements or ingredients of the detective story are brought together in one narrative. These necessary ingredients include a detective, a mystery, and the story of an investigation into the mystery, all of which are to be found in *Zadig*, *Mme Scuderi*, and even in Dickens' *Bleak House*, to take a later example (Rzepka, 2005, p. 10). What makes Poe's tale distinct is the introduction of what Rzepka calls the puzzle element, which involves positioning the reader in relation to the narrative in such a way that the reader is able to solve the mystery. The reader is no longer in the position of a passive spectator, watching inspector Bucket as he follows the track of Lady Dedlock, or laying a trap to catch her French Maid, mademoiselle Hortense, for the murder of the lawyer Tulkinghorne (Rzepka, 2005, p. 11). Rather, the reader is provided with the same clues that are made available to the detective, in the same temporal sequence, such that the reader is in a position to try to make sense of the mystery in competition with the detective (Rzepka, 2005, p. 14).

This involves two meta-rules regulating the construction of the narrative. First, that the solution to the mystery should 'employ the inductive methods characteristic of the modern sciences while conforming to the physical laws of cause and effect' (Rzepka, 2005, p. 17); second, that the solution be withheld until the reader is given access to all the information necessary for its solution (Rzepka, 2005, p. 17). This is the basis for the so-called 'fair play' conventions of the analytical detective story, which were laid down as a set of commandments for aspiring detective story writers to follow by the detective club of London in the 1920s (Haycraft, 1951; Murch, 1968; Symons, 1985; Sargent, 2008).

So the narrative must conform to the laws of cause and effect, and the process of solving the mystery must be consistent with the inductive method on which the natural sciences are based. So far, so good. But this suggests a commitment to a positivist epistemology, in which the detective story can be assimilated to the methods of the natural and social sciences (Rzepka, 2005). As we will see, however, Poe's story also involves reliance on the detective's intuitive sense, his ability to penetrate imaginatively into the inside of the events in question and to consider them from the subjective point of view of the actors involved. It is this capacity for *verstehen*, or historical imagination, which differentiates Dupin's analytical method from that of the prefect of police, and gives him such an advantage in discovering the solution to the mystery.

This intuitive aspect of the detective's method is emphasized by Poe very early in the narrative. The story begins with a discourse on analytical method. The description of the 'case' that follows is then presented by way of an illustration or case study of the previous discourse on method. The narrator observes that his companion, one Auguste Dupin, is an extreme example of the analytical reasoner, of a type we will later come to recognize in Holmes. The ideal analytical thinker, according to the narrator, combines in one person the logic of the mathematician and the imagination of the poet. Logic is necessary to scrupulously inquire into the relations between factual data, both factual data that can be obtained through direct observation, and factual data that can be arrived at by necessary inference from the data already present to our senses. But logic alone is not sufficient. Logic can only take you as far as the facts, to which you can apply your logic, will go. When the facts run out, what is the logician to do? That is the question posed by Poe's narrator. It is precisely when the evidence of the senses runs out, or when the logic of the mathematician appears to be confounded by the available evidence, that the imagination of the poet is called for.

Poe provides an instance of this tension between the mode of knowing of the logician and that of the poet in another story, *The Purloined Letter*, featuring the same triad of characters, the narrator, the detective Dupin, and the prefect of police who is confronted with an anomaly that he cannot solve – this time the search for a compromising letter known to be in the possession of a government minister, and thought to be concealed in his house rather than on his person (Poe, 1975b).[2] But, despite the prefect's best efforts, the letter has not been found, although the prefect's men have used every forensic technique known to science in the search, including microscopically examining every inch of the floor, the walls and the furniture. 'There is no square inch where that letter could be hidden that my men have not searched,' comments the prefect. When Dupin observes that the search might not have been undertaken in the correct way, the prefect only promises to redouble his efforts to locate the missing letter.

Dupin, meanwhile, sets about his own investigation in a different manner. And when the prefect next comes to see him, Dupin produces the letter, much to the prefect's mixed delight. Without going into the details of Dupin's account of how he obtained the letter, the central point is that he began his inquiry from a different research question than that which animated the prefect's search of the premises. The prefect's method was based on the scientific approach of data-gathering and analysis. His men had complete access to the premises, since the minister was much away on business; and, given that it was a matter of state importance, the prefect was provided with all the resources he could desire for the search – all to no avail.

Dupin, however, approached the problem from a very different perspective. Instead of asking where a letter of such and such a size could be hidden on the premises and then proceeding from this starting point, Dupin asked himself, reflexively, how he would set about *concealing* such a letter, if he had it in his possession, and knew that the prefect of police would probably search both his person and his premises in order to recover it.

In other words, the focus of his inquiries was not so much with the corporeal presence of the letter, but rather with the *mind* of the minister.

---

2 There is an extensive critical literature on this story. For a discussion of the numerical/geometric structure of the mystery, see Irwin, 1994, esp. pp.1–12.

He sought to imaginatively reconstruct the 'inside' of the event, the internal thought process which enabled him to understand the actions of the minister, and thereby to anticipate how the minister might have acted in the particular circumstances in which he found himself. This is an explicitly historicist approach to the problem of recreating the past, which requires the historian to understand the past in all its historical particularity, rather than seeking to explain the past by reference to general laws of material causality, human nature or social structure (Cassirer, 1972; Berlin, 1976; Hamilton, 2002).

In this instance, Dupin was familiar with the minister, and knew him to be both imaginative and intelligent, qualities of mind shared with the detective himself. So the process of imaginatively placing himself in the position of the minister was relatively easy for Dupin, certainly more so than for the prefect. The point being that it was not just that the prefect lacked the poetic imagination of Dupin; but rather that the prefect's method of investigation precluded such an approach. Imagination should have nothing to do with the process of forensic investigation, according to the prefect, who remains a stern logician to the end. For Poe's hero, the first of the analytical literary detectives whose work we are now so familiar with, the past cannot be recreated without imagination.[3]

Dupin relies on a similar critical historical method to imaginatively reconstruct the past in the case of *The Murders in the Rue Morgue*. Here the problem of how to make inferences from the sense data when the sense data runs out is presented in a very different way. The problem is not a lack of sense data, but too much contradictory sense data. How is it possible to account for the horrific events that took place inside a closed and locked room, without any obvious mode of ingress or egress other than through a single door or a window, both of which were locked and bolted from the inside? The room itself was on the fourth floor of a quiet building in a quiet street, where two women were known to live a very sequestered life. One had recently taken a considerable amount of money from the bank, which sum, 4000 francs, had been delivered to her apartment by one LeBon, whom the police have arrested on suspicion of being involved in the murders.

According to the newspaper account, the neighbours in the locality were roused at about 3 am by the sound of terrified shrieks coming from the inside of the house in the Rue Morgue. Ominously, by the time the neighbours, accompanied by a gendarme of police, managed to break open the front entrance to the building, the screaming had stopped. But the witnesses all testified that, as they mounted the stairs to the second landing, they

---

3 For a classic example of such an approach, see G K Chesterton, *The Secret of Father Brown* (1974, pp. 11), where Father Brown claims the secret of his method is that he imaginatively *becomes* the murderer, and thus is able to work out how the crime was committed.

could hear two or more 'rough voices' in contention, in the upper part of the house. But as they reached the second floor, the voices stopped. According to the depositions of the witnesses,[4] one was a gruff voice, speaking French, while the other apparently belonged to a foreigner, speaking a language none of the witnesses could confidently identify.

When the witnesses finally forced open the locked door of the fourth-floor room in which the attack took place, they found the room in a state of violent disarray. The mattress of the single bedstead had been thrown into the centre of the room, furniture was scattered and broken, and the witnesses discovered a blood-stained razor, two or three long grey tresses of human hair, smeared with blood, and apparently pulled out by the roots, together with four gold napoleons, some silver spoons, an open cash box, and two bags containing nearly 4000 francs.

Of the two women who lived in the house there was no immediate sign until one of the neighbours, noticing an unusual quantity of soot in the fireplace, looked up and discovered the body of young Mme L'Espanaye, stuffed feet first up the chimney with such force that it later took four men to pull her out. The body was fearfully mutilated, with bruising at the throat suggesting she had been strangled. The body of old Mme L'Espanaye was subsequently found in a small yard at the rear of the building, again fearfully mutilated; her neck slashed by a razor with such severity that when the body was first inspected by a witness its head fell off.

The horrific and puzzling nature of the crime thrilled the readers of the newspaper in which Dupin and the narrator first read an account of the mystery. Of the owners of the two voices all the witnesses testified to having heard arguing in the upstairs part of the house, there was apparently no trace. It was as if they had literally vanished into thin air. A full search of the premises revealed that there were no secret compartments in which anyone could have hidden, nor any other escape route from the room other than the door to the stairs, up which the witnesses were ascending, or through the fourth floor window. But the window was locked from the inside, and both window sashes were further secured by nails driven deep into the sill, such that it would have been impossible to open or close the window from the outside. (In short, the first locked room mystery.)

In the absence of any clue as to *how* the crime could have been committed and the murderers make their escape, the police focus instead on the question *why*, on the assumption that the answer to the question *why* will lead them to the answer to the question *who*. This leads them to arrest the hapless LeBon, who is the only one of the witnesses giving depositions to the police who can even remotely be seen as having a possible motive for the

---

4 As reported in the newspaper account of the mystery.

crime. As rationalists, and as followers of the positivist doctrines of Auguste Comte, they reject outright any suggestion of supernatural causality. They reason that any crime which has been caused by human agency, as this horrific crime clearly has, must have a purposive human agent behind it. And their job is to locate that purposive agent. The idea that this could be a purposeless crime, that the event in all its ferocity cannot be explained by reference to the workings of the human mind, violates their sense of the proper order of things, their belief in science, reason, progress and enlightenment. This is Paris, in the nineteenth century. We are not retrogressing to the domain of superstition, to the belief in witches and supernatural agents, who can enter into human bodies and into human buildings at will, and as secretly leave when their dark purposes have been accomplished. Their arrest of the suspect LeBon is as much a testament to their faith in reason as it is an indication of their belief in his guilt.

But Dupin is not constrained by any blind faith in reason. He is a creature of the dark. He and his companion the narrator close the shutters of their gloomy mansion on the daylight and only go out into the streets of Paris after nightfall, where they feed off the energy of the nocturnal city like intellectual vampires. For him, it is nature's secrets which need to be investigated, rather than man's purposes. Thus the question becomes not so much one of *why* did the crime take place, as *how* did it take place? How did the murderers get into the room, which was apparently closed and locked from the inside? And once having obtained entry, how did they escape without leaving any trace, other than the oral trace of their voices as deposed to by the witnesses ascending the stairs?

The method Dupin relies on to shed light on the mystery combines forensic investigative techniques with the reconstructive imagination of the historian. Having obtained permission from the prefect of police to examine the crime scene, Dupin finds it unaltered in any material respect, even to the physical condition of the bodies, which had both been placed in the room where the first body was found. He thus has the opportunity to examine the physical evidence with the same eyes as the police. But the inferences he draws from the observations he makes at the crime scene are very different from those arrived at by the police.

To the physical evidence problem – how could the perpetrators have got into and out of the room without being seen and with both doors and windows apparently locked from the inside? – Dupin provides an ingenious, but much copied, answer. The windows were fastened by a spring-operated locking mechanism. Hence, when closed (from either inside or outside), they would automatically lock on their own. However, if the window were open, even though the room was situated on the fourth floor, an extremely athletic person could have ascended a lightning rod located some feet to the side of the window, and swung laterally by means of the shutters to gain entry into the room. If, on subsequently exiting the room, the window were then closed, it would automatically appear to lock from the inside.

A greater problem was posed by the evidence of the nail, which was driven through the bottom sash of the window into the window frame, to a depth of more than an inch. This seemed to preclude the possibility that the window could have been open prior to the attack; thus negating the hypothesis that the owners of the two voices heard by the witnesses had entered and left the room by the window. Any other explanation seems to take us back in the direction of supernatural causality, which Dupin rejects with as much fervour as do the police. As he observes to the narrator: 'Madame and Mademoiselle L'Espanaye were not destroyed by spirits. The doers of the deed were material and escaped materially.' (Poe, 1975a, p. 156)

He tests further, and discovers a hairline crack in the nail, which is not visible to the naked eye when closed. The nail has obviously snapped in two at some point. But now the mystery of the window apparently being nailed shut from the inside has been cleared up. There is nothing in the physical evidence now standing in the way of the hypothesis that the attackers entered and left the room by the window. The police overlooked the possibility of the broken nail, since they were so focused on the question of motive that they had not formed any working hypothesis to explain how the attackers could have entered and left the room without being observed. Thus, they uncritically accepted the evidence of their own senses that the window was locked and nailed shut from the inside. Dupin, working on the experimental sciences' principle that views any hypothesis as only provisional until empirically tested, also subjects the hypothesis that the window is nailed shut to a critical examination, and thereby discovers the secret to the window.

Thus far, Dupin has proceeded like a strict logician, reasoning backwards from observable effects to discover their antecedent causes (Cassirer, 1972, p. 177; Bonfantini and Proni, 1983, p. 125; Harowotz, 1983, pp. 194–7). Indeed, so confident is he in his own method as to claim that he was logically convinced that the only mode of ingress and egress to the room could have been by the window. And it was this degree of moral certainty that led him to re-examine the 'evidence' of the nail, thus applying the Sherlockian maxim that when you have excluded the impossible, whatever remains, however improbable, must be the truth (Conan Doyle, 1981, p. 648; Sargent, 2008, p. 53).

However, the discovery of the secret to the window only clarifies part of the mystery. It does little to explain the extreme ferocity of the attack on the two women, or the apparent lack of motive. Nor does it shed light on one of the most puzzling aspects of the case, namely the curious inconsistency in the witness testimony regarding the two voices heard arguing in the upstairs room. While all the witnesses corroborated each other's testimony concerning the one deeper voice speaking French, there was surprising inconsistency among the witnesses concerning the second voice heard in the room, and presumably belonging to one of the murderers. It was variously described as shrill or as angry, or as the voice of a man, or of a woman. One witness speculated the language it was speaking might have been Russian, another Italian; one suggested Spanish, another English. And while a French-speaking witness thought it might have been Spanish; the Spanish witness was sure it was English, and the English witness was convinced it was German, and so on. Altogether a most puzzling and inconsistent set of witness statements. 'Did you observe anything peculiar about the testimony?' asks Dupin of the narrator. 'That it was much confused,' replies his friend. 'That was the evidence itself,' replies Dupin, not what was peculiar about it (Poe, 1975a, p. 155; c.f. Thomas, 1999, pp. 46, 48–9).

This is the point in the narrative where the imagination of the poet takes over from the logic of the mathematician. As a logician, Dupin is confounded by the absence of reliable witness statements from which to make any deductions about the identity of the owner of the second voice, or even which language it was speaking. But as a poet, he interpolates additional data from the testimony which, when combined with the traces of physical evidence found in the room, enables him to construct a hypothesis about the possible identities of the two speakers heard by the witnesses as they ascended the stairs, that goes far beyond the imaginative comprehension of even the nearest eye-witnesses to the events in question.

In this respect, Dupin's method owes much to the reconstructive historical method first developed by Giambatista Vico in the eighteenth century, namely that we can gain access to others' pasts by trying to locate ourselves imaginatively as closely as we can to what we know of their internal mental states and their particular historical circumstances, in order to understand how they might have acted (Collingwood, 1946; Berlin, 1976). From this imaginative starting point, we can then formulate provisional hypotheses about their historical motives and actions, as a basis for explaining historical events. The hypotheses must, of course, correspond with what we know from the available historical evidence. But the process of trying to imaginatively reconstruct the events from within may allow the investigator to develop an interpretation of the evidence which might not have been arrived at through the positivist methods of the police.

Vico's historical method is based on a distinction between knowledge of the natural world, and knowledge of that which man has created (Collingwood, 1946, pp. 64–5; Berlin, 1976, pp. xvi, xvii, 100–8). That which man has created is intelligible to us on a different basis from that which God has created, because we can never see into the mind of God. So we can only know that which God has created from the outside, as it registers on the senses, or through the deductive sciences of logic and mathematics. But as human purposive actors, who mentally construct the worlds we live in and act upon, we can enter into the mental worlds of other men and women who have created their own worlds in the past, and thus seek to understand their actions and their cultural practices and institutions from the *inside*, in a way which we can never do for phenomena in the natural world (Berlin, 1976, pp. xviii, 27, 28; Miller, 1993, p. 34).[5]

Moreover, in principle this should not just be possible in relation to those who are nearest to us in historical time, in culture, in world view, or in knowledge claims, but also with respect to those who are distant from us in any of these respects (Berlin, 1976, pp. 102–3). What 'man' has made is in principle intelligible to other men or women, even in very different historical circumstances, by use of their reconstructive historical imagination. By this means it should be possible, though not without great effort, to recreate the mental outlook of civilizations very different from our own, such as the Aztecs, or ancient Sumerians; and behind these even primitive man, without language or political organization (Collingwood, 1946, pp. 70, 199, 215; Berlin, 1976, p. 29).

But this cannot be accomplished by reasoning backwards from effects to their causes, or from an observable present to an unobservable past, as a natural scientist or logician seeks to do (Cassirer, 1972, p. 177). Such an approach assumes that the past can always be explained by reference to the present. But many historical events or processes cannot be understood 'from the inside' by reference to a present which is different in its internal mental workings, so to speak, from the past which is being investigated. Only if the historian or detective is able to free their imagination from the present, and to look at past events from a standpoint that is not already determined by an insistence on a strict teleological relationship to the present, will the detective or historian be able to imagine a past which is radically different in its mental outlook, than his or her own.

And this is exactly what Dupin achieves so triumphantly in his investigation of the mysterious events associated with the murders in the Rue Morgue. Interpolating from the confused testimony of the witnesses, and

---

5 Thus, to understand the behaviour of a window, one has to use one method. But to understand the behaviour of an intentional human actor, in their particular historical circumstances, one has to use another method. The question confronting Dupin is what method to use for understanding the behaviour of a man-like creature, acting in its particular 'historical' circumstances? Should it be regarded as a creature of nature, or as akin to man, from the point of view of method? This, of course, anticipates Darwin. *The Murders in the Rue Morgue* was published in 1841, Darwin's *Origin of Species* in 1859. For a discussion of evolutionary thought in fiction prior to 1860, see Henkin, 1963, chapters 1 and 2.

the equally confounding physical evidence discovered at the crime scene, Dupin imaginatively apprehends the mental world of a being whose whole mental apparatus is radically different from his own. The police, working from the premise that human nature is always and everywhere the same, look for a motive that will explain the crime, thus projecting their own mental outlook and experience onto the historical evidence. But this merely inhibits their ability to look beyond the facts to see what lies behind them.

Dupin, 'reading' the traces of the physical evidence as well as the testimonies of witnesses for clues as to the internal mental state of the actors in this particular drama, discovers something quite unexpected. Looking for evidence of mind, or purposive action, he discerns only its absence rather than its presence. He sees traces of what we may mistake for mind, such as the capacity to manipulate tools, to mimic behaviour, even to kill other human beings with a razor, or to lift bodies and push them forcefully up a chimney; also the capacity for language, or what sounds like human speech to the witnesses coming up the stairs.

And from these traces, he begins to formulate a hypothesis concerning the agency, the method and the motive of the attacks that is completely at odds with the assumptions of the police, based on their normal experience of crime. He then seeks to test his hypothesis by placing an advertisement in the paper, after completing his investigation of the crime scene. The advertisement offers the return of a large orang-utan, recently captured in the Bois de Boulogne, to its owner, who is identified as a sailor on a Maltese ship recently arrived in Paris. A step is then heard on the stairs. Quiet, says Dupin to the narrator. It is probably the very man whose testimony may help us to unravel this mystery. Close the door when he comes in and don't let him escape, and you shall learn something about the events of this mystery that may surprise you.

The trap prepared, it is sprung when the sailor enters the room. At first, he attempts to resist. But when assured that no harm can come to him by telling all he knows, he proceeds to relate the events of the night in question to the astonished narrator. It emerges that the sailor was an eyewitness to the horrific events in the room on the fourth floor of the house where the attacks took place. He was the owner of the deeper voice, which all the witnesses deposed they heard speaking French. And it was this which made him hesitant to come forward with information about the mystery, lest he be arrested for the crime. The other voice was that of an orang-utan which had been brought by the sailor on a ship from Borneo, had escaped from his lodgings that morning, and had entered the room of the two women, followed by the sailor, who had watched, horrified, while they were killed with such savagery. The razor with which old Mme L'Espanaye's neck had been severed had been carried by the beast when it escaped from the sailor's lodgings. The action itself was done in a grotesque mimicry of the sailor's morning shaving ritual.

The eye-witness testimony produced by Dupin ultimately leads to the release of LeBon, whom the police now recognize had nothing to do with the alleged crime. The mystery of the crime is thus cleared up without need of a trial – the absence of mind on the part of the beast effectively defeating the law's efforts to impose responsibility for the gruesome deaths of the two victims. Indeed, in a gesture which speaks to the gulf between the medieval trials of animals as agents of the devil (Evans, 1987) and the 'enlightened' Parisian judicial system, the orang-utan was eventually recaptured and sold by the sailor to the Jardin des Plantes in Paris, where it lived out the rest of its natural life in the service of science.[6]

The question of 'mind' and its connection with the self thus runs like an unresolved tension throughout the whole narrative. The very commencement of the tale, when the narrator discusses Dupin's uncanny ability to reconstruct his (the narrator's) internal thought processes for some 15 minutes while they walked together in silence through the streets of the city, speaks to this issue of one mind imaginatively entering into the mental state of another, which is the basis of Vico's historical method. The narrator uses this example to illustrate the method Dupin subsequently relies on to solve the mystery of the two murders.

Yet in this case, in contradistinction to the case of *The Purloined Letter*, there was no other 'mind' to enter into, no sentient historical actor whose actions or motives can be comprehended through a process of sympathetic historical imagination, unless it is the actions and motives of the sailor. Yet it is not the sailor's actions or motives we are primarily concerned with here, but the actions of the ape. This is what defeats the police in their inquiry, in the end, since not only was there no motive for the attacks, in any conventional sense, but the perpetrator of the attacks lacked any capacity for motive in the sense understood by the police or by the legal system.

The irony is that in this instance it is the police, in their search for motive, who focus on the 'inside' of the events in order to explain the 'outside' of the mystery, unsuccessfully as it transpires. While it is Dupin who works from the outside of the events to the inside, as it were. It is only from his method of critically examining the evidence, both of the crime scene (where a trace of red, non-human hair was discovered by Dupin, but apparently overlooked by the police) and of the witness testimony, that he was able to infer the existence of a perpetrator who has the physical dexterity of a human actor, but without the mental capacity to regulate it.

---

6 In sharp contrast to the fate of an elephant that killed its trainer in Erwin, Tennessee, in 1916, which was hanged for its crime (a feat requiring a crane, due to the elephant's weight).

It was this inference which led to his formulation of the hypothesis of the escaped orang-utan, and the existence of the French-speaking sailor, without whose testimony LeBon might well not have been freed. So, in this instance, it was the hypothesis that generated the testimony, not the testimony that generated the hypothesis. The police, relying on a more pedestrian approach based on interviewing and taking depositions from witnesses, could never have obtained the eye-witness testimony from the sailor, for the simple reason that they were not even aware of his existence and had no way of imagining how he could be in any way connected with the mystery.

And here one is left to speculate whether the police approach to their investigation might not have been influenced, even if unconsciously, by the spectre of the witchcraft trial, and the inquisitorial criminal procedure that led to the arrest, questioning and trial of those on whom public suspicion of witchcraft had fallen. As scholars such as Langbein (1974), Lea (1888) and Peters (1978) have shown, the witchcraft trial (as with the accusation of heresy) was always more concerned with the 'inside' of events than with their external manifestations, due to the secret nature of the crime and the assumptions about supernatural causality that underlie the accusation and trial of witchcraft. Consequently, the process of judicial reasoning backwards from observed events, such as the illness of a child, the barrenness of a wife, the destruction of crops, to the antecedent practice of witchcraft that was alleged to have caused such dire consequences had to proceed by way of presumption, rather than by a chain of physical causes. Evidence was instead required that the accused had been engaged in illicit practices of witchcraft, such as making a secret compact with the devil, or casting a spell, or night-riding with other witches. And since there were rarely witnesses to such an event, other than those who were also complicit in the act, confessional testimony was often given greater weight than evidence of circumstances, since circumstances could be made to lie, or to disguise inner thoughts. Witchcraft was therefore regarded as *crimen exceptum*, the secret nature of which was likely to render normal modes of proof inadequate (Peters, 1978, p. 152; Shapiro, 1991, p. 165).

Peters comments that the very accusation of witchcraft operated to suspend traditional procedural protections for the person accused of the crime (Peters, 1978, p. 152). Once taken into custody, a suspect could be held without charge, while being questioned by inquisitors, who were trained to look for signs of witchcraft and permitted to use judicial torture to obtain confessions, at least in continental jurisdictions, where there was sufficient presumption of guilt (Langbein, 1976; Peters, 1978, pp. 152–3). And if a suspect were to confess under torture, the confession would be entered into evidence and used against the accused person at trial, without any opportunity for cross-questioning witnesses, or of challenging the admissibility of the incriminating testimony, as might occur under the adversarial criminal trial procedure more familiar to Anglo-American readers.

While witchcraft as a separate offence, with its own modes of proof, had long fallen into disuse by the time of Poe's story, its spectral presence still haunts the narrative (Gordon, 1997), especially in view of the inquisitorial procedure followed by the Paris police, their reliance on witness testimony over forensic evidence, and their apparent lack of concern with the physical laws of cause and effect. One of the distinguishing features of the common law adversarial criminal trial procedure, as compared with the inquisitorial model of criminal trial proceedings, is its more hostile attitude towards confessional testimony, especially self-incriminating testimony generated from the accused through threat or compulsion. In this it shares with the analytical detective story a preference for external evidence of the senses, which can be independently corroborated, over uncorroborated confessional testimony (Sargent, 2010, p. 293). Thus, an accused has the right to remain silent in response to the charges brought against him or her at trial, other than to enter a plea, and cannot be forced to give testimony in his or her own defence, or otherwise be viewed as an evidentiary resource available to the court (Langbein, 2003, pp. 277–84).

By contrast, the inquisitorial investigative procedure followed by the Paris police in Poe's fictional story relies implicitly on the police power to keep LeBon in police custody without trial, and to require him to answer police questions, which can then be entered into evidence, without any right to protection against self-incrimination. The absence of evidence as to the physical or material circumstances as to how the crime could have been committed thus adds to the police pressure to obtain a confession from LeBon, since they have no other way of solving the crime, or obtaining sufficient evidence to obtain a conviction. For the police, therefore, the threat of indefinite detention in police custody does not detract from the truth value of any confessional testimony produced from the accused and entered into evidence. If anything, it adds to the reliability of the evidence on the assumption that a guilty person has a natural interest in concealing the truth, such that the truth can only be produced under pressure. For an audience familiar with the common law adversarial criminal trial procedure, just the opposite is true, that an admission that is forced out of an accused under threat or compulsion is more likely to be unreliable, precisely because it is not freely or voluntarily made.

It is Dupin who succeeds in convincing the police that LeBon could have had nothing to do with the murders, that there was another explanation of the facts that was available on the evidence which led to a strikingly different conclusion. In the end, it is the eye-witness testimony of the sailor that convinces the police of LeBon's innocence. As we have seen, the sailor's existence was inferred by Dupin from the testimony of the witnesses, all of whom heard his voice in contention with the orang-utan as they mounted the stairs, but none of whom could make sense of what they heard. It is Dupin's method of reconstructive historical imagination which supplies the missing ingredient that the police (and the witnesses) lack, namely the capacity to rearrange the evidence in his mind's eye, and thus produce a counter-narrative of events which is capable of explaining the facts in a way that raises more than a reasonable doubt about the guilt of the suspect LeBon.

Without Dupin's intervention, it is doubtful the police would have released LeBon, in the absence of any other explanation for the events in question. In this first modern detective story, we see the detective acting, not as an auxiliary to the police, seeking to impose justice on those who seek to evade responsibility for a perfect crime, but as an advocate on behalf of one who is unjustly accused of a crime he did not commit. What Dupin's intervention achieves is to test the police case against Lebon to see if it stands up to critical examination, almost in the manner of a defence lawyer at trial. In locating the mystery in Paris, and publishing it in Philadelphia for an American audience, Poe's tale implicitly generates a narrative tension not only between the rationalism of the police and the historicism of Dupin, but also between the adversarial and inquisitorial systems of proof. In their search for motive, and with their reliance on 'interior' or confessional modes of proof, rather than external evidence of circumstances, the Paris police, with all the resources of science at their disposal, could never have identified the real 'criminal.'

Conclusion

In this essay, I have tried to show that Poe's famous story, *The Murders in the Rue Morgue*, in a sense disrupts the conventional requirements of its own narrative form by incorporating elements of the uncanny, the irrational and the inhuman into what might be thought of as the central nervous system of the analytical detective story. As Rzepka (2005, pp. 11, 17) points out, the *sine qua non* of the detective story, that which makes it recognizable as a detective story, is that the mystery is presented as a puzzle that can be solved by reference to the principles of logic and inductive scientific method. Any element of the irrational, of the marvellous, of the supernatural, must be rigorously expunged from the causal explanation of the mystery, such that a rational solution can be presented to the reader. This is the primary task of the detective, who functions as an agent of rationality in the narrative (Sargent, 2008, p. 43), and is therefore less likely than the reader or the narrator to be deceived by the false glamour that the appearance of the marvellous may cast over the events being investigated.

To a later generation of mystery writers Poe's usage of a non-human agent as the hinge on which the plot turns would be considered as tantamount to cheating, as a violation of the implicit normative obligations a writer of detective stories owes to his or her readers (Porter, 1981, p. 85), akin to using doubles, or a tasteless, odourless poison hitherto unknown to science (Murch, 1968, p. 225; Symons, 1985, pp. 13, 93; Sargent, 2008, p. 42). But to Poe, writing at the end of the first third of the nineteenth century, at a moment when the positivist claims of the natural sciences seem to be on the brink of completing their colonization of the human sciences, the assumed separation between reason and the imagination, between the world as given to the senses, and the world as given to the imagination, remains very much contested terrain. Working at the borderline between the rational and the marvellous, at that creative place where the intellect and the imagination intersect, Poe's exemplary text proposes a problem that cannot be solved by analytical reason alone. Only if the results of forensic investigation can be leavened by the use of historical imagination can the detective hope to arrive at a solution to the mystery. In utilizing the tropes of the irrational, the abnormal, and the inhuman, and locating these at the epicentre of the plot structure of the narrative, Poe's story not only transgresses the conventional boundaries of the very literary genre it helped to establish, but also subtly challenges the positivist scientific foundations on which law's own claims to be able to distinguish between what is fact and what is fanciful are necessarily grounded.

References

Alewyn, R (1983) 'The Origin of the Detective Story' in G W Most and W W Stowe (eds), *The Poetics of Murder: Detective Fiction and Literary Theory* (San Diego: Harcourt, Brace, Jovanovich), pp. 62–78

Berlin, I (1976) *Vico and Herder: Two Studies in the History of Ideas* (London: Hogarth Press)

Bonfantini, M A and G Proni (1983) 'To Guess or Not to Guess?' in U Eco and T A Seboek (eds), *The Sign of Three: Dupin, Holmes, Peirce* (Bloomington: Indiana University Press), pp. 119–34

Burrell, G and G Morgan (1979) *Sociological Paradigms and Organizational Analysis* (Portsmouth, NH: Heineman)

Cassirer, E (1972 [1944]) *An Essay on Man. An Introduction to a Philosophy of Human Culture* (New Haven: Yale University Press)

Chesterton, G K (1974) *The Secret of Father Brown* (London: Penguin Books)

Collingwood, R G (1946) *The Idea of History* (London: Oxford University Press)
Conan Doyle, A (1981) 'The Sign of Four' in *The Celebrated Cases of Sherlock Holmes* (London: Octopus Books Ltd)
Esmien, A (1913) *A History of Continental Criminal Procedure: With Special Reference to France* (Boston: Little, Brown & Company)
Evans, E P (1987 [1906]) *The Criminal Prosecution and Capital Punishment of Animals* (London: Faber and Faber)
Ginzburg, C (1992) *The Night Battles: Witchcraft and Agrarian Cults in the Sixteenth and Seventeenth Centuries* (Baltimore: Johns Hopkins University Press)
Girard, R (1986) *The Scapegoat* (Baltimore: Johns Hopkins University Press)
Gordon, A (1997) *Ghostly Matters: Haunting and the Sociological Imagination* (Minneapolis: University of Minnesota Press)
Hamilton, P (2002) *Historicism* (London: Routledge & Kegan Paul)
Harrowitz, N (1983) 'The Body of the Detective Novel: Charles S Peirce and Edgar Allan Poe' in U Eco and T A Seboek (eds), *The Sign of Three: Dupin, Holmes, Peirce* (Bloomington: Indiana University Press), pp. 179–97
Haycraft, H (1951) *Murder for Pleasure. The Life and Times of the Detective Story* (New York: Appleton-Century Inc.)
Henkin, L J (1963) *Darwinism in the English Novel, 1860–1910* (New York: Russell & Russell)
Hobbes, T (1968) *Leviathan*, C B MacPherson (ed.) (Aylesbury: Penguin Books)
Irwin, J T (1994) *The Mystery to a Solution: Poe, Borges, and the Analytic Detective Story* (Baltimore: Johns Hopkins University Press)
Langbein, J H (1974) *Prosecuting Crime in the Renaissance: England, Germany, France* (Cambridge, MA: Harvard University Press)
Langbein, J H (1976) *Torture and the Law of Proof* (Chicago: University of Chicago Press)
Langbein, J H (2003) *The Origins of the Adversary Criminal Trial* (Oxford: Oxford University Press)
Lea, H C (1888) *A History of the Inquisition of the Middle Ages, Part One* (London: Sampson, Low, Marsdon, Searle & Rivington)
McAuley, F (2006) 'Canon Law and the End of the Ordeal' 26(3) *Oxford Journal of Legal Studies* 473–513
Miller, C (1993) *Giambattista Vico: Imagination and Historical Knowledge* (New York: St Martin's Press)
Murch, A E (1968) *The Development of the Detective Novel* (Port Washington, NY: Kennikat Press)
Peters, E (1978) *The Magician, the Witch and the Law* (Philadelphia: University of Pennsylvania Press)

Poe, E A (1975a) 'The Murders in the Rue Morgue' in *Complete Tales and Poems of Edgar Allan Poe* (New York: Vintage Books), pp. 141–68

Poe, E A (1975b) 'The Purloined Letter' in *Complete Tales and Poems of Edgar Allan Poe* (New York: Vintage Books), pp. 208–22

Porter, D (1981) *The Pursuit of Crime: Art and Ideology in Detective Fiction* (New Haven: Yale University Press)

Rzepka, C J (2005) *Detective Fiction* (Cambridge: Polity Press)

Sargent, N C (2008) 'Murder and Mayhem in Legal Method, or, the Strange case of Sherlock Holmes versus Sam Spade' in L Atkinson and D Majury (eds), *Law, Mystery, and the Humanities* (Toronto: University of Toronto Press), pp. 39–66

Sargent, N C (2010) 'Mys-Reading the Past in Detective Fiction and Law' **22**(2) *Law and Literature* 288–306

Schramm, J M (2000) *Testimony and Advocacy in Victorian Law, Literature, and Theology* (Cambridge: Cambridge University Press)

Shapin, S (1994) *A Social History of Truth: Civility and Science in Seventeenth Century England* (Chicago: University of Chicago Press)

Shapiro, B J (1991) *'Beyond Reasonable Doubt' and 'Probable Cause': Historical Perspectives on the Anglo-American Law of Evidence* (Berkeley: University of California Press)

Symons, J (1985) *Bloody Murder. From the Detective Story to the Crime Novel* (Harmondsworth: Viking)

Thomas, K (1971) *Religion and the Decline of Magic* (London: Weidenfeld & Nicholson)

Thomas, R R (1999) *Detective Fiction and the Rise of Forensic Science* (Cambridge: Cambridge University Press)

Watt, I (2000 [1957]) *The Rise of the Novel: Studies in Defoe, Richardson and Fielding* (London/Pimlico: Chatto & Windus).

Welsh, A (1992) *Strong Representations: Narrative and Circumstantial Evidence in England* (Baltimore: Johns Hopkins University Press)

11
Law's Life on the Screen
Richard K. Sherwin

> It is the real thing. It is the evidence. It is the incident as it's unfolding. (Cincinnati police chief referring to images shot from a police officer's head cam)
>
> Image is everything. (Canon camera advertisement)
>
> Image is nothing. (Coca-Cola advertisment)

Introduction

Law today lives in images the way images live on the screen. Visualizing law in real cases – through visual evidence and visual argument – is now becoming an increasingly routine part of legal practice in the United States, the United Kingdom and elsewhere. Viewers are used to being moved, edified and delighted (and at times titillated or even horrified) by what they see and hear on electronic screens both large and small. But what are the implications when the search for fact-based justice inside the courtroom depends upon those very responses? What does it mean for our system of law when the emotions we feel, or the sheer aesthetic delight, or the memories that are evoked, or the fantasies and desires that are activated by visual images become the motive force underlying legal judgment?

This question raises concerns not only about truth in a particular case, but also about the human mimetic capacity itself, our ability to represent the real. The latter goes to the heart of what Bruno Latour has called 'iconoclash' (Latour, 2002): we love the image, and we hate it. The image informs and enchants us. We are moved by what we see on the screen. But the image also can seduce us without reason. It cues easy stereotypes, provokes raw emotions, and stokes untamed fantasies and desires. What is more, it often works its magic beneath the surface of consciousness. This subterranean efficacy jars the tradition-bound legal mind with its insistence upon cool reason, deductive logic and careful, self-reflexive deliberation. To conceive of judgment, and of the act of law-making itself, as emanating from the unconscious would seem to subvert core assumptions about the very nature of law and the legal process.

Suffice it to say, law's migration to the screen inside the courtroom alters the familiar picture that we have of law as a dispassionate, deliberative, rationally calculating activity. I submit that the visual digital turn that is now underway worldwide calls for a very different paradigm for law than the traditional, disembodied, rational-positivist model that has served from early modernity. In short, we need a visual jurisprudence to accommodate the changing demands of the visual digital times in which we live. This is not simply a matter of changing aesthetics, though learning more about the various ways in which images persuade is also a significant part of the challenge before us. We need to understand the way visual meanings are made, cross-examined and made anew. We need new visual rhetorical handbooks (better yet, new multi-media online networks) to help make sure that lawyers, judges and the lay public alike will cultivate a level of visual literacy that is consonant with the demands of visual legal decision-making. But there is also a larger stake. The continued legitimacy of law in a world inundated with all manner of visual objects, from surveillance images to animations that digitally simulate the real, depends upon our response to law's iconoclash. Ignorance, cynicism, or indifference regarding the reliability of visual images effectively place the force of law on precarious grounds. In a time when just about anything we can imagine can be digitally pictured on a screen, it matters on what basis the state acts. It is no small thing to forcibly transfer property or impel payments or take away a person's freedom under force of law based on what viewers see and feel in response to images on a screen inside the courtroom.

Toward visual literacy and metaphysical resolve

I believe that it behooves us to apply the tools of cognitive and cultural psychology and a pragmatic ethical phenomenology to our understanding of the image. Is the image before us ontologically over-determined, or has it emptied out into mass-reproduced simulation? Does it embody something sublime, a picture whose meaning inexplicably exceeds what it shows, or does it exist as mere sensation, an offshoot of the aesthetics of formal, empty ornamentation? These possibilities describe the potential range of law's life as an image. It is my contention that there are occasions when our nerve endings are visually stimulated in a way that induces reflexive emotional reactions, and occasions when we encounter images that exact an ethical, visual demand, an 'ought' – something to which we are obliged to respond, and for which we are ineluctably responsible. In this way, we may distinguish between the aesthetic complacency of the ersatz aura of the image (mere 'eye candy') and the ethical demand of a sublime presence.

Iconoclash erodes the legitimacy of visual representation to the extent that it repudiates our sense of fealty to the real. Spectacle, pageantry, sensation – these manifestations of baroque aesthetics reflect a form of meaning-making that is largely based upon the heightening of affect. Affect, like a musical score, may be set to any number of different storylines, or political ideologies, or legal outcomes. Similarly, baroque aesthetics may back any number of preferences. In the seventeenth century, for example, baroque pageantry and spectacle well served both the state and the church. Baroque spectacle, however, is empty at its core. Its heightening of affect is meant to disguise or distract us from that melancholy reality.

Images that help to sustain our fealty to the real harbour a sublime presence. What makes them sublime is that the meaning they allow always exceeds the form in which they are represented, hence, their mystery. Iconoclash eases, therefore, not simply with the advent of visual literacy (increased knowledge about how images persuade), but also with the advent of metaphysical resolve, which is to say, with enhanced confidence in the mimetic faculty itself. The sublime image persuades not only on the basis of its form and affect, but also, and most importantly, because of what it presents, what it makes present, what it brings into being, and simultaneously withholds from view.

In what follows, I will seek to illustrate these two different ways in which images play upon mind and body. I will suggest how each of these sorts of images – both the sublime and the sensational – plays out when law migrates to the screen inside the courtroom. I will use illustrations from the arts to illuminate what distinguishes the sensational from the sublime image, and then I will correlate these distinctions with specific visuals that have been used in real law cases. We will see that the baroque aesthetic of sensation correlates well with the 'magic realism' of pop science, which is particularly evident in the way legal advocates visualize neuroscience in specific cases. This visual aesthetic has also made its appearance in the evolving jurisprudence of child pornography, where jurists are led to use visual images in the service of popular fantasies and irrational desires. Sublime images, on the other hand, arise in a far different manner. They make us shudder – at the collapse of time (for example, between the event of murder and the event of its reconstruction at trial), and in the invisible presence of a mother's incomprehensible rage, as we will see in the *Skakel* and *Borukhova* cases that follow.

Before we get to those case illustrations, however, an additional word may be in order on the subjects of visual literacy, law's iconoclash, and the aspiration to metaphysical resolve in fealty to the real.

Background: from iconoclash to the visual sublime

What, then, does visual literacy require of us with regard to law? One way to begin our response is to consider anew the core principle of adversarial justice. In the Anglo-American common law tradition, the adversarial system approaches the search for truth at trial as an evidentiary contest. Lawyers use evidence to reconstruct reality, which is to say, the historic event that is being examined and ultimately judged. In the adversarial system, the decision-maker (whether judge or juror) is supposed to test each bit of evidence that pieces reality together. When a witness is on the stand, or when a document or some physical evidence (like a fingerprint) 'testifies', jurors more or less know what it is they are seeing and hearing, and they also know what is expected of them. They are participating in a 'battle for reality' in the adversarial contest for fact-based justice. The matter is less clear, however, when judges and jurors watch videos on the screen (whether it is surveillance footage or a digital reconstruction of a crime or accident). When that occurs, it is the decision-maker who is, in effect, placed in the position of eye-witness. But that 'witness' will never be cross-examined at trial.

Visual evidence not only problematizes what it means to 'witness', but also what it means to 'testify'. Is it the camera that testifies once it has captured the scene it shows? Do the images 'speak for themselves' (as Justice Antonin Scalia and other members of the United States Supreme Court recently asserted in *Scott v Harris*)? But how could that be? We know that a camera begins and ends at a particular point in time, and that it occupies a particular place that provides its own particular (and partial) view onto the reality it shows. It also goes without saying that digital reconstructions (and digital images generally) can only show what invisible algorithmic calculations are designed to show, based on a given digital program. Who or what, then, is testifying? The image? The photographer? The camera? The digital data it contains? The underlying digital program? The engineer who designed the program?

Of course, even conventional (non-digital) images may raise similar questions. Even here it is appropriate to ask what exactly we are seeing, and what the basis is for its authority, or for the authority of the visual meaning that we make out of what we see. So should we say it is the advocate who 'testifies' when he or she edits the image or designs the montage? Is it the viewer who brings unconsciously shared cultural and cognitive templates to the screen in the visual meaning-making process?

And what if the images we see mean more than the conventional cognitive and cultural frames that we use to thematize them? What if images bear an ontological excess – what some have referred to as the 'aura' of the image, a surplus that also may be described as the image's metaphysical trace?

(Sherwin, 2011). I will say more about this presently. Suffice it to say here, the image on the screen may be either more or less than it seems. On the one hand, the delight that it yields (as a matter of pure aesthetic pleasure) may not justify the truth or belief that sensorial gratification seems to warrant. Aesthetic truth as a matter of visual delight is flat, and often empty. Where can it dwell if not on the surface of the screen? And what can it contain beyond the subjective stimuli needed for the feelings it seeks to impart? On the other hand, an invisible presence, the aura, if you will, of certain unusually potent images may carry greater weight than we can readily put our fingers on. The mysterious ontological surplus of these images is not easily explained, or dismissed.

It has often been said that the search for truth at trial is based on objective knowledge derived from precise observation by dispassionate observers. Of course, everyone knows that credibility often sounds in an emotional register (both its false notes and its true), and that the feelings that tell decision-makers that a particular witness is lying (or not), or that a lawyer's argument is hogwash (or not), are far from objective and dispassionate.

Visual images, even more than word-based stories, run on emotional currents, in large part because the meanings we draw from them are organized on the basis of associative logic rooted in our life experience. That logic usually operates subconsciously, through its emotional appeal. A viewer might be aware that an image is strongly linked to a particular emotional response without knowing or understanding just what the connection is. In this respect, then, visual images tend to capitalize on the power of people's intuitive, *gestalt* emotional responses to shape their judgments. These effects operate beneath the radar of awareness and are thus less amenable to critical scrutiny and counterargument. It is also notable that visual images tend to have more impact than non-visual expressions of the same information. This is because they tend to be more vivid, more lifelike. Studies show that people respond to photorealistic pictures as they would to the real thing. For example, viewers of an IMAX movie of a roller-coaster ride or, for that matter, of an unstable camcorder-based film like *Cloverfield* (2008), may experience a sense of dizziness that words alone could never induce.

Words are obviously constructed by the speaker and thus remain at one remove from the reality they describe. By contrast, photorealistic photographs, videos, film, as well as digital re-enactments can appear to be caused by the outside world, as if untouched by human mediation or authorial interpretation). The human brain takes in visual information all at once. This wealth of data can lead jurors to believe that they have all the information there is to be had, and thus disincline them to pursue the matter further. Held in the grip of moving images, critical thinking is discouraged, or effectively disabled; it is enough simply to keep up with the visual flow.

And since pictures cannot be reduced to explicit verbal propositions, some of their meaning always remains implicit. This represents a convenient opportunity for advocates who might well prefer to leave an intended meaning unspoken – particularly when evidentiary rules or social conventions forbid making the message explicitly.

In addition, construing visual meaning from the screen readily lends itself to what literary theorists call intertextual references (Culler, 2002, pp. 100–18). By referring to other works, other genres, even other media, screen images cue the audience's cultural knowledge and allow them to draw on that implicit knowledge in responding to what they see. Of course, words can do this, too; but pictures can do it more effectively because they do it unconsciously, in a way that embeds the borrowed cultural value invisibly in the visual representation of the picture's ostensible subject matter.

Finally, visual representations favour particularities over abstractions. This has legal consequences. For example, stories driven by particular characters and dramatic events tend to emphasize individual agency and simplified (mono-causal) explanations for the consequences of particular actions. As a result, systemic reasons for bad outcomes – such as market incentives for particular kinds of behaviour or flaws in bureaucratic decision-making processes – receive short shrift on the screen. The same may be said for more complex (multi-causal) explanations which get in the way of dramatic visual storytelling. In short, cinematic narratives mimic the often reality-distorting tendencies of mind to simplify accounts and attribute blame in precisely these ways. While we may be aware of experiencing a particular emotion in response to an image or series of images, the precise nature of the connection usually remains obscure. If we cannot account for its source, however, the emotion we experience remains less susceptible to deliberate critique and counterargument.

Skilful legal advocates, like their counterparts in politics and advertising, have learned how to exploit these features of visual communication. The rules of evidence and the ideals of deliberation that govern the legal process must now operate in the context of these audiovisual and increasingly digital communicative practices. This raises novel legal questions. For example, is a computer-generated animation (re-enacting an accident, say, or a crime) just another evidentiary illustration, or is it something qualitatively different? Might there be something so compelling about a digitally simulated reality (not to mention three-dimensional or more fully immersive simulations) that place it beyond the ordinary bounds of demonstrative evidence? Is it even within the ken of jurors' ordinary common sense to follow judicial instructions to use a visual only as illustrative of an expert's opinion rather than as documentary evidence that helps to prove a particular party's theory of the case? For example, a juror might technically obey a judicial instruction not to use illustrative visual evidence as proof of what it depicts, but can we realistically expect that juror to dispel every trace of the emotional impact that comes from 'watching' a murder, or seeming to occupy the cabin of an airplane as it crashes to earth?

In sum, to ask who or what is testifying, and with what effect, when decision-makers turn to the screen, prompts complex and deep-seated epistemological and jurisprudential issues. Indeed, it brings into question core Cartesian assumptions about what constitutes knowledge and truth inside the courtroom.

In fact, many different kinds of knowledge have consistently been called into play inside the courtroom, the archive as well as the repertoire, to use Diana Taylor's categories, which is to say, the discursive as well as the performative (Taylor, 2003). As the pictorial turn sweeps over the legal landscape, we must confront a rudimentary truth: our visual common sense resists critical reflection. The old adage still rings true: seeing is believing. When we watch, we witness. Or so it may seem. We are all naive realists in our everyday perceptions of the world around us. The cognitive psychologists are clear on this point. As it turns out, belief is our default mode (Gilbert, 1991, pp. 107–8).

Once we grasp what we see, we accept what we grasp. The speed, vividness and emotional force of our mental response to images only enhance our sense of their truth. Images have an uncanny power. Throughout history, they have struck observers as being imbued with something like an aura, a kind of halo or surplus of meaning that is irreducible to what they actually depict. Yet, the source of this uncanny effect remains elusive. Sometimes, the image seems to return our gaze, as if somehow it had absorbed and reflects back our individual and collective emotional and even erotic investments. In this sense, we may say that images can be ontologically overloaded. They sometimes shimmer with an invisible presence; a strange auratic surplus renders their impact even more vivid to the senses, even more cognitively compelling. And this remains so despite the fact that we seem ill-prepared to articulate why or how this phenomenon takes place. Yet, the mystery is not without consequence.

A recurring metaphysical anxiety has long been associated with the mysterious potency of the image. Fear lies at the very heart of the visual. After all, it is the image that is singled out for explicit prohibition in the Book of Exodus. The second commandment (which is actually the first prohibition, given that the preceding commandment asserts the oneness of God) is explicit:

> Thou shalt not make unto thee any graven image, or any likeness of any thing that is in heaven above, or that is in the earth beneath, or that is in the water under the earth. Exod. 20:4–6 (KJV)

It would seem that there is something about the creation of images that threatens the priority of God. For some, this raises the prospect of falsifying the ultimate nature of God's unmediated reality. Words, by contrast, run no such risk. They are manifestly abstract constructions. We must penetrate the word to reach the meaning it seeks to evoke. Words (except perhaps for poets and Kabbalists) are not the thing itself. Images, on the other hand, are signs that tend to deny they are signs. They readily invite the viewer to conflate the image with what it represents. This is the crux of naive realism. Images also may seem to be invested with a peculiar power, an aura that emanates from what is shown. Perhaps this has to do with the circulation of desire: the investment of the creator's desire in the creation, and the collective desire of the community out of which the image emerges, as well as the investment of desire by the one who gazes upon it.

Our current love/hate relationship with images (Latour's iconoclash) reflects a historically recurrent either/or response to the image. Either it is what it shows or it is not. Either it is a transparent frame, like a window onto reality, or it is a deceit that ought to be utterly rejected. In this way, we see that the iconoclastic impulse is parasitic upon naive realism.

Postmodern constructivism at times reflects a similar (and similarly unwitting) bond. But rather than harping on the spectacular emptiness of the image, as we find in the work of Jean Baudrillard (1994), for example, some simply yield to its allure. Faced with 'a nauseating void of signifiers', as W. J. T. Mitchell puts it, it is also possible to choose (again, in his words) 'nihilistic abandonment to free play and arbitrary will' (Mitchell, 1984, p. 503). This strategy marks the embrace of reality as endless carnival, a perpetual baroque spectacle, or masque. So, in this sense, the aura of the image might be ontologically over-determined, on the one hand, or dissipated in the endless simulations of formal or merely ornamental aesthetics, on the other.

This state of affairs harks back to anamorphic painting during the sixteenth century, and to the history of an iconic aesthetics more generally with its hyper self-reflexiveness regarding artifice in the act of representation. The classic example of anamorphic painting is Holbein's *The Ambassadors* (1533). Standing before Holbein's canvas, we behold two men, a cleric and a man of wealth who wears an elaborate fur-lined cloak. Laid out between them we see the fruits of the human arts and sciences: a globe, an open book, a mandolin. But what is that blurred image in the foreground? It rises at a forty-five degree angle from the floor like a flattened cipher. Move a few steps to the left or to the right and the mystery dissolves. The blur crystallizes into a coherent form. It is a skull. And so we see how a change in one's perspective changes everything, turning the fruits of human labour into the death-darkened shadows of *vanitas*. By triggering the invisible Christian eschatological code of redemption, Holbein's painting transforms the vanity of worldly existence into an allegory of future hope as the painting's display of pride gives way to an expression of Christian humility and renunciation. When a change in perspective brings the blurred skull into view, the normative register of the work completely shifts (from worldly values to transcendent ones).

This is deconstruction in the service of a transcendent axiological code. Without recourse to a stable code of meaning and value, however, the manifest representation may be shattered. In that case, only deconstruction, perhaps for its own sake, remains.

We witness today a similar impulse in a variety of contemporary cultural works – especially film. Consider in this regard the Wachowsky siblings' film, *The Matrix* (1999). In a critical scene, Morpheus explains the matrix to Neo, his incredulous acolyte. What is it? The Matrix, it turns out, is a computer-generated collective hallucination, a digital dream world built by an alien race to keep humanity under control. Humanity's fate is to wander, like ghosts lost in a labyrinth of empty simulacra. We witness a similar scenario unfold in Alex Proyas' *Dark City* (1998), a science fiction noir film about a dying race of aliens who abduct humans to an artificial planet and turn their lives into an unending series of experiments. The aliens endlessly rearrange their subjects' memories, personalities and professions. It is as if the wheel of rebirth had been set in super-fast motion. One day you may awaken as an artist, the next as a mass murderer. And with each transformation, amid the transient illusions of everyday life, the aliens watch for clues about the human capacity for individuality and, above all, about the human soul, which the aliens lack. So they seek it out, methodically, scientifically, as if it could be isolated like any other element of material existence.

These films (together with numerous other contemporary neo-baroque cultural expressions) share a common theme: they are infused with metaphysical anxiety. How do we know what's there, what's real? What is a dream or a digital simulation, and what is reality? How can we be certain of what we know?

The previous baroque era, which unfolded during the European Reformation, witnessed a bitter and violent clash between two opposing codes of meaning: the Protestant belief in God's essential unrepresentability, which supported the embrace of abstract (disembodied) printed text over visual image, on the one hand, and the Catholic belief in the symbolic role of images, ceremonies and icons as visual aids in the search for spiritual insight, on the other. In the current digital baroque era, by contrast, image-generating digital codes proliferate without constraint. We may deconstruct the information image to discover the algorithmic calculations that produced it, which may help us discover whether the program's input of data authorizes its visual output. But this will not tell us what kinds of images to create or how their perceptual and emotional significance should be interpreted in a particular context.

On the visual sublime in culture and law

The visual sublime, that strange excess of meaning, runs counter to the baroque recession of the real amid the mad proliferation of form. In illustration of the visual sublime, consider some typical vignettes by that most remarkable painter, Vermeer. Look: a young woman sits pensively at her writing desk, quill pen in hand, staring out toward the painter's (or viewer's) gaze; or consider the letter writer, interrupted in her task, who turns, with fingers quizzically touching her chin, toward a servant who presents her with a sealed envelope; or what about the maid who sits dozing at a table, behind a half open door, as a ray of light plays upon her face and upper torso and upon a jug and fruit-laden plate, their shadows finely cast?

Outward calm seems to prevail in these quiet domestic scenes. Except the more one looks the more one realizes that it isn't so. In fact, each painting is shot through with mystery; invisible perturbations animate these scenes with an uncanny tension. Consider the first letter writer: what is she writing, and to whom? How are we to meet the challenge of her forthright gaze? What is she thinking? The painting begs us to enter her inner world. So we gaze back at the gaze that greets us, searching a hidden reality. Or consider the equally quizzical gaze of the second writer: what are we to make of it? Does she already apprehend who the sealed letter before her is from, and what it contains? A husband away on business, or a secret lover perhaps, perhaps the very one to whom she is writing that very moment? In short, what moves us in these paintings is hidden from view. We must break the surface and plumb its depth (and our own) to crack the code of the mystery-drenched pictures we see.

In addition to manifesting itself as an uncanny absence, the visual sublime may also present itself as an uncanny presence. Consider in this regard the abstract expressionist canvases of Rothko. Faced with the colour fields that scintillate before our eyes, we are left with nothing but the amorphous, non-figural abstractions of colour, space and shape. No inherited cultural motifs remain to guide or thematize our experience of the non-figural absence before us. Yet, if we allow ourselves to open up to the strangeness of this abstract expressive field, a new register of meaning emerges. The sublime catches us again, resonating in the painterly materials of colour and brushstroke on canvas. Suddenly, we are transported to an unfamiliar field of meaning; in the moment of contact we find ourselves held fast, and constituted anew, by potent emotional tones, and obscure but equally potent spiritual undertones, perhaps of longing, that shape and inform the uncanny reality that the painting evokes. Riveted at first on the surface, we lose our balance and fall into a mysterious depth. Why is our immersion in such a field capable of evoking tears of joy? (Elkins, 2001) Why does the strange force of Rothko's paintings make one's hair stand on end? This is the uncanny ('anagogic') power of the sublime: expressing an impossible presence through a mysterious absence, enacting an inexplicable transcendence of finite form.

Uncanny presence

Now, let us shift gears again, and see if we can identify traces of the visual sublime inside the courtroom. We begin with the highly publicized prosecution, in 2002, of Michael Skakel for the 1975 murder of 15-year-old Martha Moxley. In the *Skakel* case, lawyers for the State of Connecticut used their own interactive proprietary software to display demonstrative evidence that had been shown throughout the trial, including photographs of the neighbourhood and crime scene, diagrams of the locations at which real evidence had been found, and an audiotape of a telephone interview Skakel had given to a journalist in the late 1990s. During the prosecution's closing argument, jurors heard and saw Skakel's own words appear on the oversized screen before them. As Skakel uttered the word 'panic', jurors instantly saw Martha Moxley's lifeless body appear on the bottom right of the screen, just as it was found at the crime scene some 27 years previously.

The intended association was plain. Of course Skakel experienced a 'feeling of panic' when Martha's mother asked him the next morning if he had seen Martha. The picture of Martha's battered body immediately explains the implicit meaning of his words. The viewer instantly makes the connection: Skakel panicked because he must have recalled with horror what he had done the night before. Because the jurors' screen-based emotional response to the image of Martha's body and the reality-based response (by Skakel when he realized what he had done) are comparable, the viewer's emotion is readily transferred to Skakel. The viewer 'knows' what Skakel is reacting to, and the ensuing revulsion at Skakel's horrific crime readily brings a sense of guilt to mind.

But wait. How can one be sure that the image of Martha's lifeless body is the actual source of Skakel's self-professed feeling of panic? How do we know that his panic wasn't caused by a different mental association, like the one Skakel offered in court: namely, his fear that someone might have seen him masturbating in a tree outside Martha's window on the night of the murder? The defence did not stick. It lacked the power of narrative coherence and emotional resonance that the state's evidence-based closing narrative produced. Of course he panicked. Who wouldn't have under the circumstances? By contrast, Skakel's defence not only strains credulity, but it also leaves Moxley's murder unsolved. The decision-maker's desire for narrative closure finds all that it needs in the state's visual and verbal summation of the case. The prosecution's closing multi-media montage produced a Proustian moment. A second-hand memory cued by the sound of Skakel's voice and the graphic image of the deceased strikes the viewer as if for the first time. The resuscitation of that moment causes a shudder. It is uncanny.

In a brief, but well-calibrated juxtaposition of word, image, and sound, understanding manages to transcend the ordinary barriers of time and space. The passage of years – over a quarter of a century from the murder and the morning after (in 1975) to the time when Skakel uttered these words (in 1997) up until the time they were replayed at the trial itself (in 2002) – vanishes in a flash.

In this example, the state's visual claim is authenticated by the viewer's sense of lived experience in real time (what Henri Bergson calls 'direct vision' (2010, p. 30)) and by an accompanying 'sentiment of rationality' (as William James put it (1956, pp. 63–110)) or 'deep-seated sentiment' (in Benjamin Cardozo's terms (1921)). Suffice it to say, the Skakel montage is suggestive of how the visual sublime may come into play inside the courtroom. Something that was absent was suddenly given an uncanny visual and aural presence. The juxtaposition of words, voice and image sublimely incarnated a terrible past that somehow, impossibly, haunted the present. We witness the event (on the screen), and we shudder. For an uncanny moment inside the courtroom, as the great American poet Walt Whitman put it, time and space availed not (1996, p. 307). A legal event transpired in the temporally flattened but emotionally amplified *now* time of viewing the screen. And because the understanding this visual display produced was immediate, credible and seemingly complete, the viewer experienced little reason to question what he or she simultaneously came to understand and believe. Defence counsel's purely verbal counter-narrative plainly lacked comparable explanatory or emotional power in accounting for Skakel's panic.

Uncanny absence

During the closing argument of the *Skakel* case a strange absence shone forth in the uncanny visual shimmer of a momentary *presence*. But there is something uncanny as well when an absence remains absent, but haunts the viewer's mind nevertheless. This is what occurred inside a New York City courtroom when a short video documentary transfixed the attention of judge, jurors and spectators alike. The occasion was the 2009 murder trial of Dr Mazoltuv Borukhova. Borukhova was tried and ultimately convicted of having paid a distant relative, Mikhail Mallayev, $20,000 to kill her husband,

Dr Daniel Malakov. Malakov, from whom Borukhova had been estranged for the last three years, was the father of their four-year-old daughter, Michelle.

The shooting took place on the morning of 28 October 2007, in a Queens playground in plain view of the victim's daughter, who stood nearby with her mother. The motive? Six days before, a family court judge had granted a transfer of custody from Borukhova to Malakov and this, so the state's theory ran, was something Borukhova could not tolerate. The prosecution argued that she could not accept losing custody of her only child. And, indeed, there was something exceedingly odd about Borukhova's maternal protectiveness. For example, when Michelle's father paid custody visits, Borukhova would do everything in her power to draw her daughter's attention away from her father. Michelle would remain firmly planted in her mother's lap throughout each visit, occupied with toys and sweets that her mother provided. Malakov's diminished status in his daughter's eyes (she cried whenever he sought her attention) caused him to seek help – first, from a court-appointed guardian, then from the court itself. Over time, Judge Sidney Strauss came to realize that things were not quite right with Borukhova's overweening possessiveness. She was 'smothering' the child, he explained in the judicial opinion that accompanied his order that custody be shifted from mother to father. That order, prosecutors contended, enraged Borukhova, and sowed the seed for murder.

But how do we know the state had it right? Well, among other indicators, there is a video tape, made by a professional videographer Borukhova herself hired. The assignment was to document one of her daughter's custody visits at the home of her dad. And what do we see? But perhaps we should ask not what we see, but rather what lies beneath the surface of the scene that the video unfolds. What Vermeer-like perturbations unsettle the apparent banality of a day in the life of a child of separated parents arriving at the home of her dad?

The scene opens with Michelle emerging from a car, clasped tightly in the arms of her mother. 'Here we go,' we hear Borukhova announce. Michelle immediately breaks into loud sobs. Malakov arrives from the right, smiling broadly. He takes his daughter's right arm, which had been hooked around Borukhova's neck and shoulder. Then he tries to do the same with her left. 'Very good,' he says, in an assuring tone, as Michelle screams. 'Ouch,' we hear Borukhova cry out. Then the estranged couple begin an odd dance, circling around and around, with Michelle locked between them. 'Let the hand...' says Malakov, without completing his sentence. 'Ouch,' Borukhova cries out again, louder this time. 'Why are you pushing?' Malakov asks. 'I'm not pushing,' Borukhova replies. And around they go, circling in their dance of unyielding custody. Slowly, parents and child make their way closer to the front gate of Malakov's home. 'Can you separate her legs?' he asks. Then he says it again, as the couple and child circle back onto the street outside the gate. Michelle's screams grow louder. An elderly woman in a black hat, Borukhova's mother perhaps, pushes Malakov's brother, Joseph, off to the right. We hear his plaintive voice, 'Why is she touching me?' After asking the same question five times, he cries out, 'Please don't touch me.' At the same time, a woman in a white shirt can be seen trying to get Borukhova to let go of Michelle's legs. 'You don't touch me,' we hear Borukhova say, and say again, as if echoing Joseph's words from a moment ago. Meanwhile, Borukhova still has her arms wrapped around her daughter's red corduroy pants, locked tight at the knees, though apparently Malakov hasn't noticed this. They continue to circle. Finally, Malakov realizes why mother and father have been locked into this peculiar dance. 'Why are you holding her...Let go of her feet.' He pauses, now, as if at a loss. His insistent smile at last wavers. 'Let the left side go,' he says. 'Lift your arms, I'm holding her. Lift her other arm.' Eventually, Michelle is released from her mother's grip. As father and daughter finally walk past the front gate toward an open doorway, the woman in the white shirt gazes toward the videographer. In a tired voice she says, 'Can you please shut off the camera?' 'No,' we hear Borukhova sharply countermand. 'Don't shut it off.'

What have the jurors and judge just witnessed? The images rush by quickly, and are quickly done. Yet, their brevity is belied by the depth of disturbance that they leave in their wake. There is an undercurrent here, a silent score to which couple and child have danced. In that silence viewers may discern the hidden presence of motive, its trace manifest in the irrational rage that keeps Borukhova locked in a custodial embrace, circling, unable to let her daughter go. The task of judgment this jury faces consists not simply in the effort to come to grips with the human capacity for murder. Here they must also struggle to comprehend how a mother could deprive her only child of her father. There is something utterly incomprehensible, almost Medean, in such an inhuman act. One watches, and shudders, sensing what this dance of custody foretells. The violence is already there: the dozens of phone calls (91 in all) between Borukhova and the cousin hired to kill have already been made, and the process of finalizing the details of the murder will continue, including the almost comical home-made silencer, made of a bleach bottle and duct tape, that blew off with the first shot, and remained behind after the event, lying uselessly inside the playground where the shooting occurred, though perhaps not entirely useless, for it bore the fingerprints that the shooter also carelessly left behind.

When the local news media covered the *Borukhova* trial reporters took special interest in the custody video that played inside the courtroom, and how viewers responded. As one juror would later put it after viewing the video, 'She was cold and unconcerned. She didn't try to comfort her daughter...She just wanted to show on tape how upset the child was.' (Malcolm, 2010, p. 34) Needless to say, the figure who appeared in these images was not the demure, self-possessed physician that her attorney sought to portray at trial. There was something odd, almost monstrous, about what the video showed. It was apparent to those in the room who watched, and who saw the jurors as they too watched, with fixated gazes, many eyes brimming with tears, hands lifting to mouths, heads shaking ever so slightly from left to right and back again, as if in disbelief. A shudder coursed through the courtroom. That is what happens when we encounter powerful images that we cannot fully comprehend.

As the jurors watched the Borukhova video in court they covered their mouths with their hands. Had Borukhova already set in motion a plan to murder her estranged husband, formed the intent, made the calls, as she circled around and around, choreographing the video evidence (of a murder foretold?) that would document her story in court, as she protectively (or merely possessively) clutched the child whose loss brought her unbearable pain and perhaps incomprehensible rage as well? They dance and he smiles, he smiles and they dance, mother seeking to hold onto child, father seeking to release her from mother's unyielding embrace, circling and circling around the invisible pivot of a mother's rage. And accompanying that dance a silent score plays, the phantasmal presence of implacable revenge. The jurors watch after the event, knowing what they know, and they shudder. An uncanny presence leaves a trace, a strange presence that haunts the otherwise banal images that unfold within the sanctity of the courtroom. A sublime terror provokes a visceral reaction and demands a response.

Judgment, the demand of the ethical, is all that remains to counter the twin temptations of escapism and paralysis. We judge, we pronounce judgment, and we authorize our pronouncement as a matter of law, with the full power of the state standing by to enforce it. The sublime exceeds our comprehension. Yet, at the same time, it demands something of us. We cannot fail to respond, for once having become mindful of that which calls for a response, our response becomes an unshakable responsibility. Responding is the ethical itself. Levinas calls it going 'beyond being'. That is what happens when we respond to the infinite need of the other who stands before us: 'I exist through the other and for the other...I am inspired...[My responsibility] means an openness in which being's essence is surpassed in inspiration.' (1991, pp. 114–15) In the grip of the ethical sublime, we enter a state of being-for-the-other. This is the ethically inspired state of ontological transport.

The ethical originates in this inexpressible absence, this ought for which I am responsible. In this sense, justice, as human fraternity, may turn out to be prior to freedom. The ethical is an indictment as well as a sublime transport.

It calls us into question even as it calls us beyond ourselves, in response to that which demands a response.

Visual triggers of fantasy and irrational desire: child pornography law

Risks attend the instant gratification of popular entertainment when such gratification displaces more deliberate forms of judgment inside the courtroom. This is what happens when popular aesthetics (the aesthetics of visual delight) are unwittingly internalized as the operative code for truth. There are risks as well when unconscious fantasies stirred by the visual mass media take on a life of their own. In turning our attention to these risks, consider in particular the figure of the sexual predator. In recent years, popular entertainment has exhibited a near obsession with this figure. An intriguing dynamic is at work here. Images cause viewers to react to what they see as if it were the real thing. We emote in sympathy or antipathy with what we see on the screen just as we do in response to off-screen realities. These responses include a broad spectrum of sexual fantasies and wishes. Sexual responses are particularly potent. Hence, their popularity in the visual mass media, along with violence – and judging by popularity, preferably the two combined.

Law dramas on the screen may stage a parade of legal forms on the surface, but underneath powerful unconscious forces are often at work fuelling the narrative. Film and television are desire machines regulated by familiar symbols of authority. As Freud understood, the release of powerful unconscious forces requires equally powerful prohibitions to restore psychic equilibrium. The greater the jolt of illicit titillation the more sinister is the agent who must bear the full force of law's prohibition. The vicarious fulfilment of unacceptably violent impulses requires condemnation of especially evil perpetrators, just as the gratification of unacceptable sexual desires demands condemnation of perverse sexual predators. Such predators exist, but if they didn't we might have to invent them, or at least amplify the threat they present to match our need to condemn the illicit desire with which they are associated. Like the proverbial scapegoat, someone must pay the price for the community's sins. That is what we see, at any rate, when an intra-psychic defence of this sort plays out in the public life of the community. For example, there are signs that precisely this unconscious process is at work in the realm of contemporary child pornography law.

The sexual abuse of children has been described as 'the master narrative of our culture'. It is a crime that has been described as 'worse than murder'. As Amy Adler notes, no other crime so preoccupies our tabloid culture (Adler, 2001, pp. 220–5). These popular narratives have given rise to a variety of distortions. For example, mass media depictions of child abductions and sexually motivated murders promote the belief that children are at great risk from predators lurking in schoolyards and playgrounds. Studies have shown, however, that the vast majority of child sexual abusers are well known to their victims (Katz-Schiavone, 2008, p. 291)

According to one study, approximately 34 per cent are family members and 59 per cent are acquaintances (US Department of Justice, 2000). The similarly pervasive fear of recidivism among sexual offenders has led to the proliferation of laws calling for indefinite civil commitment once criminal sentences have expired. The empirical data do not support prevalent fears and beliefs concerning the perverse other among us. What accounts for such a gap between belief and reality?

Terror management studies have shown that terror prompts a heightened tendency to blame and punish. Punishment re-establishes social stability by restoring confidence in a pre-existing 'steady state' of conventional values and beliefs which undergird and authorize the punitive impulse. It has been suggested that since fantasies help to constitute what we fear, they may be useful to those whose objective it is to stage the efficacy of the state's power to manage fear. Punitive measures restore confidence in the community's ability to police and effectively prohibit dangerous contaminants. Whether or not one accepts such a theory, the fact remains that the public and in particular the legal attention paid to violent and especially sexually violent child predators is disproportionate to what the actual data show. Such wildly exaggerated claims alert us to the supernumerary presence of a highly over-determined psychic phenomenon. In a word, some strange fantasies are afoot.

Consider in this regard the bizarre accounts of sexual and often satanic ritual abuses in day-care centres in the 1980s. This prompted a slew of criminal prosecutions. Perhaps most notorious was the *McMartin* preschool trial in Los Angeles. The trial ran for two years, making it the longest criminal trial in American history. No convictions resulted. Many of these day-care cases claimed that the alleged sexual abuses were undertaken in order to produce child pornography. None was ever found. Throughout this period of 'crisis' and 'moral panic', the empirical data seemed to contradict the need for such exceptional concern and such extraordinary legal remedies. Yet, the public's obsession with the child predator continues.

Indeed, these days popular images of the sexual predator have migrated from the visual mass media to various public fora involving law enforcement and legislation. Consider, for example, this public notice from a local law enforcement website:

> The predator can be anyone from any social standing in life.
> From the doctor, who we admired for his manner, to the race

car driver, whose public persona was filled with the embraces of a multitude of female fans it become apparent that there is no 'typical' profession with which to associate him to. He (or she) no longer hides on the boundaries of our school playgrounds but now exists within the confines of the Internet as well. Where he was once a transient he is now the vice president of a corporation. Where he was limited in choice as to where he 'operated' he now resides in anonymity within a largely unregulated medium. (Law Enforcement Division, 2003)

This kind of official notice has helped to fan public fears, which in turn have motivated expansive prosecutions, more stringent laws and even vigilantism. For an example of the latter, consider the formation of citizen groups, such as Perverted Justice, which have initiated their own efforts to hunt down sex offenders. Volunteers for Perverted Justice trawl the internet pretending to be underage boys and girls in an effort to catch prospective sex offenders. These efforts have been aided by partnering with the hit reality television show called *To Catch a Predator*. The concept for the show debuted in 2004, on the television news magazine *Dateline NBC*, which featured a series of hidden camera investigations aimed at identifying and detaining alleged paedophiles who sought out minors on the internet for sex. The predators were then lured by sexually explicit communications supplied by the show's staff writers to meet with a decoy in a staged (televised) undercover sting operation.

It has been noted that the fear of moral contagion may prompt a community to seek to uncover and root out the source of the infection. In some societies, this is undertaken by way of a public ritual of symbolic purification. (We see something of this sort depicted in film-maker Andrew Jarecki's riveting documentary, *Capturing the Friedmans* (2003).) A significant shift in current American child pornography laws may be driven by a comparable animus. In this instance, however, the contagion (of illicit sexual desire) has been incorporated into the law itself. This was not always the case. At the outset, child pornography laws were created because of concern about the harm suffered by underage victims of sexual abuse. As the Supreme Court put it in the seminal case of *New York v Ferber*, the state's compelling interest in the well-being of minors trumps the first amendment claim that child pornography is a protected form of free speech.

The court's withholding of constitutional protection included *non-obscene* as well as obscene forms of child pornography, thus making child pornography a new and independent category of unprotected speech. Subsequent legal developments in this area, however, reflect a marked change of emphasis. Instead of actual harm, the new laws now target the *illicit fantasies* on which child pornography allegedly feeds and in turn fuels in the minds of its viewers. It is these fantasies which the law condemns based on the fear that they might lead to the harm of children *in the future*. In other words, as the perceived social evil has shifted from actual to prospective harm (in the event that a paedophile might use child pornography to seduce future victims), the law's focus has likewise shifted to the paedophilic fantasies that might spur child abuse in the future. It is the forbidden gaze itself (from which perverse fantasies are said to arise) that has been outlawed. By taking aim at the forbidden gaze the law seeks to avoid the 'perception of children as sexual objects'. The paradoxical outcome, however, is that it achieves precisely the reverse of what it sets out to do.

If the evil of pornographic images (which express or inflame impermissible desires) consists in the forbidden gaze, according to this juridical logic, by prohibiting that gaze the sexual purity of children will be protected. The problem is that (aside from its puritanical and clinically disputed denial of children's sexuality) the law cannot effectively prohibit pornographic images in this way for the simple reason that it cannot determine the existence of pornographic images based on the forbidden gaze itself. For one thing, the illicit desire the law seeks to proscribe may or may not have been present at the time the targeted image was created. Indeed, such desires may readily be brought to an entirely innocuous image.

Experts have observed that it is precisely the sexual innocence of the child in view that often prompts the paedophile's sexual arousal. By asking judges to focus on the forbidden gaze, the law invites them to re-enact the paedophile's process of arousal. In this way the law encourages the creation of the very evil that it purportedly sets out to suppress. Only by emulating the paedophile's forbidden gaze may the law against child pornography (so defined) be implemented. The more judges entertain prohibited fantasies whilst they look the more prohibited pornography they will find. As Amy Adler puts it, the current child pornography regime teaches jurists to 'transform the world into a pornographic place'. If pornography lies in the eye of the beholder, the beholder must assume the persona of the predator he or she condemns in order to authorize the law's prohibition. Without the illicit fantasy there is nothing to prohibit. Law's prohibition thus remains parasitic upon the desire it condemns.

This paradoxical state of affairs, in which law constitutes the very evil it seeks to avert, brings to mind Freud's insight into the way the human unconscious operates: 'Whatever is expressly forbidden must be an object of desire.' (Freud, 2008, p. 46) In other words, the very act of prohibition tempts transgression. Thus, the cycle commences: prohibition escalates desire which in turn calls for greater prohibition, which in turn escalates desire even further. The forbidden desire that stares back from the prohibited image is the one the viewer projects onto it. This is what happens when law migrates to the screen: it lives there as other images do, which means sometimes it internalizes the visual mass media's own logic of desire.

Conclusion

Law's life on the screen is an occasion for iconoclash – a state of affairs in which the reliability of the image and, indeed, of the mimetic faculty itself, the human capacity to represent reality, have fallen under a cloud of suspicion. It is this state of affairs that leads me to describe our contemporary culture as the digital baroque, for it is the hallmark of the baroque to channel and express a deep metaphysical anxiety concerning the nature of reality. Are we living in a dream? A shared hallucination? An interactive digital program – as depicted in *The Matrix*? What is real?

The challenge of iconoclash, and of the digital baroque in general, requires an aesthetic, cognitive and metaphysical response. Cognitive and cultural heuristics (those mental short cuts – the story forms, genres and other meaning-making templates – that we use to make sense of everyday life) help us to understand what we see on the screen. This is how we 'mind the image'. For its part, phenomenology helps us to understand what we are responding to (how image embodies mind – as well as how mind embodies image). This approach invites us to ask, how do we think with visual objects? Visual literacy invites more sophisticated visual discernment and better judgment. Are we moved by sheer visual delight or by the sublime presence of an ontological excess that we experience as an ethical demand, an ought for which we are responsible?

Law today lives in images the way images live on the screen. We need a new rhetorical toolkit and a new jurisprudence – a visual jurisprudence – that can help us live the life of law in the digital age, a life that increasingly unfolds as images on the screen.

Cases cited

New York v Ferber, 458 US 747 (1982)
Scott v Harris, 550 US 372 (2007), www.law.cornell.edu/supct/html/05–1631.ZO.html

References

Adler, A (2001) 'The Perverse Law of Child Pornography' **101** Columbia Law Review

Baudrillard, J (1994) *Simulacra and Simulation* (Ann Arbor: University of Michigan Press)

Bergson, H (2010 [1946]) *Creative Mind* (Dover: New York)
Cardozo, B (1921) *The Nature of the Judicial Process* (New Haven, CT: Yale University Press)
Culler, J (2002) *The Pursuit of Signs* (Ithaca, NY: Cornell University Press)
Elkins, J (2001) *Pictures and Tears* (New York: Routledge)
Freud, S (2008) *Totem and Taboo* (Lawrence, KS: Digireads.com).
Gilbert, D (1991) 'How Mental Systems Believe' **46** *American Psychologist*
James, W (1956) *The Will to Believe* (Dover: New York)
Katz-Schiavone, S (2008) 'Myths and Facts about Sexual Violence: Public Perceptions and Implications for Prevention' **15** *Journal of Criminal Justice and Popular Culture*
Latour, B (2002) *Iconoclash* (Massachusetts: MIT Press), available at www.bruno-latour.fr/livres/cat_icono_chap.html
Law Enforcement Division (2003) Child Abuse Unit, Long Island, New York, http://childabuseunit.com/p_information.cfm
Levinas, E (1991) *Otherwise Than Being, or Beyond Essence*, A Lingis (trans.) (Dordrecht and Boston, MA: Kluwer Academic)
Malcolm, J (2010) 'Iphigenia in Forest Hills: Anatomy of a Murder Trial' *The New Yorker*, 23 May, p. 34
Mitchell, W J T (1984) 'What is an Image?' **15** *New Literary History*
Sherwin, R K (2011) *Visualizing Law in the Age of the Digital Baroque: Arabesques and Entanglements* (New York: Routledge)
US Department of Justice (2000), Bureau of Justice Statistics, 'Summary Findings: Violent Crime', available at, www.ojp.gov/bjs/cvict_c.htm
Whitman, W (1996) 'Crossing Brooklyn Ferry' in J Kaplan (ed.) *Walt Whitman: Poetry and Prose* (New York: Library of America)

Index

Adler, Amy 207, 210
adoption 116
aesthetics 44, 46, 56, 137, 193, 199
  baroque 194
  iconic 199
  and the law 12
  popular 207
agency 4, 10, 68, 70–1, 74, 77, 80, 107, 150–2, 157–8, 160–3, 165, 180, 184, 197
  gendered 71, 73
  moral 161, 163
  narrative 107
Amsterdam, Anthony 3, 7, 18, 102, 107
Antier, Edwige 118
asylum politics 77

Baader-Meinhof Group 20, 24
Baudrillard, Jean 199
Berti, Simone 106–07
Binder, Guyora 18, 89, 94
Borukhova, Mazoltuv 203–6
Brook, Peter 118–19, 124–5, 129–30
Brooks, Peter 18
Brown, Wendy 69, 77
Bruner, Jerome 3, 7, 18, 66, 102, 107
Butler, Judith 17, 19

Cadoret, Anne 118
Cardozo, Benjamin 134, 136–7, 203
carnival 199
Chinese art 9, 85, 88
Christian Democratic Party 90
Civil Code 11, 105, 117
Collier, Stephen 86, 88
Collingwood, R G 171–4, 182–3

custody 126–8, 204–5
  police 186, 187

De Riedmatten, Adrien 85
Del Don, Alan 106–7
Descartes, René 143–4
desire 56, 72, 109, 117, 121, 127, 177, 192, 194, 199, 203, 207, 209–11
detective fiction 10, 170–2
digital baroque 11, 200, 211
discourse 2, 4, 12, 66–8, 70–4, 78–9, 91–2, 99, 103, 108, 176
  gendered 28
  legal 19, 88
  literary 139
  moral luck 157
  national 110
  political 87
  tolerance 69
  victim 67, 69, 73–4, 77, 81
Dormann, Rosemarie 90–1
Dupin, Auguste 170, 176–85, 187–8

epistemology 9, 153, 176
evidence 11, 33, 36, 58, 154, 157, 161–2, 166, 171–2, 174, 177, 181–2, 185–8, 192, 195, 197, 202
  forensic 10, 170, 187
  hearsay 172
  physical 173–4, 180–2, 184, 195
  video 206
  visual 43–4, 45, 192, 195, 198
Ewick, Patricia 19, 50, 89, 98

factum 145–6
federalism 107, 109, 111–13
Feeley, Malcolm 51–4, 60

female circumcision 8, 73 *see also* female genital cutting
female genital cutting (FGC) 8, 67–80
fertility clinic 125
FGC *see* female genital cutting
Foot, Philippa 153
freedom of research 2, 9, 86–99
Freud, Sigmund 164, 207, 210

Gadamer, Hans-Georg 142–3, 145
gay rights 122, 124, 127, 129
Gieryn, Thomas 92
Goldhagen, Daniel 161–3, 166
Gottweis, Herbert 86, 88, 99
Gross, Martine 118, 128
Gschwend, Hanspeter 104

hermeneutics 136, 142, 145–6, 154
Holbein 199–200
Huber, Fabiola 118

iconoclash 192–5, 199, 211
imagination 3, 68, 108, 133, 144, 151, 162, 176–8, 182, 183, 189
  historical 174, 176, 180, 183, 185, 188, 189
  legal 134

Jannidis, Fotis 89
Judge Judy 56–57, 60
judges 4, 7, 18, 25–7, 32, 33–44, 45–6, 50, 52, 56–7, 59–60, 63–64, 141, 195, 210
judiciary 7, 31–2, 38, 45, 46, 106
  and authority 36
  images of 33–44, 45

Kaim, Stéphanie 120
Kley, Andreas 91
Kunstmuseum Bern 85 *see also* Ruan

Lakoff, Andrew 86
Lalli, Chiara 118
Latour, Bruno 89–90, 192, 199
laws
  on asylum 70
  on child pornography 209
  and civil unions 127
  on counter terrorism 22
  on female circumcision 8
  on gay parenting 2, 127
  on the minaret ban 12
  on research on humans 87, 90, 116
Leemann, Ursa 118
legal consciousness 7–8, 50–53, 61, 63
legislation 8, 66, 73, 78
  and asylum 78
  biomedical 9, 87, 95–7, 99
  and direct democracy 90
  and female genital cutting 67, 72–3, 77, 79–80
  minaret ban 4
  and the Other 67
  and queer fatherhood 116
  and research on humans 87, 94
  and sexual predators 208
LGBTQ (lesbian, gay, bisexual, transgender and queer community) 117–18, 124
litigiousness 52–53

Macklin, Ruth 91
Malakov, Daniel 204–05
Margolis, Susanna 128
masculinity 7, 18, 21, 23–5, 28, 70
matrix 79
Matrix, The 200, 211
Mazzoleni, Oscar 103, 110
Mécary, Caroline 117
Merry, Sally 50, 55–6, 59, 60, 61
Merryman, John 6

Miéville, Ariane 106
minarets 1, 2, 4–6, 12, 67, 79
moral luck 10, 150–1, 157–8, 162, 163, 164, 166
Moxley, Martha 202–3
Müller, Jakob 17–18, 20–22

narratives 8, 18–20, 66, 69, 77, 80, 207
 of dilettantism 21, 28
 gendered 7, 17–18
 identity 113
 of law 18–19, 143, 146
 personal 89
 quest 102, 109
nationhood 7, 66, 79, 113
Nnaemeka, Obioma 72
non-lieu 9, 116–19, 125–6, 128–9 *see also* non-space
non-space 9, 116, 118 *see also non-lieu*

Ong, Aihwa 88

paedophiles 209–10
Papke, David 31
Parry, Bronwyn 88
Perez-Perdomo, Roger 6
Peyceré, Mathieu 128
Plattner, Gian-Reto 90
Poe, Edgar Allen 10, 170–2, 174–8, 181, 187–9
pornography 210
 child 194, 207–10
Porsdam, Helle 51, 53, 57, 59, 61–2
Posner, Richard 134–5, 137
postmodern 199

Reader, The 10, 151–4, 157–60, 163–4, 166–7
 reception 160, 161, 166

Red Army Faction (RAF) 17, 20
Reubi, David 88
Roduit, Guillaume 93, 96
Rothko 201, 202
Ruan 8, 85, 87, 90, 92, 94, 98 *see also* Kunstmuseum Bern

Sanna, Federica 105–6
Sarat, Austin 5, 51
Schiff Berman, Paul 114
Schlink, Bernhard 151–2, 154–7, 160–1, 163–4, 166
Schwander, Verena 91
Seibert, Thomas 18
semiology 44
sexual abuse 207, 208
sexual abusers 208
sexual offenders 208
sexual predators 207–8
Sherwin, Richard 6, 11, 51–53, 141, 192, 196
Silbey, Susan 19, 50, 52–3, 55, 89, 98
Skakel, Michael 194, 202–3
Smith, Courtney 70–2
space
 domestic 112
 legal 119
 narrative 7, 18
 political 23
spectacles 2, 36, 56, 59, 194, 199
 baroque 194, 199
Sprumont, Dominique 93, 96
Steinberg, Jonathan 103
Strah, David 128
sublime 11, 193–4, 201–2, 206
 visual 195, 201–3
supernatural 175, 180–1, 186, 188
surrogacy 116–18, 127
 international 120, 122, 125
 legality of 9

Switzerland 1, 4, 6–12, 17, 19, 22, 28–9, 67, 73–81, 85, 99, 102–4, 108, 111, 113–15
  and direct democracy 12, 78
  and the EU 11, 70, 103, 113
  and gender 22–23, 67, 69, 77–8
  and research on humans 86, 87, 88, 89, 90, 91, 95–7
  and strikes 9, 105–6, 113
  and terrorism 17–18, 21
  and xenophobia 1, 8, 67, 78– 9
syndi-courts 51, 56–59, 62 *see also* television courts

television courts 50–2, 56, 58–9, 61, 64
terror 154, 206, 208
terrorism 7, 17, 20–3, 28
terrorists 7, 17, 18, 20–6, 28, 42, 153
Tervonen, Tania 120, 126
thought experiments 10, 150–1, 153–5, 157–8, 163, 166

uncanny 144, 185, 188, 198, 201–3, 206

Valsangiacomo, Nelly 104, 112
Vico, Giambattista 133–4, 141, 143–6, 182, 185
video 195–6, 203–6
visual 6, 7, 11, 31–32, 33, 34, 35, 38, 43–6, 69, 141, 193–4, 196–8, 200–3, 207–8, 211
  and jurisprudence 11, 193
  and literacy 6, 11, 193–5
  and meaning 193, 195, 197
von Hagen, Gunter 93–4
Vorverständnisse 142

Watt, G 140
Watt, Ian 10, 171
Weibel, Ewald 92, 93, 94
Weisberg, Richard 137, 160
Weisberg, Robert 18, 89
Williams, Bernard 157–8, 164–5
witchcraft 170, 175, 186–7

xenophobia 67, 79–80

Yu, Xiao 9, 85, 92, 93, 98